D1189093

ALASTAIR SAWDAY'S
SPECIAL PLACES TO STAY

FRENCH
HOLIDAY HOMES

Design:	Caroline King
Maps & Mapping:	Bartholomew Mapping, a division of HarperCollins, Glasgow
Printing:	Canale, Italy
UK Distribution:	Portfolio, Greenford, Middlesex
US Distribution:	The Globe Pequot Press, Guilford, Connecticut

Published in 2004

Alastair Sawday Publishing Co. Ltd
The Home Farm Stables, Barrow Gurney, Bristol BS48 3RW
Tel: +44 (0)1275 464891 Fax: +44 (0)1275 464887
E-mail: info@specialplacestostay.com   Web: www.specialplacestostay.com

The Globe Pequot Press
P.O. Box 480, Guilford, Connecticut 06437, USA
Tel: +1 203 458 4500 Fax: +1 203 458 4601
E-mail: info@globe-pequot.com   Web: www.GlobePequot.com

Second edition

ISBN 1-901970-42-6 in the UK
ISBN 0-7627-2856-6 in the US

Printed in Italy on Megamatt paper: 50% recycled and de-inked fibres. There is no use of chlorine in the de-inking process.

A WORD FROM ALASTAIR SAWDAY

We all know how beautiful the buildings of France can be – so it is no surprise to find some stunners within these pages.

There's a convent school in the Lot, beautifully converted by two painters, a cottage in the grounds of a Burgundian château, an old bergerie deep in a forest, a farm in the Loire with 40 goats and its own cheese. Many places have open fires and wood burning stoves, and some even have underfloor heating.

Since we first wrote about 'self-catering' places in France there has been a minor revolution in the way they are seen by the French themselves. Gîtes (literally, 'shelters') – once the resting place of cast-off furniture – were expected to be treated with abandon but now there is a new awareness of how sensible it is to make them as lovely as possible. The influx of foreigners into the gîte scene has, perhaps, given it a boost, with Dutch, British and other nationality owners waving their wands over buildings that were thought to be beyond imagination. The French have joined in with their particular élan and the results, as you can see, are sometimes breathtaking.

There is a castle whose moat has become a swimming pool. A school has been transformed into a place of peace and luxury. There are entire hamlets available, not to mention the huge and wonderful houses that can take whole tribes. We have found tiny boltholes for two, apartments in Paris and other cities, and exquisite buildings in deep countryside. You can live in huge style or in charming, rural simplicity; you may be a minimalist or a traditionalist.

There is little more discouraging than to trek across the country to arrive, hopes high, at a grim, mean-spirited cottage in which you had planned to spend a week. I've done it. So we inspect these places and it is we who write about them, an unusual phenomenon in the world of self-catering. If you know about Special Places then you won't need convincing that this is a gem of a book for anyone planning to do their own thing in France. A week away is far too important to be left to chance.

Alastair Sawday

ACKNOWLEDGEMENTS

No book such as this one can appear without Herculean efforts on the part of many people. If only it really were a case of one or two happy souls criss-crossing spring-time France in an open-topped turbo-charged Citroen 2CV. The reality is hundreds of phone calls from a frost-bound UK office. Then comes a frenzied bout of inspecting, and the detailed work of compilation.

The goddess behind the scenes – the *deus ex machina* – has been the ineffable Emma Carey. Her humour, patience and efficiency, added to the hard-work of Philippa Rogers – without whose loyal support and talent the book could not have been done – have been formidable allies and have made the book what it is – bigger, better and more gorgeous than our first edition.

We also owe much to Viv Cripps and Tom Bell, two of our star writers. These places are not easy to write about, for human beings play a lesser role than in B&Bs, but they have conjured marvels of descriptive writing. To Jo Boissevain we owe thanks for writing and proofing and 'pulling together'. Jess Hughes did brain-boggling quantities of administration and our trusty team of inspectors pulled rabbits out of strange hats in odd places.

The sheer beauty (and 'efficiency') of the book owes all to the production team, named below. It's a hell of a job and they have done it brilliantly.

Alastair Sawday

Series Editor:	Alastair Sawday
Editor:	Emma Carey
Editorial Director:	Annie Shillito
Assistant to Editor:	Philippa Rogers
Production Manager:	Julia Richardson
Web & IT:	Russell Wilkinson, Matt Kenefick
Editorial:	Sarah Bolton, Roanne Finch, Jessica Hughes
Copy Editor:	Jo Boissevain
Production Assistants:	Rachel Coe, Paul Groom, Beth Thomas
Accounts:	Jenny Purdy
Sales & Marketing & PR:	Siobhan Flynn, Paula Brown, Sarah Bolton
Writing:	Tom Bell, Jo Boissevain, Viv Cripps, Anne Woodford
Inspections:	Emma Carey, Philippa Rogers, Richard & Linda Armspach, Helen Barr, Lillian Bell, Jo Bell Moore, Alyson & Colin Browne, Jill Coyle, Meredith Dickinson, Sue Edrich, John Edwards, Valerie Foix, Georgina Gabriel, Denise Goss, Anne Guthrie, Diana Harris, Heather Nears Crouch, Clarissa Novak, Viki Rainsford, Penny Rogers, Carol Waugh, Elizabeth Yates

A special thank you, too, to the other inspectors who saw just one or two houses for us.

WHAT'S IN THE BOOK?

CONTENTS

CONTENTS

CONTENTS

CONTENTS

INTRODUCTION

What is a
Special Place

We look for owners and houses that we like – and we are
fiercely subjective in our choices. Those who are familiar
with our Special Places series know that we look for comfort,
originality, authenticity. We reject the banal, the insincere and
the anonymous.

Finding the right
place for you

Do read our write-ups carefully – we want to guide you to
a place where you'll feel happy. If you are staying on a farm
don't be surprised to have tractors passing early in the morning,
or the farmer calling his cattle for milking.

Many of these properties have all mod cons but an ancient
building may have temperamental plumbing and be less than
hermetically sealed against draughts; a remote hilltop
farmhouse may have power cuts.

Use our descriptions as a taster of what is on offer and have a
conversation with the owners about the finer details. Perhaps
we've mentioned a pool and you might want to check that it
will be open at Easter, or you want to know whether the bikes
will be available on your particular weekend. If you do find
anything misleading in our books please tell us. And do discuss
any problem with your hosts at the time, however trivial.
Owners always say "if only we'd known" when we contact them
on readers' behalf after the event.

If the entry mentions other gîtes or that the owners do B&B, do
realise that you may not be in total isolation, but will perhaps be
sharing the pool and garden with other guests and their families.
This shouldn't spoil your holiday but, if absolute peace is vital, ask
the owners how many other people are likely to be around.

Some of our properties have owners who live nearby; others live
far off. If it matters to you, check when booking (though there will
usually be someone you can turn to should you lose your key).

How to use
this book

Our maps

The general map of France is marked with the page numbers
of the detailed maps, as are the individual entries. The entry
numbers on the detailed maps show roughly where the holiday
homes are and should be used with a large scale road map.

The address

We give only an abbreviated address for the property. Owners
will supply complete addresses when you enquire or book.

INTRODUCTION

How many does it sleep?

In some instances we give two figures, divided by a dash. The first figure is the number of adults the house sleeps comfortably; the second is the number of people who can actually fit in, but the extras may need to sleep on sofabeds or on mezzanine floors and privacy may be compromised.

If you squeeze in the second number of people, don't be surprised if it feels cosy. If you want to bring extra people, you absolutely must ask the owner first.

Some places offer special rates if you are fewer people than the number shown. Often this only applies out of season.

Bedrooms

In this book a 'double' means one double bed, a 'twin' means two single beds. A 'triple' is three single beds. 'Family rooms' include at least one double bed. Extra beds and cots for children, sometimes at extra cost, can often be provided, so do ask. We also give total numbers of bathrooms and shower rooms. We don't give details about which bathrooms are 'en suite' but many are so please check with the owners if this is important to you. We only mention wcs if they are separate from the bath and shower rooms which generally have their own wcs.

Facilities

If it is important to you that your holiday home has a dishwasher/ TV/CD-player/barbecue – or central heating in winter, check with the owners first. Most properties will have a washing machine, we try to mention where they don't, but again it is worth double-checking.

Prices

Prices are in euros and/or sterling, according to the wishes of the owner.

All prices are per property per week, unless we say otherwise. We give a range from the cheapest, low-season price to the highest, high-season price. Most owners offer weekend/short-stay rates out of season and these places carry a Weekend Break symbol. Check with the owner and confirm in writing the price for the number of your party. Remember that in ski resorts, high season is February.

INTRODUCTION

Prices are for 2004 and may go up in 2005 so please check with the owner or on their web site if they have one. A few properties offer a reduction if you stay for more than a week but don't expect any deals during peak season. Some places require you to stay a fortnight during these months.

Winter lets

Some holiday homes can be rented all the year round, some close during the winter, while others close during the winter but open for Christmas and New Year. The winter months are often a good time to glimpse the real France; the weather in the South can be very pleasant, and rates are normally extremely reasonable. In some cases, but not all, we tell you if winter lets are available, so please check with owners.

Symbols

Symbols and their explanations are listed inside of the back cover. They are based on the information given to us by the owners. However, things do change: bikes may be under repair or a new pool might have been put in. So please use the symbols as a guide rather than an absolute statement of fact and double-check anything that is important to you. In particular look out for '*B&B also*' at the end of the write-up as this indicates that there may be other guests on the premises.

Practical Matters

When to go

Families with school-age children will generally take their main holiday in July and August, which is when the French en masse will be taking theirs. For these months particularly it is essential to book well in advance. If you can holiday outside those busy months, do so: it'll be slightly cooler; it'll be cheaper; you're less likely to get snarled up in traffic jams, especially on arrival and departure days (avoid 15 August, the Assumption bank holiday, at all costs); and you have a better chance of seeing France going about its everyday life. May and June are the best months for flowers, for temperatures suitable for walking, and for visiting the Mediterranean coast. If mushrooms are your thing, then September's the time. Temperatures in autumn can be ideal, and the winter months, when you often get clear fine days, are well worth considering too (see Winter Lets above). A word of warning, though: some restaurants in rural areas only open in July and August. Some markets too, but they tend to be the touristy, less authentic, ones anyway. Many restaurants close in the winter.

INTRODUCTION

How to book

Contact the person listed on the entry under 'Booking Details'. (You'll know what language to speak according to whether there's an 'English Spoken' symbol or not.) They will normally send you a Booking Form or Contrat de Location (Tenancy Contract) which must be filled in and returned with the deposit, and commits both sides. The owner will then send a written confirmation and invoice, which constitutes the formal acceptance of the booking. Contracts with British owners are normally governed by British law.

Remember that Ireland and the UK are one hour behind the rest of Europe. Folk can be upset by enquiries coming through late in their evening.

Deposits

Owners usually ask for a non-refundable deposit to secure a booking. It makes sense to take out a travel insurance policy with a clause to enable you to recover a deposit if you are forced to cancel. Your policy should also cover you for personal belongings and public liability.

Many owners charge a refundable security/damage deposit, payable either in advance or on arrival.

Payment

The balance of the rent, and usually the security deposit, are normally payable at least eight weeks before the start of the holiday. (If you book within eight weeks of the holiday, you'll be required to make full payment when you book.) A few owners take credit cards and have our credit card symbol. Otherwise you will need to send a euro cheque, or a sterling cheque if the owner has a British bank account.

What payment covers

In most cases this covers electricity, gas and water. In some cases, the electricity meter will be read at the start and end of your stay and you will have to pay separately.

Our linen symbol shows where linen is provided but at extra cost. Even where linen is provided free of charge, towels often are not, so please check when booking.

In some case owners charge for the cost of cleaning and you will have to pay this whether or not you are willing to clean the place yourself. At other places you can either clean yourself, or pay someone else to do it. In some cases tenants only have to pay for cleaning if they leave the house needing it; the cost is deducted from the security deposit.

Changeover day

Usually this is a Saturday and where it is not we have tried to mention it in italics. Many owners are flexible outside of the high season so, again, it is worth checking. Normally you must arrive after 4pm, and depart by 10am. Don't arrive earlier as your house may not yet be ready and you will wrong-foot your busy owners.

Consider taking...

Electrical adaptors: virtually all sockets now have two-pin plugs that run on 220/240 AC voltage.

Electric kettles are a rarity in French-owned homes, so if you can't manage without, bring your own (with adaptor plug).

Children

Our symbol shows where children of all ages are welcome. If there's no symbol, it doesn't mean the owner doesn't like children but may mean there is an unfenced pool, a large boisterous dog or some steep stairs. If you are convinced that your impeccably behaved five year old can cope, the owner may allow you to bring her – but at your own risk.

Pets

Our Pets symbol tells you which houses generally welcome them but you must check whether this includes beasts the size and type of yours; whether the owner has one too (will they be compatible?); and whether you can bring it in the house or must keep it in an outhouse. Your hosts will expect animals to be well-behaved and obviously you must be responsible for them at all times.

Telephoning/Faxing

All telephone numbers in France have ten digits, e.g. (0)5 15 25 35 45. The initial zero is for use when telephoning from inside France only, i.e. dial 05 15 25 35 45 from any private or public telephone.

INTRODUCTION

• From another country to France:

From the UK dial 00 33, omit the zero in brackets, then the rest of the number given.

From the USA dial 011 33, omit the zero in brackets, then the full number given.

• Numbers beginning (0)6 are mobile phone numbers.

• When dialling from France to another country: dial 00 followed by the country code and then the rest of the number without the first 0. When dialling ASP from France, the UK no. 01275 464891 becomes 00 44 1275 464891.

• To ring Directory Enquires in France dial 12.

Télécartes (phone cards) are widely available in France and there are plenty of telephone boxes, even in the countryside, where you can use them. Few boxes now accept coins, and many take credit cards. Many of our holiday homes have telephones from which you can ring using a card.

Business days and hours

If you get up late and stroll to the shops at midday hoping to pick up some tasty morsels for lunch, you'll be disappointed. France closes down between midday (or sometimes 12.30pm) until around 2pm or 2.30pm for the all-important business of lunching. Some post offices have a crafty habit of closing early for lunch, so don't get caught out. Most shops and banks open from 8am or 9am on weekdays, and food shops normally stay open until around 7.30pm. Many food shops open on Sunday morning but close on Mondays.

Environment

We try to reduce our impact on the environment by:

• publishing our books on recycled paper

• planting trees. We are officially Carbon Neutral®. The emissions directly related to our office, paper production and printing of this book have been 'neutralised' through the planting of indigenous woodlands with Future Forests

• re-using paper, recycling stationery, tins, bottles, etc.

• encouraging staff use of bicycles (they're loaned free) and car-sharing

INTRODUCTION

- celebrating the use of organic, home and locally-produced food
- publishing books that support, in however small a way,
  the rural economy and small-scale businesses.

Subscriptions   Owners pay to appear in this guide. Their fee goes towards
the costs of the inspections and producing an all-colour book.
We only include places and owners that we find positively special.
It is not possible for anyone to buy their way into our guides.

Internet   Our web site (www.specialplacestostay.com) has online pages
for all of the places featured here and from all our other books
– around 4,000 Special Places in Britain, Ireland, France, Italy
Spain, Portugal, India and Morocco. There's a searchable
database, a taster of the writeups and colour photos. For more
details see the back of the book.

Disclaimer   We make no claims to pure objectivity in judging our Special
Places to Stay. They are here because we like them. Our
opinions and tastes are ours alone and this book is a statement
of them; we hope you will share them.

We have done our utmost to get our facts right but apologise
unreservedly for any mistakes that may have crept in.
Sometimes, too, prices shift, usually upwards, and new
buildings get put up. Feedback from you is invaluable and we
always act upon comments. With your help and our own
inspections we can maintain our reputation for dependability.

You should know that we don't check such things as fire alarms,
swimming pool security or any other regulation with which
owners of properties receiving paying guests should comply.
This is the responsibility of the owners.

And finally   Do let us know how you got on in these houses, and get in
touch if you stumble across others which deserve to be in our
guide – we value your feedback and recommendations
enormously. Poor reports are followed up with the owners in
question. Recommendations may be followed up with
inspection visits. If yours leads to a place being included in a
future edition, you will receive a free guide.

There is a report form at the back of the book or you can
e-mail frenchholidayhomes@sawdays.co.uk

Emma Carey

explanations

Abbreviated address
...ot to be used for correspondence.

Italics
...entions other relevant details e.g.
...B also, or when changeover day for
...lf-catering is not Saturday.

sleeps
...e lower number indicates how
...any adults can comfortably sleep
...re. The higher is the maximum
...mber of people that can be
...commodated.

price
...e price shown is per week
...d the range covers low season
... high season, unless we say
...herwise.

rooms
...e give total numbers of each type
...bedroom e.g. double, triple, and
...tal numbers of bathrooms. We give
...c details only when they are separate
...om bathrooms.

closed
...hen given in months, this means for
...e whole of the named months and
...e time in between.

map & entry numbers
...ap page number; entry number.

symbols
...e the last page of the book for
...planation.

sample entry

WESTERN LOIRE

La Maison Aubelle - Tour, Gaudrez & Jardin
Montreuil Bellay, Maine-et-Loire

A 16th-century nobleman's house in an old country town. It stands in secluded gardens flanked by high stone walls, renovated by craftsmen, thoughtfully equipped by Peter and Sally. The original apartments are Tour, Jardin and Gaudrez. Tour – in the tower, as you'd expect – is one flight up a spiralling stone stair; it has a beamed living room/kitchen with trim red sofas and wraparound views (below). The garden apartment, with terrace, is as neat as a new pin; white walled Gaudrez has a 16th century window, discovered during restoration. The feel is airy, relaxing, comfortable; crisp linen, central heating and daily cleaning are included and the quality is superb. There's a terrace and games room for all and an appropriately large pool. If you can't face cooking, let the Smiths do it for you: they whisk up delicious meals five times a week, cheerfully served in the dining room in winter, on the terrace in summer. Peter and Sally are also on hand to advise, translate or leave you in peace. They run French courses, too. *Apartments rented separately or together. Children over 12 welcome. Shared laundry. Min. three nights.*

sleeps	Tour & Gaudrez: 4. Jardin: 2.
price	Tour & Gaudrez €775–€1,000; Jardin €675–€925.
rooms	Tour: 2 doubles, 2 shower rooms. Gaudrez: 2 doubles, 2 shower rooms. Jardin: 1 double, 1 bathroom, 1 separate wc.
closed	Rarely.

booking details

Peter & Sally Smith
tel	+33 (0)2 41 52 36 39
fax	+33 (0)2 41 50 94 83
e-mail	maison.aubelle@aubelle.com
web	www.aubelle.com

entry 71   map 7

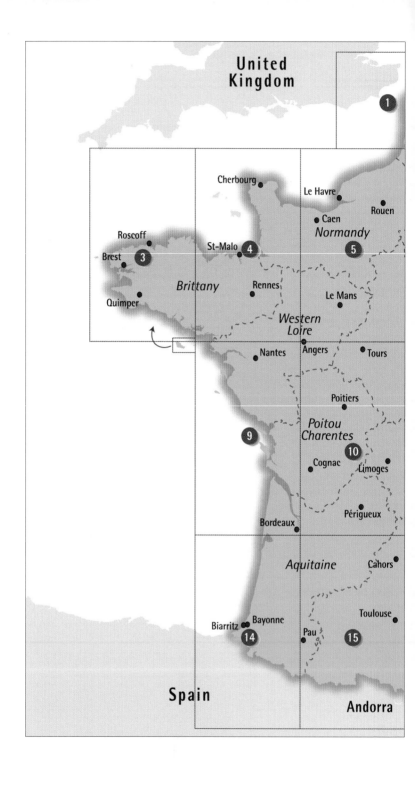

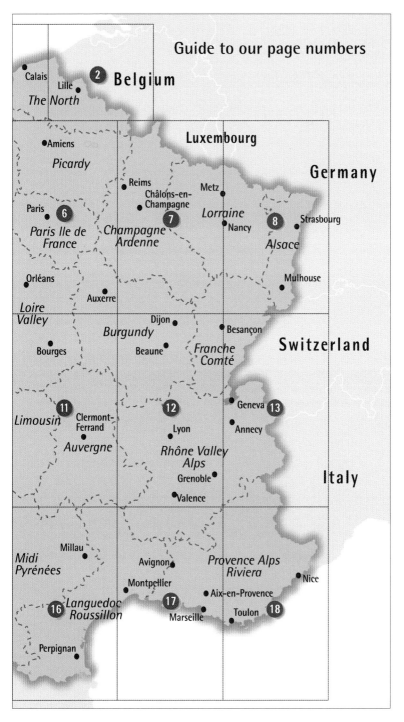

Guide to our page numbers

©Bartholomew Ltd, 2003

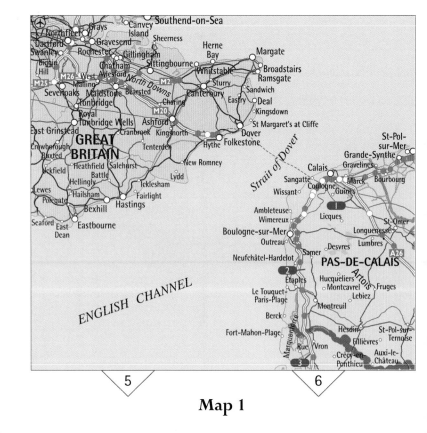

Map 1

Scale for maps 1:1 600 000

Map 2

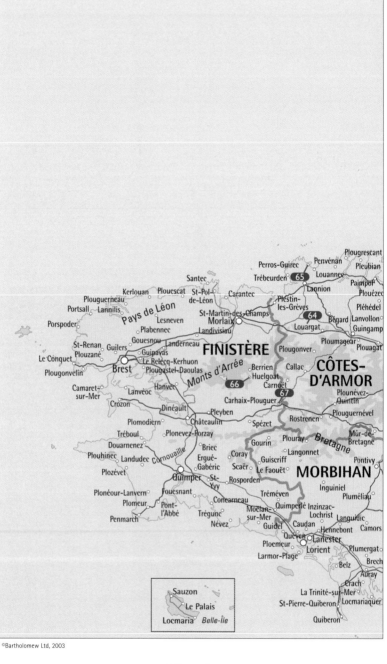

Map 3

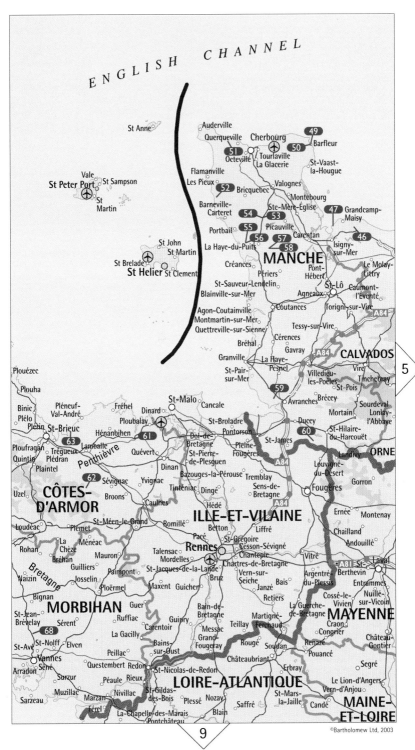

Map 4

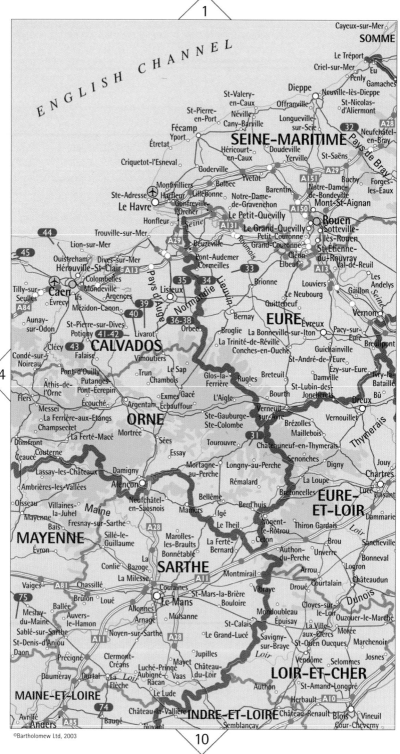

ENGLISH CHANNEL

SOMME
Cayeux-sur-Mer
Le Tréport
Criel-sur-Mer
Penly
Eu
Gamaches
Dieppe
Neuville-lès-Dieppe
St-Nicolas-d'Aliermont
Offranville
Neufchâtel-en-Bray
St-Valery-en-Caux
Néville
Cany-Barville
Longueville-sur-Scie
32
Pays de Bray
A28
St-Pierre-en-Port
Yport
Fécamp
SEINE-MARITIME
Doudeville
Yerville
St-Saëns
Étretat
Héricourt-en-Caux
Forges-les-Eaux
Buchy
Criquetot-l'Esneval
Goderville
Yvetot
A151
Notre-Dame-de-Bondeville
A29
Montivilliers
Bolbec
Barentin
Mont-St-Aignan
Ste-Adresse
Harfleur
Lillebonne
Notre-Dame-de-Gravenchon
A150
Gonfreville-l'Orcher
Le Havre
Le Petit-Quevilly
Rouen
44
Honfleur
Seine
Le Grand-Quevilly
Sotteville-lès-Rouen
A131
Petit-Couronne
St-Étienne-du-Rouvray
Trouville-sur-Mer
A29
Beuzeville
Grand-Couronne
Cléon
Val-de-Reuil
45
Lion-sur-Mer
Pont-Audemer
Elbeuf
Les Andelys
Ouistreham
Dives-sur-Mer
Cormeilles
Roumois
33
Gaillon
Hérouville-St-Clair
Tilly-sur-Seulles
Colombelles
35
34
Brionne
Louviers
Vernon
A84
Caen
Ifs
Mondeville
Argences
Lisieux
Pays d'Auge
Normandie Lieuvin
Le Neubourg
Seine
Évrecy
Mézidon-Canon
39
Quittebeuf
EURE
Évreux
Pacy-sur-Eure
Aunay-sur-Odon
St-Pierre-sur-Dives
40
Bernay
Breuilpont
Potigny
41-42
Livarot
36-38
Broglie
La Bonneville-sur-Iton
Guichainville
Ézy-sur-Eure
Clécy
43
CALVADOS
Orbec
La Trinité-de-Réville
St-André-de-l'Eure
Ivry-la-Bataille
Condé-sur-Noireau
Falaise
Vimoutiers
Conches-en-Ouche
Damville
Bû
Glos-la-Ferrière
Rugles
Athis-de-l'Orne
Pont-d'Ouilly
Le Sap
Breteuil
St-Lubin-des-Joncherets
Dreux
Flers
Putanges
Chambois
Bourth
Pont-Écrepin
Trun
Verneuil-sur-Avre
Vernouillet
Messei
Écouché
Exmes
Gacé
L'Aigle
Brézolles
La Ferrière-aux-Étangs
Argentan
Échauffour
Maillebois
Thymerais
Champsecret
Mortrée
ORNE
Ste-Gauburge-Ste-Colombe
31
Châteauneuf-en-Thymerais
Dompront
La Ferté-Macé
Tourouvre
Senonches
Digny
Jouy
Ceaucé
Couterne
Sées
Essay
Longny-au-Perche
La Loupe
Luce
Chartres
Lassay-les-Châteaux
Damigny
Mortagne-au-Perche
Rémalard
Bretoncelles
EURE-ET-LOIR
Toisant
Ambrières-les-Vallées
Alençon
Bellême
Berd'huis
Dammarie
Oisseau
Villaines-la-Juhel
Neufchâtel-en-Saosnois
Mamers
Igé
Thiron Gardais
Mayenne
Maine
Fresnay-sur-Sarthe
A28
Le Theil
Nogent-le-Rotrou
Brou
Sancheville
Bais
MAYENNE
Sillé-le-Guillaume
Marolles-les-Braults
La Ferté-Bernard
Authon-du-Perche
Unverre
Logron
Bonneval
Évron
Conlie
Bonnétable
Arrou
Châteaudun
La Bazoge
Montmirail
Courtalain
Vaiges
A81
Chassillé
La Milesse
SARTHE
A11
Vibraye
Droué
Dunois
75
Brûlon
Loué
Coulaines
St-Mars-la-Brière
Cloyes-sur-le-Loir
Ouzouer-le-Marché
Meslay-du-Maine
Ballée
Auvers-le-Hamon
Le Mans
Bouloire
Mondoubleau
La Ville-aux-Clercs
Morée
Marchenoir
Sablé-sur-Sarthe
Arnage
Muisanne
St-Calais
Épuisay
St-Ouen Oucques
St-Denis-d'Anjou
Noyen-sur-Sarthe
A28
Le Grand-Lucé
Savigny-sur-Braye
Loir
Vendôme
Selommes
Josnes
Daon
Précigné
Clermont-Créans
Jupilles
LOIR-ET-CHER
Daumeray
Durtal
Aubigné-Racan
Mayet
Château-du-Loir
Authon
St-Amand-Longpré
MAINE-ET-LOIRE
La Flèche
Vaas
La Loir
Herbault
A10
Avrillé
74
Le Lude
Château-la-Vallière
INDRE-ET-LOIRE
Château-Renault
Blois
Vineuil
Angers
A85
Baugé
Noyant
Semblançay
Cour-Cheverny

©Bartholomew Ltd, 2003

Map 5

Map 6

©Bartholomew Ltd, 2003

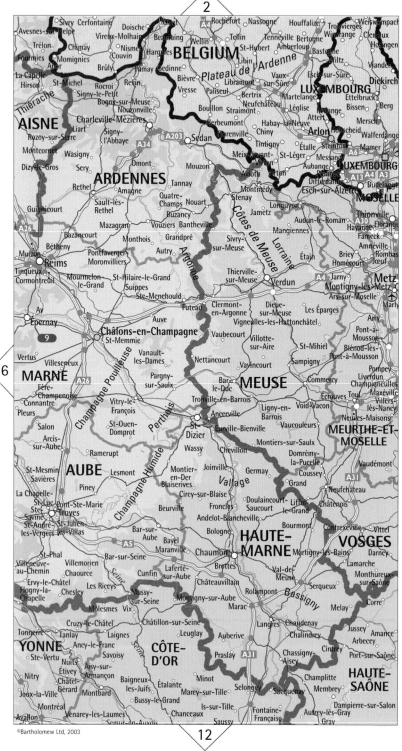

Map 7

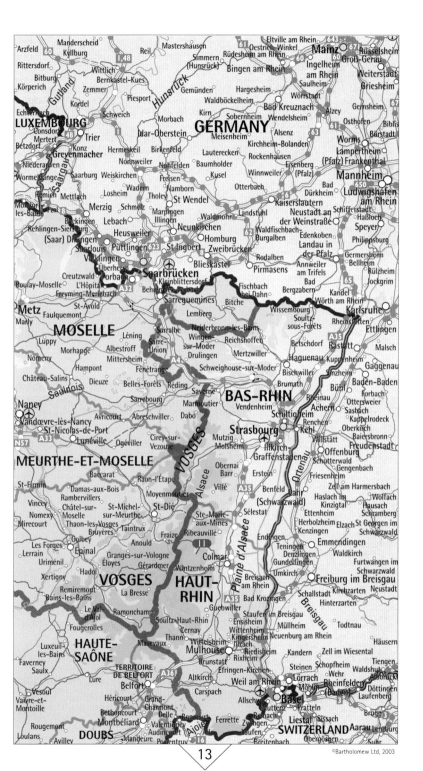

13

Map 8

©Bartholomew Ltd, 2003

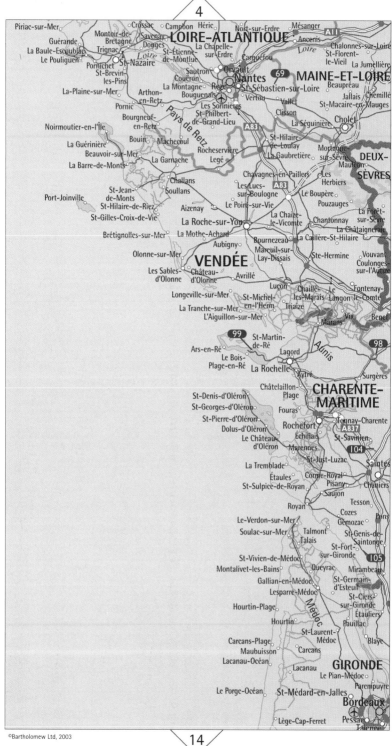

Map 9

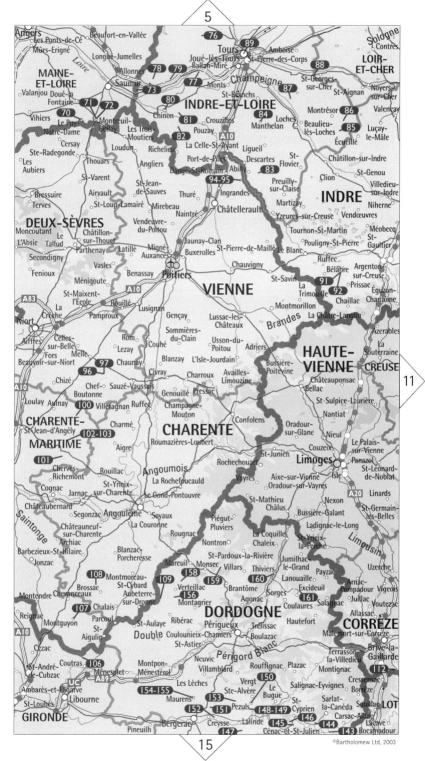

Map 10

©Bartholomew Ltd, 2003

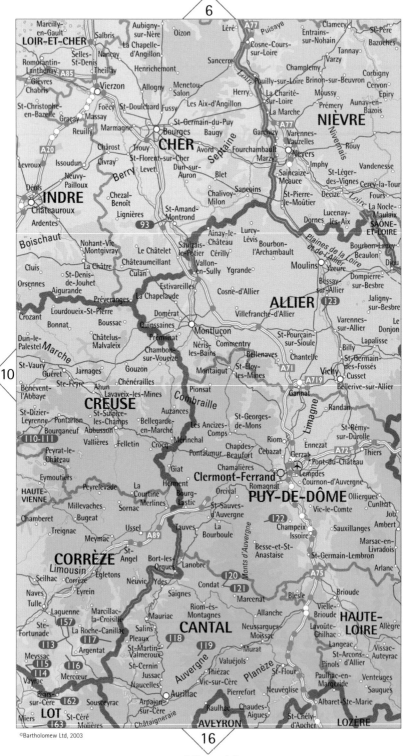

©Bartholomew Ltd, 2003

Map 11

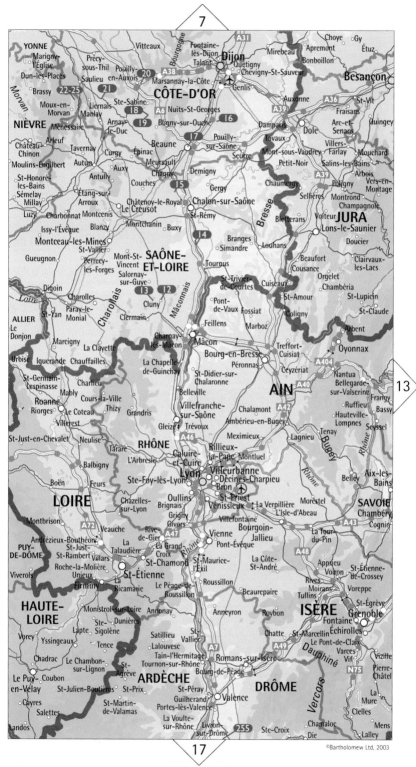

©Bartholomew Ltd, 2003

Map 12

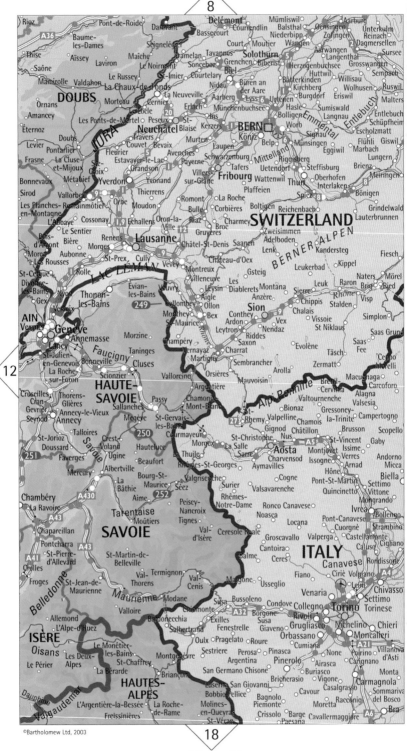

©Bartholomew Ltd, 2003

Map 13

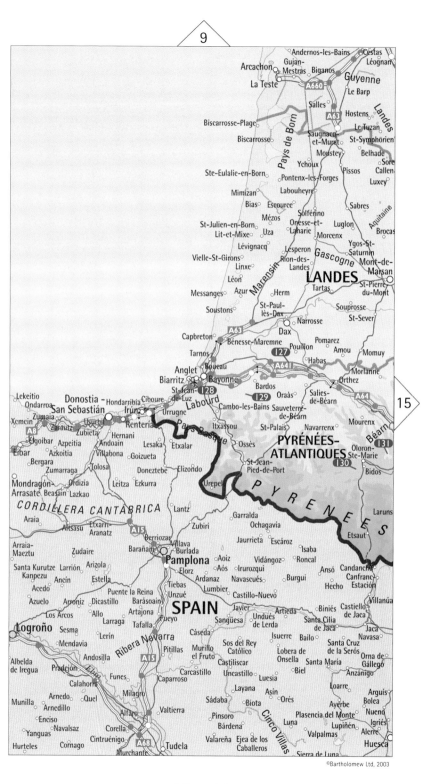

15

©Bartholomew Ltd, 2003

Map 14

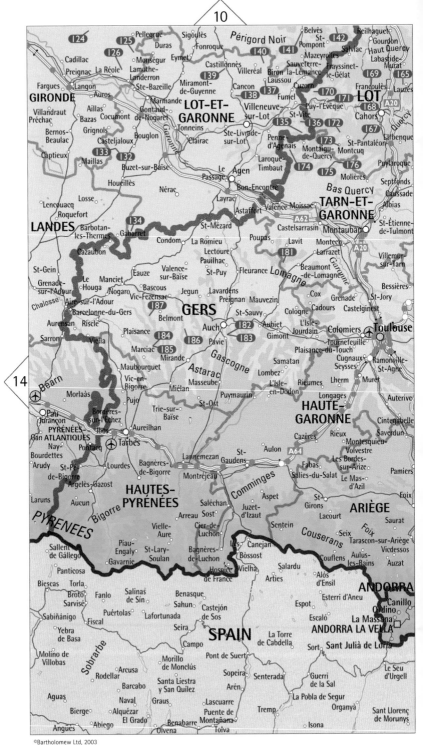

Map 15

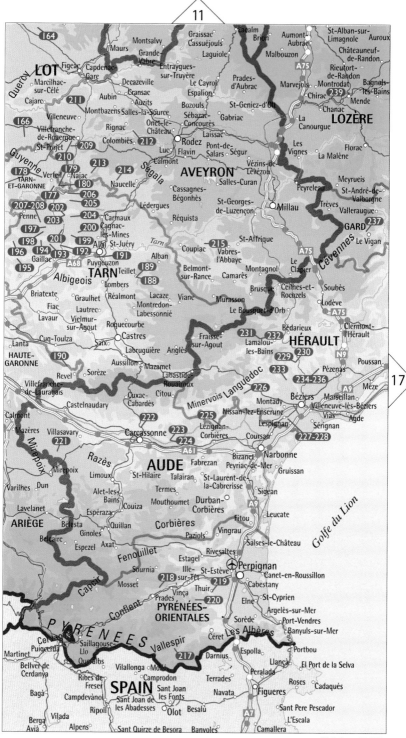

Map 16

©Bartholomew Ltd, 2003

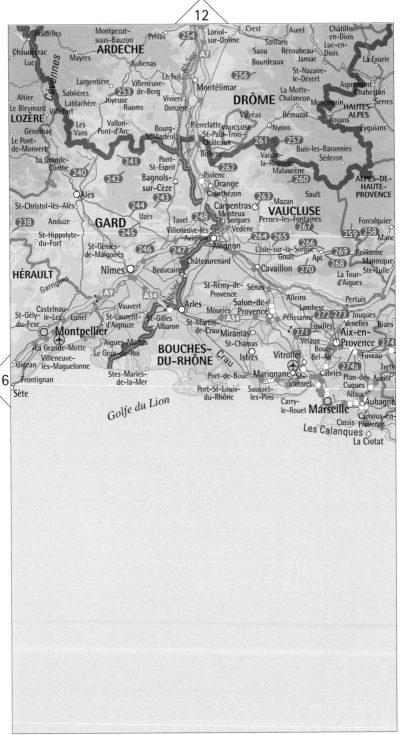

Map 17

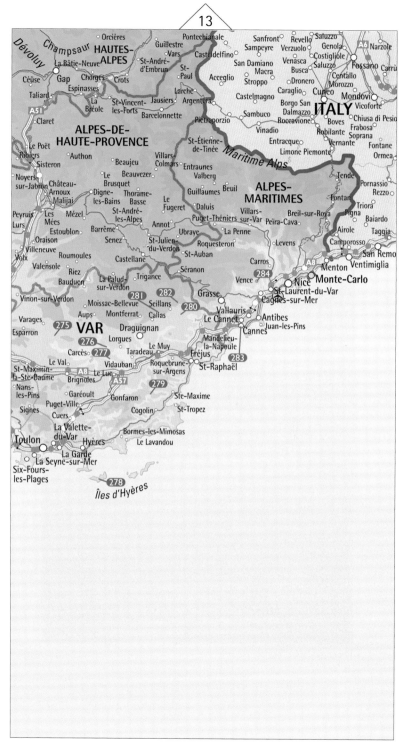

Map 18

Photography by Michael Busselle

the north, picardy,
champagne-ardenne,
alsace, burgundy
& paris-ile de france

Le Manoir de Bois en Ardres

Ardres, Pas-de-Calais

Come to commune with nature. The 1776 farmhouse is hidden by hedges and trees in the Manoir de Bois' 15 wooded acres. Françoise and Thierry, a warm, eager couple – she the artist, he the earthy do-er – do B&B in the main house; you are totally independent in your modest home, yet your hosts are there when you need them. This is a one-storey gîte furnished with bright checks and wicker chairs – a neat retreat from which to explore the region. It's just right for two, though you could – just – squeeze in two more. There's a barbecue for summer meals, ping-pong at the manor, and a shed in your big, green, gated garden with two bikes; why not spin off to the little market town of Ardres that overlooks the coastal marshlands of Calais. Ardres is the sort of place that wins awards in France's annual Ville Fleurie competition, delightful by day and peaceful at night. Its ancient market is still held every Thursday, and you have plenty of shops and restaurants to discover. You are also walking distance from Ardres' lake (created out of marshland by peat diggers) where you can hire a boat and fish. *B&B also.*

sleeps	3-4.
price	€ 300–€ 380.
rooms	2: 1 double, 1 single, extra bed available, 1 shower room.
closed	Never.

booking details

Françoise & Thierry Roger

tel	+33 (0)3 21 85 97 78
fax	+33 (0)3 21 36 48 07
e-mail	roger@aumanoir.com
web	www.aumanoir.com

Halinghen Home
Halinghen, Pas-de-Calais

This would be a first-rate holiday home for two or more families, and just across the channel – you could be here in time for lunch. There's a huge garden and orchard to play in, with swings; table tennis, table football, snooker and games keep everyone happy on rainy days. The rooms are homely, with an English feel, big and light with a cosy medley of furniture – it is perfect for families. The open-plan living area has French windows so you can spill onto the terrace, scented with honeysuckle on summer evenings. Beds are comfortable, bathrooms are carpeted and there are spectacular countryside views from every window. Merelina swapped London for this gentle French village and lives in one self-contained side of the house. She is warm and helpful, and will rustle up a celebration cake on request. Hardelot Plage is a 15-minute drive; its wide beaches, fringed with sand dunes and pines, have turned it into a popular sand-yachting centre. Le Touquet, too, is nearby, and there are over 100km of gorgeous sandy beaches on the Côte d'Opale. *Babysitting & hairdressing available. Flexible changeover day & length of stay. B&B also.*

sleeps	8–17.
price	€ 1,200; € 380 for three days.
rooms	4 (+ 2): 1 double with 1 set of bunks & wc, 3 family rooms for 3, 2 shower rooms. (2 additional doubles on request).
closed	Never.

booking details

	Merelina Ponsonby
tel	+33 (0)3 21 83 04 80
e-mail	merelina@wanadoo.fr
web	www.france-short-breaks.co.uk

map 1   entry 2

Le Thurel
Rue, Somme

Apurist's paradise. Outside, it's aristocratic and ever-so-white; inside, a minimalist's dream, life stripped to the bare essentials. This farm cottage will delight those who enjoy clutter-free living, sobriety and space. Scrubbed floorboards and perfect white walls are enriched by the odd splash of colour from ethnic rug or table-cover. The huge living/dining room is decorated in ivories, creams and beiges, in beautiful contrast with the smokey blue-grey window frames, the antique dining table and chairs and the odd Flemish oil painting. There are views of the courtyard and a stunning red-brick barn to the front; behind, the large leafy garden which you share with the Bree-Leclefs' B&B guests; there's boules, too. Bedrooms are white (of course) with fabulously luxurious linen. Glamorous, welcoming Patrick and Claudine will go out of their way to initiate you into the local lore. No surprise to learn he is an interior architect; she is an ex-teacher of Italian and concocts divine suppers which you're welcome to share; just book first. *Cleaning charge supplement. B&B also.*

sleeps	6-7.
price	€840–€882.
rooms	3: 1 double, 1 twin, 1 family room for 3, 1 bathroom, 1 separate wc.
closed	January.

booking details

Claudine & Patrick Van Bree-Leclef

tel	+33 (0)3 22 25 04 44
fax	+33 (0)3 22 25 79 69
e-mail	lethurel.relais@libertysurf.fr
web	www.lethurel.com

26 rue Principale – Cottage & Studio
Creuse, Somme

The soft light filters through the trees of the big, luxuriant garden, with corners for all and bantams about. With its neatly tended beds to the front, and rough, wild area behind, the garden will inspire anyone who stays in these 200-year-old stables. Eat out on the terrace, snooze on the lawns. The studio, like a nest in the roof, has been stylishly converted by French owner Monique who lives in the timbered manor house next door (and holds painting classes). It's snug, neat and simple, with a colour scheme of marine and white, and pure white walls offset by a solid antique table and modern, gilt-framed paintings. The cottage lies below (you share a hall) and B&B guests sleep in a neighbouring room, but you're unlikely to be disturbed. Here, rooms are decorated in country style with a perfect mix of antiques and pretty checked or soft ivory fabrics. The fresh, doll's house kitchen has all you need... there's a mood of sober, uncluttered elegance. Amiens' 13th-century Gothic cathedral – the largest in France – is a must and its Saturday morning riverside market overflows with produce of the area's fertile land. *B&B also.*

sleeps	Cottage: 4. Studio: 2.
price	Cottage: € 275–€ 305. Studio: € 150–€ 180.
rooms	Cottage: 1 double, 2 single beds in living room, 1 bathroom. Studio: 1 double, 1 shower room.
closed	Never.

booking details

	Mme Monique Lemaître
tel	+33 (0)3 22 38 91 50
fax	+33 (0)3 22 38 91 50

map 6   entry 4

Les Gîtes de l'Étang

Mons en Laonnois, Aisne

A fine estate set in 50 acres of wooded parkland, with majestic trees, vast lawns and a delightful lake. This old coach house has been converted into two roomy gîtes, neat as a new pin. The original gates through which the coaches passed are now vast windows, the style is simple, uncluttered and stylish, and light creams and honey-whites give a cosy, warm feel. Bedrooms have padded bedheads, pretty floral bed linen and views onto the park; bathrooms are small, neat and clean. Downstairs, a large sitting/dining room is open plan and has all you'll need: sofas and armchairs, a white-tiled floor and a working fire. The kitchen is in the corner, compact but modern with *tout confort*. Big glass doors open to a terrace with table and chairs, separated from your neighbours by a big new fence – a fine place to eat out. Madame and Monsieur, a retired NATO official, lived in England and speak the language well. They are courteous, welcoming and available, and live in the main house close by. Beyond the gates is the pretty village, holding all you need. Keep going and you'll discover Laon, its medieval quarters and fine cathedral. *B&B also.*

sleeps	2 gîtes for 6.
price	€310–€430 each.
rooms	Gîte 1: 2 doubles, 1 twin, 2 shower rooms. Gîte 2: 1 double, 2 twins, 2 shower rooms.
closed	Never.

booking details

Mme P Woillez

tel	+33 (0)3 23 24 18 58
fax	+33 (0)3 23 24 44 52
e-mail	gitemons@aol.com
web	www.gitenfrance.com

Verneuil – Gîte de Moussy

Vendresse-Beaulne, Aisne

It's deep in the country, surrounded by copses and fields – a peaceful, isolated little farmhouse. After the devastation of the World War I, when all that remained of the village were the wash-house and church (a triumph for cleanliness and godliness?), this farm was the only one to be rebuilt. Play at being the farmer and his wife as you contemplate grazing Salers cattle and acres of wheat, barley, peas and sunflowers. There are seats, swings and a barbecue in the garden; the outbuildings are still used to store farm equipment. Your house is bigger than it looks, with fresh, white-walled rooms and fairly minimalist furnishing – the whole place has a new and spotless feel. One end of the living room has pretty, original tiling and rustic dining furniture; the other, dark polished boards, an inviting sofa and wicker chairs. Black and white floor tiles gleam on the hall floor and the square, airy kitchen is designed to provide all you need. Upstairs are simple, pleasant bedrooms and a plain bathroom. There's a Sunday morning market nearby and a whole range of First World War museums, monuments and cemeteries to visit.

sleeps	6.
price	€230–€380.
rooms	3: 1 double, 2 twins, 1 bathroom, 1 separate wc.
closed	Never.

booking details

Bruno & Blandine Cailliez

tel	+33 (0)3 23 24 41 44
fax	+33 (0)3 23 24 43 55
e-mail	blandine.cailliez@wanadoo.fr
web	www.gitedeverneuil.fr.st

map 6   entry 6

Ferme de Ressons
Mont St Martin, Aisne

Feel the simple country lives which have been played out within these old walls. There's nothing fancy or pretentious about this rustic farm cottage, with its ancient beams, neat brick fireplace and almost secret access. Come for deep peace, soothing views and champagne vineyards and, if you wish, join Valérie and Jean-Paul and their B&B guests for excellent and convivial dinners cooked in the grand farmhouse across the gardens (just book in advance). Or gather around the old square wooden table in your simple kitchen with its incongruously grand Henri II dresser and all mod cons. Other rooms have an eclectic mix of antique and modern furniture, including one of the bedrooms with its horizontally-striped wallpaper in red, green and blue, green quilted bed and butter-yellow curtains. You may fish on the lake; ask Valérie about permits and rods before you arrive. Restaurants and shops are two miles off. The hilly forests of the Montagne de Reims, south-east of here, provide unexpectedly rich walking and a sharp contrast to the flat vineyards, and the beech woods at Verzy are believed to be over 500 years old. *B&B also.*

sleeps	6.
price	€230–€305.
rooms	3: 1 double, 2 twins, 1 bathroom.
closed	Never.

booking details

	Valérie & Jean-Paul Ferry
tel	+33 (0)3 23 74 71 00
fax	+33 (0)3 23 74 28 88

Le Point du Jour
Mont St Martin, Aisne

Valérie, the French owner, is an architect and has left her creative stamp on the house's attractively simple rooms, with their wonderful wide views over the champagne vineyards. This 19th-century village house, two kilometres from the Ferry's farm, exudes light, space and homeliness. The big living room has beams, a new fireplace, an old piano and a modern, round glass and chrome dining table. Upstairs, parquet floors, pretty woven cotton curtains with floral patterns and a splendid, ornately carved 19th-century Portuguese bed. One slopey-ceilinged twin has more sober country-style beds, with sunflower-yellow covers and curtains. Dine out on the south-facing terrace or in the garden, from where you can stride straight out into fields and woods. Your hosts do B&B a mile away, and are ready with help and advice. They'll probably recommend you head for one of the many champagne *maisons* in Reims, a 20-minute drive, for a tasting of the bubbly stuff. Those of Mumm, Taittinger and Piper-Heidseick allow you to join (paying) tours without an appointment, including a *dégustation*. B&B also.

sleeps	6.
price	€275–€380.
rooms	3: 1 double, 2 twins, 1 bathroom, 1 shower room, 1 separate wc.
closed	Never.

booking details

	Valérie & Jean-Paul Ferry
tel	+33 (0)3 23 74 71 00
fax	+33 (0)3 23 74 28 88

map 6   entry 8

Gîte de Cramant
Cramant, Marne

A simple little cottage in a village in Champagne. It is distinctly homely, French without the frills, a little like a doll's house – one you can live in very comfortably. The Charbonniers, who do B&B on the spot, are a delightful couple and work hard to keep everyone happy; you may even arrange to have breakfast with them if you prefer. Cosy bedrooms are upstairs and share a neat little bathroom; the double comes in yellow and blue and has a couple of beams, the twin has small beds dressed in patchwork quilts, perfect for children. Downstairs, an open-plan kitchen/sitting/dining room with a tiled floor and neatly beamed ceiling – simply decorated, typically French. There's a round dining table and a decorative fireplace, too, and lots of pretty china. Outside, a postage-stamp lawn is flanked on one side by an old stone wall up which creepers clamber, and there are chairs, a café table and a barbecue, so you can eat outside. Epernay is seven kilometres away and has a fine market and lots of champagne; if you overdo it, head to Reims and its cathedral to beg forgiveness. *Babysitting available. B&B also.*

sleeps	4-6.
price	€260.
rooms	2: 1 double, 1 twin, 1 sofabed in sitting room, 1 bathroom.
closed	Never.

booking details

	Éric & Sylvie Charbonnier
tel	+33 (0)3 26 57 95 34
fax	+33 (0)3 26 51 60 23
e-mail	eric-sylvie@wanadoo.fr
web	www.ericsylvie.com

Auprès de l'Église

Oyes, Marne

Artist Julia Morison fell in love with this peaceful old place, then restored in her inimitable style. She has left some interior walls as she found them with the mason's scribbles intact; the house is full of surprises. Upstairs bedrooms and the bathroom are separated by bookcases and an attic stair; the ground floor is a mix of country house and Julia's modern art. Kitchen, dining and living rooms merge into one airy space that overlooks Oyes church on one side, the courtyard on the other. Sit out in the sun and sip the local champagne – it's delicious – as you wait for the barbecue to smoulder. Quirky objects from brocantes abound, like zinc containers in all shapes and sizes, and there is no shortage of mod cons: dishwasher, washing machine, DVD. Two further bedrooms lead off the hall, one with a painted ceiling, and beds are king- or queen-size. This is an atmospheric house in an undiscovered area. Oyes is on the doorstep, charming Sezanne a 20-minute drive, and the surrounding marshlands (now drained, but an unwelcome surprise for the invading soldiers of World War I) are a birdwatchers' paradise.

sleeps	8.
price	€ 800–€ 1,450. Heating supplement € 70 in winter.
rooms	4: 2 doubles, 1 twin/double, 1 twin, 1 bathroom, 1 shower room downstairs.
closed	Christmas.

booking details

	Sally Velvin
tel	+64 4 476 3472 (New Zealand)
fax	+64 4 476 3472 (New Zealand)
e-mail	villachampagnefrance@xtra.co.nz
web	www.aupresdeleglise.com

map 6   entry 10

Les Hirondelles
Orbey, Haut-Rhin

Nature lovers will find it hard to leave. Swallows and redstarts nest in the eaves, deer populate the forests, and all around, breathtaking views stretch across the valley to the Black Forest beyond. Your little granite barn is inviting and cosy with pine-panelled walls, wooden or carpeted floors, good, plain furniture and central heating for the cold months. In summer walk into the mountains from the front door, in winter don your skis; at any time of year follow the Route de Vin to sample the area's delicious wines. Some of the fiercest fighting in both world wars took place here, and you can see World War II bullet-holes in the farmhouse next door where John, the friendly English owner, runs a B&B. The front-line trenches from World War I and a museum are a 10-minute drive away. In summer the locals compete for the best scarecrow and you'll see them in all shapes and sizes in the local villages... Orby, just up the road, has everything you need, including a cinema. Try Munster cheese from the farm shop opposite – it's wonderfully pungent – and don't miss out on the stunning medieval walled village of Riquewihr. *B&B also.*

sleeps	4-7.
price	€462.
rooms	2: 1 family room for 3, 1 twin, 1 sofabed, 1 shower room.
closed	Never.

booking details

John Kennedy
tel +33 (0)3 89 71 34 96
fax +33 (0)3 89 71 34 96
e-mail jhken1@aol.com

La Maison Tupinier

Cluny, Saône-et-Loire

A huge, elegant apartment for two in a hugely civilised town. Luc owns an antique shop and lives in this 16th-century house of a judge. He has the first floor, you have the second, and there's a bakery next door for your croissants. A spiral stone stair leads up to stately quarters: high ceilings with decorated beams, gleaming terracotta floors, a Louis XIV fireplace, a marble wash basin. A large, light hall opens to the living room, distinguished with pale sofabed, painted upholstered chairs, a big old cupboard that hides the linen, a walnut dining table under windows with fine drapes. The bedroom has perfect proportions and is painted the colour of corn; the kitchen has ornate tiles and a cream farmhouse table (dishwasher and fridge/freezer, too). The bathroom has an *oeil de boeuf* window and a radiator for your towels. On a lower floor a door leads onto an open-roofed gallery that looks onto Luc's courtyard and garden: the ideal spot for those just-baked croissants. It is surprisingly peaceful here, in the centre of town, yet almost everything is outside your door. Very special. *Free parking nearby. Flexible changeover day.*

sleeps	2-4.
price	€ 750–€ 850.
rooms	1 double, 1 sofabed in sitting room, 1 bathroom.
closed	January-February.

booking details

Luc du Mesnil du Buisson
tel +33 (0)3 85 59 27 67/30 81

map 12   entry 12

Le Nid

Château, Saône-et-Loire

Another artist-owner, another dreamy place. This is an 18th-century Burgundian farmhouse that neatly divides into three apartments. There is an understated elegance, as if everything has been designed, but quietly so. Wander at will: here are old stone floors, exposed limestone walls, high ceilings, colour added in small doses – a crisp sense of light and space. In the largest living room, a cream sofa, two blue armchairs, books, candles, clever lighting, a big fireplace. Two apartments have kitchenettes; Rouge-Gorge's kitchen has table and chairs to serve a multitude, and every modern thing. A broad stone stair leads from here to a hallway and delightful bedrooms. Good art hangs on the walls – sketches, old oils, watercolours – while Karen's sculpture is dotted about the grounds. The pool bathes in the sun, encircled by loungers and lawn. Beyond, fields and woodland stretch across the hills. This part of France has been compared to Tuscany, only it is less busy, and your hosts, who do B&B in the big house next door, will cheerfully help you discover the region – and give cookery lessons in French. *B&B also.*

sleeps	Rouge-Gorge: 4. Le Pinson: 2-6. La Chouette: 2-4. Whole house sleeps 10-11 + cot.
price	RG € 690–€ 785. LP € 495–€ 645. LC € 425–€ 535. Whole house € 1,500–€ 1,800.
rooms	RG: 2 doubles, 2 baths. LP: 1 twin, 2 sofabeds, 1 bath, 1 shower. LC: 1 double, 1 sofabed, 1 bath.
closed	Never.

booking details

	Marc & Karen Keiser
tel	+33 (0)3 85 59 18 02
fax	+33 (0)3 85 59 86 98
e-mail	info@lenid-france.com
web	www.lenid-france.com

Abbaye de la Ferté

St Ambreuil, Saône-et-Loire

The Thenards have been here since the Revolution; they not only kept their heads but their château too. It is a jaw-dropper, with ornate arched windows and a wonderfully aristocratic feel. You get the old stables, once the mill; behind the house water spills over the weir and into the lake. You can fish here, even swim… or walk your socks off in the château's gorgeous parkland grounds and discover the ancient abbey. The setting is impossibly pretty, with sunlight filtering through the graceful branches of tall trees and bouncing off water lilies at anchor on the lake. The gîte – attractive, uncluttered, welcoming – is a great little spot for a family stay. You have exposed beams, wooden floors, generous windows; the double bedroom, reached via an outdoor stair, has an old armoire; the long, thin triple room comes in pretty yellows with beds running against the walls on both sides. There's a kitchen for eager cooks and a terrace on which to sit and relish the results. Venture beyond the gates and you'll find horses and bikes to ride – or head to Beaune for a glass of something special. *B&B also.*

sleeps	4-5.
price	€ 331–€ 618.
rooms	2: 1 double, 1 triple, 1 shower room.
closed	Never.

booking details

	Jacques & Virginie Thenard
tel	+33 (0)3 85 44 17 96
fax	+33 (0)3 85 44 17 96
e-mail	thenardjacques@aol.com
web	www.abbayeferte.com

map 12   entry 14

La Griottière

Fontaines, Saône-et-Loire

The *maison bourgeoise* dates to 1900 and was once part of a dairy farm. It is a little French gem, formal yet pretty, with two stone staircases leading up to the front door and blue-shuttered windows on both sides. Within, nothing fussy – just a cool, clean elegance that runs throughout. In the bedroom you have pale stripes on the walls, African-themed covers and cushions on the bed. The dining room and sitting room, on the same level, have polished floorboards dressed with rugs, a glass coffee table, a red-checked sofa with matching fauteuil. The kitchen is small, modern, well-equipped; the laundry room and shower room are below. Dine in summer under grand trees at the foot of the stone stairs and look out on the pretty, well-kept garden and orchard. Monsieur and his wife do B&B next door; he is utterly charming – cheerful, knowledgeable, welcoming – and still helps out on a local wine estate (happy to arrange visits and tastings). A canal flows through the village and a cycle path follows it for miles – borrow the bikes. Good walks, fine gardens and local markets all wait. *B&B also.*

sleeps	2-4.
price	€ 385–€ 420.
rooms	1 double, 1 sofabed, 1 shower room, 2 separate wcs.
closed	December.

booking details

Serge Doumenc
tel +33 (0)3 85 91 48 47
e-mail lagriottiere@infonie.fr
web www.griottiere.com

Les Hêtres Rouges
Argilly, Côte-d'Or

The mood is traditional, the furniture antique, and the gardens full of flowers stretch serenely as far as the eye can see: little would seem to have changed since the Duke of Burgundy came here at weekends to hunt. Madame, who looks after her B&B guests in the hunting lodge next door, used to run an antique shop and the past is something in which she is well versed. Restoring old buildings is her passion and she has put her artistic talent to good use in renovating and decorating this lovely wisteria-draped outbuilding. Downstairs rooms are a festival of warm ochres, pinks and blues which enhance the lovely antique furniture, and there's a fine working fireplace. The upstairs bedroom has a handsome brass bed, rich colourful fabrics and interesting *objets*. If you're a wine buff you'll know the names of the surrounding villages like Nuits Saint Georges and Pommard already; visit their *caves* for a tasting if your purse allows, or explore the pretty Côte d'Or along the GR7 and GR76 footpaths. There are plenty of restaurants within a 15-minute drive. *Flexible changeover day. B&B also.*

sleeps	2-3.
price	€ 770 for 2, € 920 for 3.
rooms	1 double with extra single bed, 1 bathroom.
closed	Never.

booking details

	Jean-François & Christiane Bugnet
tel	+33 (0)3 80 62 53 98
fax	+33 (0)3 80 62 54 85
e-mail	leshetresrouges2@wanadoo.fr
web	www.leshetresrouges.com

map 12   entry 16

15 rue Maizières
Beaune, Côte-d'Or

Loft-house living meets 12th-century France. This exquisite apartment was part of the Abbey de Maizières until the Revolution and is entered via a 500-year old spiral stone stair. It stands on a medieval street near the town ramparts, one of the oldest buildings in an ancient city – an architectural masterpiece spread over three levels, renovated with dazzling, contemporary economy. Floors are of polished stone and oak parquet, walls of exposed stone and shining limewash, and bedrooms have beds dressed in white linen scattered with silk cushions. There are nuances of colour from honey to pink, funky armchairs in black and white, stiff curtains of purple taffeta. Halogen lighting soothes, the stereo music system is discreet, there's a curved screen of light oak to separate sitting room from dining room and the kitchen is stylish in stainless steel and granite. There's even a cellar in which to store your new acquisitions: Beaune is the centre of the Burgundy wine trade and vineyard tours can be arranged. The market place is a three-minute walk, yet the district is one of the quietest in town. Exceptional. *Free parking three-minute walk.*

sleeps	4.
price	€ 840–€ 1,145.
rooms	2 doubles, 1 bathroom, 1 separate wc.
closed	Never.

booking details

Penny & Ben Martin

tel	+33 (0)3 80 20 19 13
fax	+33 (0)3 80 20 19 13
e-mail	beaune-apart@club-internet.fr
web	www.beaune-apart.com

Rose Cottage

Painblanc, Côte-d'Or

The best of Burgundy: vineyards, gastronomic eateries and the Morvan National Park are within easy reach. Here in tranquil Painblanc (literally, 'white bread') you get a taste of French village life – the main event of the week is the visit of the butcher's and baker's vans. Prettily draped in wisteria and roses, this 19th-century stone village house has been attractively restored by English owners Penny and Ben who live in a nearby village and will be there to settle you in. The centrepiece is the kitchen: sunny and homely, with a large wooden table to gather around for feasts in front of the woodburner. Logs are thoughtfully provided. The original hexagonal terracotta floor tiles (cosy with rugs), handsome oak beams and open fire are all intact, as are the endearingly sloping floors of the apricot and cream bedrooms. On the floor of the bathroom downstairs, the painted feet of humans and geese! Take lazy, long lunches under the enormous willow tree in the garden and orchard – scented with honeysuckle, roses and wisteria, replete with pond full of vocal frogs. Shop in pretty Bligny sur Ouche, a five-mile drive.

sleeps	6-7 + cot.
price	€450-€600.
rooms	3: 1 double, 1 twin, 1 triple with cot, 1 bathroom, 1 shower room, 2 separate wcs.
closed	Never.

booking details

	Penny & Ben Martin
tel	+33 (0)3 80 20 19 13
fax	+33 (0)3 80 20 19 13
e-mail	benpenny.martin@club-internet.fr

map 12   entry 18

Well Cottage
Painblanc, Côte-d'Or

So pretty here in early summer, with the cowslips, lady's smock and wild orchids. In autumn there are the golden colours of the woods and vines, and deer, red kite and buzzards to spot. Whenever you come, you'll love this 19th-century cottage, with its long lazy views over the garden to fields and the upper part of the tranquil village. Among a cluster of cottages and farm buildings on a quiet side street, the gîte, deceptively large, has been attractively restored by English owners Penny and Ben. Oak beams, old and vast, dominate the large living/dining room/kitchen which has attractive features like a little stone alcove and a window seat. There's a modern terracotta tiled floor, primrose-yellow colours, a comfy sofa, a *chaise longue* and a woodburner (logs free of charge). An open oak staircase leads to simple carpeted bedrooms with sloping beamed ceilings and velux windows. The garden (with slide) is sun-filled from early morning to mid-evening in summer – a private space and you are not overlooked. Make time for some serious gastronomy – and for wine-tasting in the famous Burgundy vineyards of the Côte de Nuits.

sleeps	4-5.
price	€ 340-€ 490.
rooms	2: 1 twin, 1 family room for 3, 1 shower room, 1 separate wc.
closed	Never.

booking details

	Penny & Ben Martin
tel	+33 (0)3 80 20 19 13
fax	+33 (0)3 80 20 19 13
e-mail	benpenny.martin@club-internet.fr

Chateau de Créancey
Créancey, Côte-d'Or

In the grounds of a breathtakingly beautiful château, with a moat running past the kitchen door and, opposite, its own dovecote with resident owl, this listed 14th-century tower is a truly special place. Fiona – ex-Sotheby's – and her French husband, Bruno, have restored it with impeccable taste and passionate respect for the building's original materials and character. Arrow slits – surprisingly light – are your windows, and an old wooden staircase twists its crooked way upstairs. French country furniture, quarry-tiled floors, muted pink walls and an open log fire create a mood of warm elegance in the spotless living/dining room, and in the double bedroom upstairs are the original 14th-century beams. There's a small oak-fitted kitchen with flagstone floors, very well-equipped. Eat on the terrace by the moat to the sound of hoopoes as you quaff those Burgundy wines. Fiona is delightful, does B&B in the château and will advise you on the region: discover the rugged Côte d'Or – and its wine-tasting châteaux – on foot or by bike. *Because of moat, children must be able to swim. B&B also.*

sleeps	4.
price	€ 480–€ 640.
rooms	2: 1 double, 1 twin, 1 shower room.
closed	Never.

booking details

	Fiona de Wulf
tel	+33 (0)3 80 90 57 50
fax	+33 (0)3 80 90 57 51
e-mail	chateau@creancey.com
web	www.creancey.com

map 12   entry 20

Hameau de Nailly – La Maison de Grand-mère

Liernais, Côte-d'Or

The stoneware crockery was made by the owners who run a pottery in nearby Vandenesse-en-Auxois; their artistic touch is evident in the colourful, simple furnishings of this lovely farmhouse. They follow a long tradition of craftsmanship, for the house once belonged to the clog-maker – you'll see his bench in the old workshop. Unwind after a day's walking or birdwatching around the farmhouse table in the homely terracotta-floored dining room/kitchen, with cheerful ceramic wall tiles, the original stone sink and bread oven and a dresser-full of games and books. There's no shortage of mod cons either. The Williams have skilfully and unselfconsciously kept the feel of a 1920s farmhouse; there's a glass-fronted stove and the bedrooms still have the original rose-sprigged wallpaper, antique beds and (new, handmade) patchwork bedcovers. Children have a play area in the loft and an acre of walled garden with orchard, hammock, barbecue, even a playhouse where the chickens once lived. Foodies, too, will be in heaven: Saulieu, with its famous Côte d'Or restaurant, is nearby, as are numerous Burgundy wine *caves*.

sleeps	4-6 + cot.
price	€340-€610.
rooms	2: 1 double, 1 family room for 4, 1 bathroom.
closed	Never.

booking details

Mary Williams

tel	+33 (0)3 80 49 29 19
fax	+33 (0)3 80 49 29 19

Domaine de La Chaux – Le Château

Alligny en Morvan, Nièvre

La Chaux is more village than domaine. Rent a small part of it – or the whole gorgeous place for an anniversary or wedding. Madame de Chambure lives in the middle of it all, sparkles with energy and exercises a benign rule, delighting in bringing families and friends together. The peace enfolds you and the magnolias and the ancient trees are beautiful in spring. The old hunting lodge, or château (below), is where Madame herself once lived, and its vast warren of rooms has barely changed over the years – in spite of the happy addition of new kitchen, modern plumbing and some elegant wrought-iron furniture. Two dining rooms, two salons, all with open fires: a warm, ample place for a large party. It has that wonderful French feel, with stippled, faux-marble walls, fine furniture dating from Louis XV onwards, polished parquet – a gentle elegance touched with eccentricity. Eleven bedrooms, several bathrooms and a dressing room share the top two storeys; views swoop over parkland and hills; you have everything you could possibly need, from a library full of books to TV, table tennis and loungers. *See next page.*

sleeps	Château sleeps 15.
price	€ 1,900 per week.
rooms	11: 3 doubles with wcs, 1 double, 7 singles, 3 bathrooms, 3 shower rooms, 3 separate wcs.
closed	Never.

booking details

	Alice de Chambure
tel	+33 (0)3 86 76 10 10
fax	+33 (0)3 86 76 10 10
e-mail	giteslachaux@wanadoo.fr

map 12   entry 22

Domaine de La Chaux – Moines & Roses

Alligny en Morvan, Nièvre

Moines is great fun, and its monk-ish name is reflected in the décor – there's a refreshing, monastic simplicity. Bedrooms on the second floor, in a row of monks' cells, have two *salles d'eau* between them – each graced with three unmonastic sinks set in granite. Showers are downstairs on the ground floor, so you may suffer a bit… The two main bedrooms have wcs and basins en suite. It's a big, delightful space where you could happily hole up for a week with friends. Warm colours, solid beams, terracotta floors, three stairs; you have a library and a *salle de séjour* (above) with antique trestle tables and rush-seated, ladderback chairs. A carved statue of the Virgin Mary stands in one corner, two cream-coloured fauteuils pull up by the fire. And what a hearth – it's big enough to fit a small tree, and can belt out quite a heat on winter days. Across a small meadow is Roses (below), a very charming gite with four bedrooms (two in the attic) and another lovely fireplace. With its fine trestle table and wood-panelled walls it has a similarly medieval feel, but is smaller, cosier and perfect for six. *Shared laundry.*

sleeps	Moines: 15-18. Roses: 6.
price	Moines € 1,335. Roses € 540.
rooms	Moines: 3 doubles, 1 twin, 1 single, 1 family room for 3, 1 family room for 6, 2 shower rooms, 3 separate wc. Roses: 1 double, 1 twin, 2 singles, 1 bathroom, 1 separate wc.
closed	Never.

booking details

Alice de Chambure

tel	+33 (0)3 86 76 10 10
fax	+33 (0)3 86 76 10 10
e-mail	giteslachaux@wanadoo.fr

Domaine de La Chaux – Chèvrefeuille & Glycines

Alligny en Morvan, Nièvre

These two gîtes are a step apart – Chèvrefeuille (Honeysuckle) with its farmhouse feel, and the more modern Glycines (Wisteria), custom-made for wheelchairs, and with its own washing machine. Both sleep six. Glycines' rooms are on the ground floor of the last stone cottage in a row of four (above) – clean lines, pale beech, dark wicker. Chèvrefeuille has two storeys and a charming outside stone stair; its floors are new and tiled, its furniture a mix of country antique and good modern, with a big squishy sofa and russet muslin drapes (below). There's ping-pong on the estate, trout-fishing in crystal-clear creeks beyond, kayaking on the Cure. You are bang in the middle of the Morvan National Park, a wild area of central France distinguished by vast forests of beech and oak, moorland and lakes. Criss-crossed by rapids, the area is a dream for white water enthusiasts. The walking, too, is exceptional, so take maps and go off the beaten track. Come for red and roe deer, wild boar and badgers, buzzards and woodpeckers. In the gentler, more pastoral north, there are carpets of wild flowers in spring. *Shared laundry.*

sleeps	Chèvrefeuille: 6. Glycines: 6.
price	Chèvrefeuille €540. Glycines €550.
rooms	Chèvrefeuille: 2 doubles, 1 twin, 1 bathroom. Glycines: 2 doubles, 2 singles, 1 shower room, 1 separate wc.
closed	Never.

booking details

Alice de Chambure

tel	+33 (0)3 86 76 10 10
fax	+33 (0)3 86 76 10 10
e-mail	giteslachaux@wanadoo.fr

map 12   entry 24

Domaine de La Chaux – Iris & Clemetis

Alligny en Morvan, Nièvre

Every house in La Chaux has its own individual touch, but there's one feature they share: a huge country fireplace stacked with logs. So winter stays are as much of a pleasure as those of summer, and the logs are provided (at extra charge). Ground-floor gîtes Iris (above) and Clemetis sit opposite each other, with a good stretch of grass in between – they would be ideal for a family and grandparents on holiday together. Clemetis's raised fireplace dominates the main bedroom (below), giving this lovely, pale-walled, red-tiled room a country feel. The living area is open plan with the kitchen in the corner (stocked with all you need, dishwasher included); the second, bigger bedroom has three beds. Iris, too, is terracotta-tiled, with russet-brown drapes and good country furniture. Every house in the domaine has a barbecue and garden furniture, including loungers: summers are long and hot in the Haut Morvan. A visit to the Lac des Settons, the biggest man-made lake in Europe, will cool you down: sail, swim, waterski, windsurf or pedalo. And there's a magnificent *bateau mouche* for the less sporty. *Shared laundry.*

sleeps	Iris: 2. Clemetis: 4-6.
price	Iris € 240. Clemetis € 480.
rooms	Iris: 1 sofabed, 1 shower room, 1 separate wc. Clemetis: 1 double, 1 family room for 4, 1 bathroom, 1 separate wc.
closed	Never.

booking details

	Alice de Chambure
tel	+33 (0)3 86 76 10 10
fax	+33 (0)3 86 76 10 10
e-mail	giteslachaux@wanadoo.fr

1 place de la Fontaine

Arcy-sur-Cure, Yonne

A simple but charming one-up, one-down in a perfect Burgundian village – once the village bakery. You are right next door to the well and close to the ancient church that was on the pilgrim trail to St Jaques de Compostella. There is no garden, but the idea is that you plonk the table and chairs outside the front door, sit out French-style and indulge in a little local gossip. Or watch the passers by (and count the cars – there will be few). You are at the end of a wooded valley and it is wonderfully peaceful. The stone-flagged downstairs is dominated by the old bread oven, with woodburner – though our inspector also found three corkscrews. (Well, this is Burgundy and Chablis is only 20km away.) A quaint little stair leads to a fresh, white bedroom: a beautiful, simple, antique French bed, a bright rug on a stripped pine floor, two little windows with the loveliest views. There is also a single bed for a child, and, downstairs, a sofa to accommodate one more – though four could feel squashed on a rainy day. You eat at a blue and white check-clothed table: it's homely and inviting. Roger runs hot-air ballooning trips, so why not book a trip?

sleeps	2 + 2 children.
price	€ 305–€ 380.
rooms	1 double, 1 bathroom; children's beds available
closed	Never.

booking details

Roger & Naomi Bishop

tel	+33 (0)3 86 33 93 19
e-mail	rogerbishop@wanadoo.fr
web	www.burgundypropertyservices.com

map 6   entry 26

Maison de la Reine

Ligny le Châtel, Yonne

Stay here and follow in the steps of royalty: Marguerite de Bourgogne, Queen of Sicily and Jerusalem, lived in this stunning, listed *maison de maître* several centuries ago. Ceilings are high (with beams of course), colours warm and welcoming, rooms big and airy. Recline on the *chaise longue* in the living room and gaze onto the wisteria – glorious in May; behind is a massive walled garden, with fountain, box hedges and flowers. Children can paddle in the gently gurgling stream – a raging torrent in the rainy season! – which was once the millrace of the mill next door; the owners (who live an hour away) plan one day to install a pool. The kitchen is beautifully equipped and the bedrooms most comfortable, with good modern lighting and the odd French armoire. Thoroughly Gallicised, the Roses are both artists – she does still-life drawings while he paints classic and modern cars; you'll see their paintings around the house. You overhear the village church and are 10km from Chablis in one of the top wine producing areas of the world; be sure to plan some serious *dégustations. Children by arrangement.*

sleeps	12.
price	€ 1,600–€ 2,500.
rooms	6: 3 doubles, 3 twins, 6 bathrooms.
closed	Rarely.

booking details

	Stanley & Avril Rose
tel	+33 (0)3 86 81 06 81
fax	+33 (0)3 86 81 06 81
e-mail	avril.rose@free.fr
web	lavie.enrose.free.fr

Gare de l'Est

Paris

A quick run from the Eurostar platform yet in a quiet bourgeois street where a good solid church rubs shoulders with lots of trees and two restaurants, here is a deeply civilised place in which to stay and be Parisian. The rather scruffy staircase is soon to be redecorated; the space, art and smart comfort inside the second-floor flat are a surprise. It is fascinatingly hung with prints, engravings and paintings from 15th to 20th centuries. An eclectic choice of good furniture – quite a lot from the Far East – adds yet more personality. Beyond the hall is the blue-shelved dining space with its generous table; off it all other rooms lead: a snug little double with purple blinds and a wall of cupboards, a perfectly-equipped corridor kitchen, a modern white and steel bathroom... and a triple-windowed bedsitting room over the street where a fine Chinese screen shields the high square bed from the deep and tempting sofa. Glorious to wake to birdsong, rustling leaves and church chimes. All carpeted in biscuit tones, this is a very adult and interesting home that's ideal for transport to anywhere in the city.

sleeps	2–4.
price	€ 500; € 850 per fortnight.
rooms	2: 1 double, 1 double bed in sitting room, 1 bathroom.
closed	Never.

booking details

	Lindsay Sharp
tel	+44 (0)20 7942 4003
e-mail	l.sharp@nmsi.ac.uk

map 6   entry 28

Montparnasse district
Paris

No, that little white-faced blue-shuttered terrace house in a stunningly quiet cobbled alley is not a country village dream, it's a most delectable place that can be yours for a good, long summer stay in the centre of sophisticated Left Bank Paris. The hall, which also leads to another flat upstairs, welcomes you with shelves of books. To the left, a good square bedroom with a pleasingly eclectic mix of warm fabrics, honeycomb tiles, old chest and contemporary paintings. The new white and pine bathroom has space, all mod cons and good cupboards. To the right is the pretty, wood-ceilinged and very well-equipped kitchen/diner. Beyond lies the richly French sitting room – modern art alongside antiques, an alcove stuffed with music and books – and the inestimable privilege of the little patio with its table, chairs and plants. The second big bedroom is at the back with its smart bathroom. Public transport abounds, so do shops, restaurants and cafés. This is an ideal way to mix peace and quiet in a Parisian home with sightseeing and shopping, night life... or academic research. *B&B only October-June.*

sleeps	4.
price	€ 1,000.
rooms	2 doubles, 2 bathrooms.
closed	October-June.

booking details

	Janine Euvrard
tel	+33 (0)1 43 27 19 43
fax	+33 (0)1 43 27 19 43
e-mail	euvrard@club-internet.fr

Domaine des Basses Masures

Poigny la Forêt, Yvelines

There are riding stables nearby, so you can saddle up and go deep into the Rambouillet forest; it encircles this peaceful hamlet. Madame, who is friendly and informal, takes care of several fine horses. They graze in the field behind the house – do introduce yourself. The house is an old stables: long, low and stone-fronted, built in 1725 and covered in Virginia creeper and ancient wisteria. Madame lives in one end and does B&B; the gîte is at the other end. It is a homely little place with a cosy cottage feel. Whitewashed bedrooms are up in the eaves, carpeted and cosy, with sky-light windows and the odd beam. New beds are dressed in crisp cotton and fat pillows. The sitting room downstairs has a cheerful blue sofa that opens to a bed, a big oriental rug, modern wicker armchairs, an open fireplace and white-painted beams. There are views to the back of the surrounding fields. The kitchen, more functional than aesthetic, has a round dining table and is very well equipped; it leads into the garden, with outdoor furniture. Versailles is only 20 minutes, Paris 45 and there's excellent walking from the door. *B&B also.*

sleeps	4-6.
price	€ 600.
rooms	2 doubles, 1 sofabed, 2 bathrooms.
closed	Never.

booking details

Mme Walburg de Vernisy

tel	+33 (0)1 34 84 73 44
fax	+33 (0)1 34 84 73 44
e-mail	domainebassesmasures@wanadoo.fr
web	www.domaine-des-basses-masures.com

map 6   entry 30

Photography by Michael Busselle

normandy
& brittany

L'Onglée

L'Home Chamondot, Orne

A converted 19th-century barn that stands next to the Normandy farmhouse in which Alan and Jackie live. Rural France wraps itself around you. There are open fields to the front, woodland behind, and red squirrel, deer and buzzard nearby; follow the paths out from the house and you may see them. The cottage has been renovated from top-to-toe. There's a beamed ceiling, thick stone walls and a woodburner in the fireplace. The feel is light and airy, relaxed and user-friendly with all the comforts you need, from TV and CD player to dishwasher; books, videos, games and jigsaws, too. Outside are a good wooden table and chairs, parasol, barbecue and pool. The latter you share with B&B guests, but your garden is private and secluded. Bedrooms are pretty and beds are made up when you arrive. And if you don't feel like cooking, join the folk in the farmhouse for sociable dinners on the terrace. Jackie and Alan keep lots of rare-breed chickens, so eggs may be available. There's boules, table tennis, a raised pool; a field for football here, golf at Bellême. *B&B also.*

sleeps	6.
price	£225–£495.
rooms	3: 1 double, 2 twins, 2 shower rooms.
closed	Never.

booking details

Alan & Jackie Ainsworth

tel	+33 (0)2 33 73 81 46
fax	+33 (0)2 33 73 81 46
e-mail	jackieainsworth@hotmail.com

Château Le Bourg
Bures en Bray, Seine-Maritime

The 1860 *petit château* has tall windows, a grand position in the middle of the village and was once owned by the mayor of Dieppe. You get the top floor to yourself and with it the best views – of the village, church and surrounding low hills. The interior comes in comfortable, homely, château-style: high slanting ceilings (you are up in the eaves), colourful stylish fabrics, vibrant quilts, polished wooden floors. The odd beam runs from floor to ceiling and there are skylights and dormer windows. The master suite is big, the twin room smaller, one room has a mural and the beds are excellent. A spacious sitting room has sunny yellow walls, comfy sofas and much colour. Léonora, a retired lawyer from Hereford, is an excellent cook and you are welcome to join her for sumptuous dinners – 'bistro' or 'gastronomique'. Relax in the dining room decorated in the grand style: old oils, period wallpaper, candelabra on a mahogany table. And there is a garden to share, with barbecue and trees for your children to climb. Beyond, cows mow the meadows and the market town of Neufchatel is close. Wonderful. *B&B also.*

sleeps	6 + child.
price	€ 750.
rooms	3: 1 twin/double, 2 twins, 1 children's room, 1 bathroom, 2 shower rooms.
closed	Never.

booking details

	Léonora Macleod
tel	+33 (0)2 35 94 09 35
fax	+33 (0)2 35 94 09 35
e-mail	leonora.macleod@wanadoo.fr

map 5   entry 32

La Vallée Blonde
St Georges du Vièvre, Eure

You might expect Hansel and Gretel to step out of this fairytale, half-timbered cottage, deep in the Normandy woods. The only passers-by are the cows in the neighbouring fields, the only sounds that of the owl, cuckoo and woodpecker. Peace is yours as you eat out in the grassy glade under the geraniums; walks start from your tiny sky-blue front door. The house, once a bakehouse, has been simply furnished by its English owners; they have kept the wooden beams, brick and stone skirting and oak floor boards, and added local country furniture, interesting bric a brac and a kitchen with mini oven, hob and fridge. There's a traditional enamel Godin woodburner – with logs – in the sitting/dining room, and a bedroom in the rafters up a steep stair. Rouen and Honfleur are less than an hour away, the magical Abbaye de Bec Hellouin much nearer; be sure to visit the Château de Launay with its breathtaking Renaissance dovecot. There are shops in St Georges du Vièvrehere and a restaurant/bar in the nearby village; eat and be merry, then roll down the hill and up to bed. *No washing machine. Bring own linen.*

sleeps	2.
price	€ 273–€ 413.
rooms	1 double, 1 shower room downstairs.
closed	December–February.

booking details

Jennifer Murray
tel	+44 (0)1273 888033
fax	+44 (0)1273 245855
e-mail	jenmurray@20powis.fsnet.co.uk
web	www.normandy-cottage.co.uk

Clos Vorin

Triqueville, Eure

This blue and white timbered doll's house cottage is so pretty, and the idyllic apple orchards in which it stands so lush, you have to pinch yourself to believe it's real. Even when you've crept inside the blue-framed front door, the fairy tale continues: enchanting, embroidered voile curtains, colourful beams and, everywhere, clean pure space. This magical single-storey cottage is the creation of Eddy and Delphine, who live in the half-timbered house across the garden and who run the village newsagent's. There's a light and airy living room with lovely pale wooden floors and white walls which perfectly offset the dark antiques – piano included – and richly coloured handwoven rugs. Furniture is a successful mix of old and new, expensive and budget, and there's a wonderful baroque-style antique bed in the cosy bedroom. Drink in the peace of inland Normandy from the hammock suspended between the apple trees. Explore the area's half-timbered houses, walk its meadows and forests, and taste its tempting cheeses, creams and ciders.

sleeps	2-4.
price	€ 250–€ 330.
rooms	1 double, 1 sofabed in living room, 1 shower room.
closed	Never.

booking details

	Eddy & Delphine Cayeux
tel	+33 (0)2 32 56 53 15
fax	+33 (0)2 32 56 53 15
e-mail	gite.closvorin@wanadoo.fr
web	travel.to/giteclosvorin

map 5   entry 34

La Baronnière
Cordebugle, Calvados

A 200-year-old barn in the grounds of a manor house; nine lush acres and a forest encircle it, silencing the outside world. The barn once stood elsewhere; the Fleurys dismantled it piece by piece, then reassembled it 20 paces from the lake. (It had, apparently, been moved twice before.) It is a stunning colombage and brick building, renovated with boundless verve and sublime style. Pristine white walls soak up Normandy light, exposed beams and sand-blasted timber frames stand out like architectural ribs. Uncluttered bedrooms have garden views, trim carpets, contemporary wooden beds, maybe a hi-fi; nothing disappoints. The Fleurys run painting and cookery courses. You can gorge on a four-course feast at the manor house if you don't wish to cook, and they'll do your shopping for you before you arrive – just ask. Escape your private paradise and visit Monet's garden at Giverny, or stay put and watch koi carp commuting in the lake. You can also fall asleep to the sound of water; the stream that feeds the lake tumbles over a sluice gate close by. Too much camembert and calvados is inevitable – why resist? *B&B also.*

sleeps	6–8.
price	€400–€650.
rooms	3: 2 doubles, 1 twin, 1 bathroom, 1 shower room, 1 separate wc. Extra double and shower room available with separate entrance.
closed	Never.

booking details

	Christine Gilliatt-Fleury
tel	+33 (0)2 32 46 41 74
fax	+33 (0)2 32 44 26 09
web	www.labaronniere.connectfree.co.uk

La Boursaie – Le Pressoir

Livarot, Calvados

You can almost smell the intoxicating aroma of fermenting apples as you dine in the groove where the great granite wheel of this old cider press once turned. Apples and cider have made this superb cluster of half-timbered buildings tick since medieval times, and English owner Peter and his German wife Anja have done a remarkable job restoring them. Ancient cider barrels, wheelbarrows and apple baskets have been used around the grounds, and the interiors of what are now five holiday cottages are decorated with 'ciderabilia' Peter has bought over the years. The large open-plan living/dining room and kitchen have the biggest beams you've ever seen, an attractive terracotta-tiled floor, and quaint baroque-style pink velvet armchairs. Bedrooms have seagrass floors, and one is painted shocking raspberry. You won't be alone here, among the other guests, but with 65 acres of land there's room to roam. Watch the hovering buzzards from your private patch of garden, drink in the fabulous valley views, join the apple harvest in autumn. The Davies are happy to put up wedding parties, too, and can host and dine. *B&B also.*

sleeps	7.
price	€ 550–€ 1,165.
rooms	4: 2 doubles, 1 twin, 1 single, 1 bathroom, 1 shower room, 1 separate wc.
closed	February half-term.

booking details

Anja & Peter Davies

tel	+33 (0)2 31 63 14 20
fax	+33 (0)2 31 63 14 20
e-mail	laboursaie@wanadoo.fr

map 5   entry 36

La Boursaie – Le Trou Normand

Livarot, Calvados

Even the ducks and chickens live in a half-timbered cottage: no modern building disrupts the black-and-white beauty of this tranquil farmstead, hidden like a buried treasure in a fold between rolling hills. Couples will love this tiny cottage, where once calvados was distilled, with its long views of apple, cherry and pear orchards; relax by the cosy fire in the winter and enjoy a glass of home-produced cider. Décor is simple and clean, and cream walls are enhanced by deep-red tiled floors and softly beamed ceilings. You can see the original copper still downstairs, and there's a pretty bedroom under the rafters with a pale blue bed. If you love walking, join the Tour du Pays d'Auge GR footpath which runs almost from the door; there's riding at Deauville, on the beach (a half-hour drive) and the gardens of the Château de Vendeuvre nearby. Camembert, too, is a short drive, and the cheese's creator, Marie Harel, whose promotion campaign included sending free samples to Napoleon, is commemorated with a statue in the next-door village of Vimoutiers. *B&B also.*

sleeps	2.
price	€300–€460.
rooms	1 double, 1 shower room.
closed	February half-term.

booking details

	Anja & Peter Davies
tel	+33 (0)2 31 63 14 20
fax	+33 (0)2 31 63 14 20
e-mail	laboursaie@wanadoo.fr

La Boursaie – La Grange

Livarot, Calvados

You'll spot deer in the early mornings, and foxes, badgers and the occasional wild boar roam the magical woods. The hamlet takes its name from *bource*, the old Norman word for source. Drink in the ancient beauty of this cider farm under the shade of the 300-year-old walnut tree, which towers and protects like a friendly giant. Anja and Peter will bring walnuts, apples and pears to your cottage, and you can buy their home-produced cider and calvados. La Grange, with its stupendous views over the courtyard, duck pond and lush valley beyond, was formerly the hayloft, and has been attractively converted into a split-level first-floor apartment. Old beams have been skilfully used to divide the space, and blend well with the antique and new pine furniture and seagrass matting. Downstairs Peter has his watercolour and pastels studio – his work is on display in the cottages – and there's a dining room where the couple, both ex-catering, entertain guests to a weekly feast: Norman cooking at its best. They also hold art and cookery courses in spring and autumn. *B&B also.*

sleeps	4.
price	€ 450–€ 890.
rooms	2 twins, 1 shower room, 1 bathroom.
closed	February half-term.

booking details

	Anja & Peter Davies
tel	+33 (0)2 31 63 14 20
fax	+33 (0)2 31 63 14 20
e-mail	laboursaie@wanadoo.fr

map 5   entry 38

Les Petits Matins Bleus

Ste Marguerite de Viette, Calvados

This little red and black brick cottage with a romantic name was once a distillery where cider bubbled into calvados in an alembic on the fire. Now French windows lead to a neat, brick-paved terrace complete with pergola, climbing roses and vines. Pictures and ornaments, magazines and books, TV and hi-fi give the living room a homely yet uncluttered air. There's an old stone fireplace, a sofa, cane armchairs with cushions and a built-in cupboard with glasses for champagne and bowls for nibbles. The kitchen has piles of plates, plenty of pots and pans, good kitchen knives; even dishwasher tablets are provided. One bedroom is on the ground floor, made up with pretty blue and white checked sheets; a second bedroom is under the roof, thrillingly reached by wooden loft ladder – rickety but safe! Anne's welcome to her guests may include fresh flowers, wine, home-backed apple tart or fresh herbs. She also plans to put on themed weekends in the future. A place to relish. *B&B also.*

sleeps	4-5.
price	€170-€405.
rooms	2: 1 double, 1 twin/double with extra single available, 1 shower room.
closed	Never.

booking details

	Anne Bourbeau
tel	+33 (0)2 31 20 62 88
e-mail	matinsbleus14@wanadoo.fr

Les Aunaies – La Ferme des Rosiers & Le Pressoir
Mittois, Calvados

Bursting at the beams with character, La Ferme des Rosiers is poised on a wooded hillside overlooking the lovely Pays d'Auge. Lavish restoration has not turned it into a showpiece but a welcoming, family home; there are many personal touches, such as the the pretty plates on the dining room dresser bordered with lavender, sage and roses. One surprise is the small library with deep fuschia walls, leather-backed books, stripey French sofa and chairs, another is the hideaway gallery above the sitting room, comfortable with armchairs and reading lamps. A wealth of roof beams, joints and colombage – and an open fire – creates a superbly cosy, country feel. The kitchen has all that's needed for 12-14... including an electric kettle, not a priority in France! Bedrooms are reached via the gallery or a narrow stair. In the Pressoir: beams, good paintings, pretty curtains, rugs on tiled floors, a wooden stair up to carpeted bedrooms with wrought-iron beds. Both would be perfect for families: warm in winter, a big shared garden for summer – you may pluck the soft fruits – and safe, sandy beaches a 25-minute drive. *May be let together.*

sleeps	La Ferme 8-9 + cot.
	Le Pressoir 6-8 + cot.
price	La Ferme £460-£847.
	Le Pressoir £305-£610.
rooms	La Ferme 4: 2 doubles, 1 twin,
	1 triple, 1 bathroom, 2 shower rooms.
	Le Pressoir 3: 2 doubles, 1 twin,
	1 sofabed in living room, 1 bathroom,
	1 shower room, 1 separate wc.
closed	Rarely.

booking details

Ann Watts

tel	+44 (0)1992 575026
fax	+44 (0)1992 575026
e-mail	normandydream@yahoo.co.uk
web	www.geocities.com/normandydream

map 5   entry 40

La Ferme de l'Oudon – Les Tulipes
Berville, Calvados

This stone farmhouse has a pigeon tower and dates in parts from the 15th century. Although the days of farming have long gone, free-range hens survive, as do the ducks, who sail upon their pond with highfaluting grace. Monsieur and Madame have horses; guests can bring theirs. They are hands-on owners, do B&B in the main house, will provide picnic baskets on request and are extremely welcoming. Madame is learning English with the local Chamber of Commerce while Monsieur runs a kitchen-and-bathroom design company. His work is on view in the old dairy, now Les Tulipes – a light, bright, sunny, one-bedroom gîte sited at the far end of the courtyard. It is a well-nigh perfect ground-floor conversion that has been carried out with great flair and a consummate eye for detail. In the open-plan living area find colourwashed walls, an L-shaped sofabed, warm colours, wicker chairs and a corner kitchen *par excellence*. You have your own enclosed garden with table tennis, barbecue, furniture and darts, there's a potager where you can pick herbs and salads, and bicycles to rent. *Plans to enlarge gîte for 2004. B&B also.*

sleeps	2-4.
price	€230-€335.
rooms	1 double, 1 sofabed, 1 shower room.
closed	3-23 January.

booking details

Patrick & Dany Vesque-Mikaleff

tel	+33 (0)2 31 20 77 96
fax	+33 (0)2 31 20 67 13
e-mail	patrick.vesque@wanadoo.fr
web	www.fermedeloudon.com

La Ferme de l'Oudon – Le Pressoir

Berville, Calvados

Another enchanting farm building at Oudon, another fine restoration. This was the old cider press, its ground floor now a vast, light living space, comfortable and contemporary. You have red leather sofas, beautiful floor-to-ceiling curtains and a brand-new woodburning stove. A well-equipped kitchen leads to a private garden; there's a big sunny bedroom and a paved terrace; even the outdoor tables and chairs are ultra-stylish. Walls are white plaster or creamy exposed stone, floors are pale-tiled, there are old beams and joists and new windows to pull in the light. Ascend the new staircase with tiled treads to find a mezzanine with sofa and three skylit bedrooms under the eaves, one large, all delightful. Bathrooms shine. The friendly Vesques give you a bottle of cider, homemade jam and farm eggs on arrival, and everything is included: linen, electricity, logs. Twice a week there's *table d'hôtes* – a chance to meet the B&B and other guests over a civilised meal. The orchards, rich pastures and half-timbered manor houses of the Pays d'Aube are yours to discover. Superb. *B&B also. Shared pool ready August 2004.*

sleeps	6.
price	€ 590–€ 750.
rooms	3: 2 doubles, 1 twin, 2 bathrooms.
closed	Never.

booking details

Patrick & Dany Vesque-Mikaleff

tel	+33 (0)2 31 20 77 96
fax	+33 (0)2 31 20 67 13
e-mail	patrick.vesque@wanadoo.fr
web	www.fermedeloudon.com

map 5   entry 42

Manoir de Laize – Le Pressoir

Fontaine Le Pin, Calvados

Apples used to be pressed for cider and calvados in this grandiose, medieval *pressoir*. Across the lawns, pretty with blossoming apple trees in the spring (redolent with fruit in the autumn) is the 15th-century manor farmhouse where the owners live. Horses graze in the meadows, dogs and cats doze in the barns, and David and Emily do B&B. They're there when you need them, happy to give you advice on exploring this lovely, lush area. Inside, much country charm: ceilings are beamed, walls are soft-coloured, floors new-tiled, there are several antiques and plenty of space. The living area is open plan, with a kitchen in the corner, well equipped; French windows lead down a step to the walled patio with barbecue. Upstairs: new beds dressed in crisp white linen, a bathroom filled with soft towels. Central heating means you're a warm as toast in the winter. In summer, eat on the patio, relax on the front lawn, drink in the peace – the setting is heavenly. Stock up at the weekly market in Falaise – birthplace of William the Conqueror; cycle or canoe down the gorge of the Orne; pick wild flowers in spring. *B&B also. Babysitting.*

sleeps	6-7 + cot.
price	£275-£450.
rooms	3: 2 twins, 1 double with extra single bed & cot, 1 bathroom, 1 separate wc.
closed	Never.

booking details

David & Emily Lloyd
tel +33 (0)2 31 20 93 74
e-mail emlloy@aol.com

Le Clos St Bernard – Les Camelias & Les Fuchsias

Reviers, Calvados

The very first farmhouse built in this Normandy village – well placed for countryside and coast – has been transformed into two gîtes, and sits in the walled courtyard opposite the owner's house. Les Camelias, on the ground floor, has a living/kitchen room with exposed stone and beams, cane armchairs, floral drapes, a sofabed and dining table. There's an array of equipment in the kitchen, including a raclette machine and electric mixer. An open tread stair leads to carpeted blue and white bedrooms; the double has the original stone sink with spout, now a display unit, and a fitted pine wardrobe; the twin has English style pillows. A corner of lawn in the courtyard has been set aside for this gîte, complete with sun loungers, parasol, table, chairs and barbecue. Visitors can drive in to unload, then park safely outside; gates are securely locked at night. Les Fuchsias, on the first floor, is reached via a stone stair. It has a charmingly beamed kitchen/sitting room with pretty tiles and curtains and a white tiled floor; again, it is very well-equipped, even sporting a fondue set! *Electricity not included. B&B also.*

sleeps	Les Camelias: 5. Les Fuchsias: 2-4.
price	Les Camelias: € 244–€ 355. Les Fuchsias: € 275–€ 385.
rooms	Les Camelias: 3: 1 double, 1 twin, 1 single, 1 shower room. Les Fuchsias: 1 twin, 1 sofabed, 1 bathroom.
closed	July-August.

booking details

	Nicole Vandon
tel	+33 (0)2 31 37 87 82
fax	+33 (0)2 31 37 87 82
e-mail	nicole.vandon@free.fr
web	le-clos-st-bernard.st.bernard.ifrance.com

map 5   entry 44

Manoir des Doyens

Bayeux, Calvados

If military history is your thing, this 17th-century stone farmhouse is for you. Bayeux, with its famous tapestry, medieval cathedral and military cemetery, is within walking distance, the Normandy landing beaches are a short drive away, and Lt-Colonel Chilcott, the owner, is a military historian and will take you on a private battlefield tour if you are interested. He and his gentle wife moved here from the Isle of Wight and run a B&B in the main part of the farmhouse (once the property of the Deans of Bayeux, according to the Lt-Colonel). But even if military history isn't for you, you'll love the peace and space of this farm with its grassy courtyard, animals and ancient stone pond. The wing, where you lodge, also has its own walled garden for meals out, and you may use the barbecue. The kitchen and living room are plain but functional and furnishings basic and somewhat worn – but improve as you ascend: pretty antiques mingle with the modern furniture in the interconnecting gabled bedrooms upstairs. Perfect for a family with children. *B&B also.*

sleeps	2-7.
price	€ 198-€ 304.
rooms	2: 1 family room for 3, connected to 1 twin, sofabed downstairs, 1 bathroom, 1 separate wc.
closed	Never.

booking details

	Lt-Col & Mrs Chilcott
tel	+33 (0)2 31 22 39 09
fax	+33 (0)2 31 21 97 84
e-mail	chilcott@mail.cpod.fr

La Commune

Cricqueville en Bessin, Calvados

La Commune is well named – there is an easy feel to the place. It is not designer-decorated, preferring a low-key, easy-going style. One wall is rag-rolled orange, the roof above the kitchen is open to the ceiling and there's a bedroom on the landing. The house, a former stables and hay barn, has the odd exposed stone wall and is eclectically furnished: an old church pew, a card table topped with green baize, a hi-fi system that refuses to play pirated CDs. The whole of the downstairs is open plan, with a bar kitchen and a terracotta-tiled floor; French windows open to a decked terrace (with barbecue) shaded by roses climbing over a pergola-style roof. Upstairs, bedrooms are quite simple, and one has views of the front garden, others over neighbouring fields. The Goupils live next door and have lavished love on the garden: large, lush, lawned, with a small natural pond in one corner – the star of the place. The setting is glorious, and La Commune is ideal for a free-range family who like a little style but not too much formality. The travelling baker passes by each morning at about 10.30, so late breakfasts are obligatory.

sleeps	4-6.
price	€ 310–€ 495.
rooms	3: 1 double, 1 double on mezzanine, 1 twin, 1 bathroom, 1 separate wc.
closed	Never.

booking details

	Jehan-François Goupil
tel	+33 (0)2 31 22 66 82
e-mail	jehan-francois.goupil@wanadoo.fr

map 4   entry 46

Manoir de la Rivière

Géfosse Fontenay, Calvados

It was once the watchtower for this medieval fortified farm and you can still see the loopholes through which the guards kept an eye on the enemy. All you'll spy today are the Leharivels' 80-odd dairy cows, munching on the lush pasture of the rugged Cotentin peninsula. Isolated at the end of the manor house walled garden, this doll's house gem is the ultimate lovers' getaway. Arrive in winter and owner Isabelle will have lit a fire for you in the woodburner; come in summer and you'll dine on a sun-drenched terrace before trotting up the outside stone steps for a siesta. In the bedroom, pristine exposed stone walls and matching bedcovers and curtains in red and white create a mood of light and calm. A steep staircase leads down to the tiny beamed living room, just big enough for a sofa to snuggle up in by the fire, and there's a kitchenette in one corner. The beach is a stroll away, and the D-day beaches, including Pointe du Hoc on Omaha beach, where you'll still see German bunkers and shellholes in the cliffs, are nearby. Bliss. *Second gîte in manor house. B&B also.*

sleeps	2.
price	€ 230–€ 330.
rooms	1 double, 1 shower room.
closed	Rarely.

booking details

	Gérard & Isabelle Leharivel
tel	+33 (0)2 31 22 64 45
fax	+33 (0)2 31 22 01 18
e-mail	manoirdelariviere@mageos.com
web	www.chez.com/manoirdelariviere

Porte à Cabin

Tout près de l'arbre, Val-d'Oise

Our photographer, after a heroic trek across wooded hills, found the place boarded up – a shame, for the surprises are all inside. The owners have taken minimalism to a new level, providing a startling contrast between the richly textured exterior – with part-exposed brick-and-plaster walls and original wooden shutters – and the plain, sparkling interior. It is one open space, a sea of stainless steel and polished wood upon which float islands of function: kitchen units, cupboards and furniture able to glide on air at the touch of a button, and move elsewhere according to whim. Even the beds do it, providing an experience that few have had: the hover-bed. The photograph of the front door does it scant justice; note the inclusion of a few old Roman bricks in the supporting wall. If you look carefully you can see the well-preserved bullet holes from the day the house was first opened to the self-catering public. The first renter found the house shut and vented his fury on the door. Oh well – such is life in the 'hospitality' business. *For improved lighting, bring a torch or a hammer.*

sleeps	Anyone.
price	A lot for a little. It doesn't seem fair really...
rooms	None – just a bed, tethered to a post.
closed	All the time, hence the bullet holes.

booking details

	M Jacques Le Chac
tel	118811118118811
fax	12
e-mail	y@il-quelqun.la?
web	www...jenemesouviensplus...

map 0   entry 48

La Fèvrerie No 1

Ste Geneviève, Manche

The creeper-clad 16th-century house was a farm labourer's cottage; the other half is rented out too (see opposite), and each has its own private front garden, divided by a high hedge. The owners are a delight: she charming, bubbly and elegant, he full of kindness; together they've grown vegetables on their farm near the sea for as long as they can remember. They're now retired and run an idyllic B&B 50 yards down the lane. Madame's passion is interior decoration, and it shows: ancient-beamed rooms are furnished with solid, comfortable sofas and chairs, beautiful country antiques, plain or checked drapes. The kitchen is both practical and pretty, and a wooden, open-tread stair leads from the large open-plan living/dining room to charming bedrooms above. The tiny fishing village of Barfleur is just across the fields, and the invasion beaches a short drive to the south. In summer you can pop over to the nearby island of Tatihou for atmospheric concerts. Don't forget to taste the local oysters. *Supplement for cleaning at end of stay. B&B also.*

sleeps	4–5.
price	€285–€475.
rooms	2: 1 twin, 1 triple, 1 bathroom.
closed	Never.

booking details

	Marie-France & Maurice Caillet
tel	+33 (0)2 33 54 33 53
fax	+33 (0)2 33 22 12 50

La Fèvrerie No 2

Ste Geneviève, Manche

The old stone cottage is buffered from the rugged rocky Normandy coast by a swathe of dreamy fields, where Monsieur Caillet's racehorses graze. The owners are a sparkling and cultivated couple who have given up vegetable farming and full-time racehorse breeding to run a successful B&B nearby, although Monsieur still breeds a few horses every year. Inside the large living/dining room, a magnificent stone fireplace, chunky beams, exposed stone or whitewashed walls, French windows with cheeful yellow drapes that lead to a small patio for dining out. A delicious retreat, whose pretty carpeted bedrooms have dark antique furniture, charming French wallpapers and tranquil views over surrounding fields. Explore the Cotentin peninsula on foot, visit the weekly markets at Barfleur and St Pierre Église, or stroll along the bay in attractive St-Vaast-la-Hougue where Edward III landed on his way to Crécy. There are some excellent seafood restaurants in little Barfleur, a two-mile drive, and in Saint-Vaast. *Supplement for cleaning at end of stay. B&B also.*

sleeps	4-5.
price	€ 285-€ 475.
rooms	2: 1 twin, 1 family room for 3, 1 shower room, 1 separate wc.
closed	Never.

booking details

	Marie-France & Maurice Caillet
tel	+33 (0)2 33 54 33 53
fax	+33 (0)2 33 22 12 50

map 4   entry 50

Capel

Urville Nacqueville, Manche

Michel, keen sailor and builder of submarines, wanted a view of the sea; Éliane craved an old house built in traditional Normandy stone. *Et voilà!* this 200-year-old spinner's cottage in a friendly hamlet on the north-west tip of the Cotentin peninsula offered both – and convenience too: the cross-Channel ferry at Cherbourg is just 12km away. (If you arrive car-free, Élaine will pick you up and drop you off – happily.) One day Michel and Éliane plan to retire here – they currently live nearby – but Michel will be delighted to take you off sailing if you ask in advance. Landlubbers and seafarers alike will love the views of the glistening bay from the north side. There's a sheltered south-facing patio; steps lead up to steep-sloped, shrub-filled garden. Inside, white walls, dark old beams, a fine stone fireplace in the living/dining room; tiled floors are modern and furniture a mix of old and new. Pick your bedroom according to whether you want views of sea or garden. After a day on the beach, eat out on the patio, or in the restaurant 500m away. *B&B also.*

sleeps	5.
price	€223–€451.
rooms	3: 1 double, 1 twin, 1 single, 1 shower room downstairs, 1 separate wc.
closed	Never.

booking details

	Michel & Éliane Thomas
tel	+33 (0)2 33 03 58 16
fax	+33 (0)2 33 03 58 16
e-mail	thomas.eudal@wanadoo.fr
web	www.chez.com/lahague/hebergem/gite/thomas.htm

Les Sources
Surtainville, Manche

A maze of narrow lanes between high banks and hedges bring you at last to Les Sources. Hydrangeas and old-fashioned roses surround the early 19th-century longère, newly restored and thoughtfully equipped by Roger and Sandra. They used to own a Michelin-starred inn in Gloucestershire and understand perfectly what makes a good holiday home. They'll also cook dinner one evening – just ask. The rooms are beamed and attractively furnished, and the big granite fireplace in the sitting room is just the place to curl up by with a book. Open-tread stairs lead to the first floor (the bathroom is on the ground floor) with a landing bedroom with a single bed and a child's crib screened by a heavy curtain. One of the other bedrooms, up a couple of steps, has a big roof window overlooking the garden. It's a lovely place – nearly an acre of lawns, trees and shrubs, with a stream forming the boundary on one side. There's a herb garden, too, and an orchard full of cherry trees, plums and apples. All around are fields and the sea is less than two miles, with deserted sandy beaches and a view of Jersey. *Babysitting available. French cookery courses.*

sleeps	5-6.
price	£250-£475.
rooms	3: 1 double, 1 family room, 1 single on landing, 1 bathroom downstairs, separate wc.
closed	Never.

booking details

	Roger & Sandra Bates
tel	+33 (0)2 33 52 12 89
e-mail	rogersandrabates@wanadoo.fr

map 4　entry 52

Le Bas du Parc – The House

St Sauveur le Vicomte, Manche

Off the old courtyard, next to The Cottage (see opposite), looking onto shared gardens, a farmhouse sleeping 11. The two houses together would be perfect for families aiming to be close, but can be rented separately. The whole place is child-friendly – high chairs, cots, babysitting – and the coast a mere 20 minutes: bring the buckets and spades. You have a wooden-floored parlour with ceiling-to-floor drapes, sofa and chairs; a charming dining room/kitchen wonderfully equipped, four easy chairs round the fireplace and a *cuisine arrière* (dishwasher, washing machine, freezer). Up the wooden staircase to three sunny bedrooms on the first floor: a beautiful antique carved bed, an oak armoire, white linen, fat pillows. More bedrooms in the attic, cosy for kids. Bathrooms are spotless and white. You'll be very snug in winter, with logs crackling in the old fireplace downstairs, and central heating throughout. Kathleen lives in a cottage next door, has done for years, and is there whenever you need her. Birds, squirrels, flowers, peace – a wonderful place. *Highchair. Babysitting available. Bring your own linen.*

sleeps	9–11.
price	€ 510–€ 1,050.
rooms	5: 2 doubles, 1 twin, 1 single, 1 quadruple, 2 bathrooms, 1 shower room.
closed	Never.

booking details

Kathleen Byles

tel	+33 (0)2 33 41 39 22
e-mail	lebasduparc@hotmail.com
web	www.lebasduparc.com

Le Bas du Parc – The Cottage

St Sauveur le Vicomte, Manche

You leave a country lane, follow a track through the woods, cross a bridge and when the road runs out... Le Bas du Parc awaits in deepest Normandy. It's stylish, too: Kathleen has given her 18th-century barn a 21st-century makeover. Old stone walls are festooned with hollyhocks and roses, while inside, the odd wall has come down to give it all an open-plan feel. You have pale wooden beams, rugs on tiled floors, white walls, old pine doors. China plates and good prints adorn the walls, and the fabrics – curtains, bedspreads, tablecloths and upholstery – are the work of Kathleen's exceptionally gifted hands: gently floral curtains here, a bedcover in *toile de Jouy* there. The quaint, country-style sitting room has a video and TV, the modern kitchen a dishwasher, and there are heaters for winter. Upstairs: three simple but pretty bedrooms overlook the garden or the courtyard; one has a wisteria mural. French windows open to a patio, and the garden runs into a field where paths have been mown through the long grass – perfect for dens. *Highchair. Babysitting available. Bring your own linen.*

sleeps	5-7 + cot.
price	€ 290-€ 650.
rooms	3: 1 double, 1 twin, 1 single with bunkbeds, 1 bathroom, 1 separate wc downstairs.
closed	Never.

booking details

	Kathleen Byles
tel	+33 (0)2 33 41 39 22
e-mail	lebasduparc@hotmail.com
web	www.lebasduparc.com

map 4   entry 54

La Bergerie

St Rémy des Landes, Manche

After a day on the dunes, cook your dinner, Norman-style, in the great inglenook fireplace, then wash it down with a flask of local cider. All is wooden inside this ancient farmhouse, from the gorgeous panelling around the hearth to the inviting oak settle and heavy ceiling beams. The high-quality, personalised furnishings make this feel like a much-loved home rather than a holiday let – probably because it *is* a home much of the year. Even though the Lea family won't be here when you are, they'll make you feel welcome on arrival by leaving you food and drinks. Enjoy serene views over the house's eight acres of fields from the huge, south-facing master bedroom; children will be in heaven in the carpeted, primrose-coloured dorm. There's a games room if it's wet; if not, head for nearby Portbail to swim, sail or ride. If you're not persuaded to cook (despite the lovely Paul Bocuse range in the well-equipped kitchen), try the *moules* in the town's many restaurants. Ideal for two families holidaying together – beaches and sailing are no distance at all – and temptingly close to Britain.

sleeps	8-12 + cot.
price	£350-£675.
rooms	4: 3 doubles, 1 twin with bunkbeds & sofabed, 2 shower rooms, 1 bathroom.
closed	Never.

booking details

	Oriana Lea
tel	+44 (0)1963 359234
fax	+44 (0)1963 351433
e-mail	oj.lea@btinternet.com

La Valette – La Grange

St Rémy des Landes, Manche

Hospitality comes naturally to Jacqueline, the British owner, who bought this 17th-century farmhouse and barn several years ago. She is thoroughly integrated into the life of this pretty Norman hamlet and works in the tourist office in nearby Portbail; you'd be hard-pushed to fine a better source of advice on places to visit. Her passion is herbs and she's created a special herb garden for the converted barn where you stay. With its delicious views of the orchard and garden, the house has been sympathetically furnished and is spotless. Relax after a day on the dunes by the woodburner – it sits in an imposing stone fireplace in the living room, full of personal touches and comfy sofas. Downstairs is modern tiled, upstairs is carpeted, and bedrooms have simple pine furniture and velux windows. Rooms are generous both in comfort and stylish cosiness. Eat out in the garden, take a picnic to the beach three kilometres away, visit the waterside church of Notre-Dame in Portbail and shop at its Tuesday market.

sleeps	4-6.
price	€ 399–€ 669 (£250–£450).
rooms	2: 1 double, 1 twin, 1 sofabed in living room, 1 bathroom, 1 shower room.
closed	Never.

booking details

Jacqueline Livock
tel +33 (0)2 33 07 27 17

map 4   entry 56

La Merise

Gerville la Forêt, Manche

Another impossibly pretty cottage, with rambling pink roses by the front door.
The house basks on the sunny side of Mont Castre, an island of stone in a sea of
green. You are in a national park: marshland, coastal dunes and woodland burst with
diverse populations of birds; wild flowers flourish. Back at the ranch John and
Valerie, two ex-pat Aussies who do B&B, have brought to life a colourful organic
garden; you have your own private piece, with barbecue, and can eat out at night.
Your semi-detached gîte is encased within 300-year-old walls: simple, homely, ideal
for two and very good value. The front door opens to a sunny kitchen/living room,
small but cosy, and a dear little mezzanine bedroom, reached via an Everest stair.
There are bicycles to borrow and old railway lines to cycle along. In summer, grab
the boogie boards and head for the beach. There's a local market for each day of the
week, or you can try the fisherman's cooperatives for oysters, mussels, lobster, crab.
Lessay with its abbey is well worth a visit; its September festival is the oldest
country fair in Europe and has been going for over 900 years. *B&B also.*

sleeps	2-3.
price	€215–€270.
rooms	1 double, 1 shower room. Extra single bed available.
closed	Never.

booking details

	Valerie & John Armstrong
tel	+33 (0)2 33 45 63 86
e-mail	the.armstrong@libertysurf.fr

Les Pommiers

Gerville la Forêt, Manche

The local farmer is also the mayor; he makes calvados from the apples that fall in the orchard. You are in the middle of nowhere: a narrow lane skirts the forest and leads across open farmland to this 200-year-old stone barn. It was converted by Don, Gilly's husband, an English builder who sits on the Comité de Fêtes. Local artisans helped him out and their fine handiwork is evident: there are tiled floors, exposed beams and ceiling joists. The feel is warmly rustic with all the comforts you'd hope for: a big family kitchen, a woodburner, a balcony in the first-floor sitting room with views over the orchard. Bedrooms are excellent. The downstairs room is huge, lovely and sunny, and has bunk beds and two singles; upstairs, yellow walls, more exposed timbers and a pretty stained-glass window in the large double. Outside, a 500-year-old oak casts generous shade, while paths lead out into the forest; if you're lucky you'll see buzzards resting on the fence posts. In April and May the lane teams with foxglove and in summer orchids flourish. There are long sandy beaches close by, too. Perfect for young families.

sleeps	8-10.
price	€375–€740 (£250-£495).
rooms	3: 2 doubles, 1 family room with 2 sets of bunkbeds & 2 singles, 2 bathrooms, 1 shower room, 1 separate wc.
closed	Never.

booking details

	Gilly Turner & Anne Corden
tel	+33 (0)2 33 21 35 95 (Gilly)
	+44 (0)1730 829277 (Anne)
e-mail	gacorden@btopenworld.com

map 4   entry 58

Hotel la Ramade – Gîte Country Garden

Marcey les Grèves, Manche

In a courtyard to the back of the hotel run by kind Véronique, a little granite one-storey house originally built for Grand-mère. It is a comfortable resting place for two, or four, and a baby if desired (cots are available). From a wooden-slatted patio with pots, enter a tiled living room furnished with black leather convertible sofa, two recliners, a dining table and a wrought-iron shelving unit filled with knick-knacks and radio. Wall heaters give year-round warmth. The kitchen – white, brand new and well-equipped – has a door to the grounds: yours to share, full of mature trees that give privacy from the road. And if you're a reluctant cook, there's a crêperie you can walk to and more restaurants in Avranches. You can also eat at the hotel – just book in advance. Véronique serves delicious food: *salade aux gésiers* in the spring, perhaps, followed by *navarin de veau* and early Breton strawberries. With such privacy and grounds this would be a good place for young children, if you feel like squeezing them in; you are 100 yards from the river and a short drive from Mont St Michel and the sea. *B&B also.*

sleeps	2-4.
price	€ 240–€ 380.
rooms	1 double, 1 sofabed in living room, 1 bathroom.
closed	Rarely.

booking details

	Véronique Morvan
tel	+33 (0)2 33 58 27 40
fax	+33 (0)2 33 58 29 30
e-mail	vmorvan@wanadoo.fr
web	www.laramade.fr

La Cahudière – Marguerite, Coquelicot & Bleuet
St Martin de Landelles, Manche

The lane runs out at La Cahudière: expect peace and quiet in the rolling folds of deep country. A family venture, this 100-year-old stone farmhouse with hay barn has been neatly converted into three neighbouring gîtes. Window boxes brim with colour, butterflies come for the peach trees, you may munch the fruit. There are white walls and new pine, shuttered windows, pastel fabrics and tiled floors... Stone fireplaces and woodburners give winter warmth, thick walls keep you cool in summer. Pretty bedrooms are spotless and come with check curtains, cane furniture, good beds. There are big double rooms for adults and bunk rooms for children. Sit out front and watch the cattle graze; spot deer, even badgers, in the woods. There's badminton in one of the fields, tennis and fishing nearby and a video library for the horizontally-inclined. Children have masses of space to run around in safely, and there's a private patio for each gîte. The village, a mile away, has good little shops and a restaurant for lunch. Mont St Michel is within striking distance; Canale, a pretty coastal town, is known for its oysters. *Shared laundry.*

sleeps	Marguerite 4. Coquelicot 4-7. Bleuet 8-11.
price	£165-£645.
rooms	Marguerite: 1 double, 1 twin, 1 bath. Coquelicot: 1 double, 1 single with adult bunks, 1 sofabed, 1 bath. Bleuet: 2 doubles, 1 single with bunks, 1 room with bunkbed, 1 twin on mezzanine, 1 bath, 1 shower.
closed	Never.

booking details

	Michael, John & Margaret Atherton
tel	+33 (0)2 33 49 30 45 or +44 (0)1204 657413
e-mail	enquiries@lacahudiere.co.uk
web	www.giteholidays.com

map 4   entry 60

La Channais
Plouër sur Rance, Côtes-d'Armor

No frills but plain comfort in this 18th-century terraced cottage in a quiet back lane 500 yards from the river Rance. Guests are asked to mow the badminton court and clean the house before they go but this seems fair exchange for the use of four new bikes and an eight-foot dinghy on the river. Inside, a fully equipped IKEA kitchen sits on a grey, slate floor. There's ample seating in the cosy sitting room, an old Breton armoire, two oak ship's timbers in the ceiling, and a granite wall at the foot of the steep, stone spiral stair. A spliced and knotted rope handrail – 'Turkshead' for those in the know – hauls you up to the landing and the pretty iron balcony on the front of the house. Plain bedrooms – blue and white for the double room, red and white for the bunk beds – overlook woods and gardens. And it's a garden for living as well as playing in, being part terraced and part large lawn enclosed by hydrangeas and shrubs. There's teak furniture and a barbecue, plentiful instructions and advice for visitors and logs for your fire. Plouër is up the road for shops, supermarket, two restaurants and several sports.

sleeps	6-7.
price	€285-€570.
rooms	3: 1 double, 1 twin, 1 room with double bunkbeds (+ small extra bed), 1 bathroom.
closed	Never.

booking details

	Neil & Pamela Millward
tel	+44 (0)1803 782981
fax	+44 (0)1803 782391
e-mail	pamela@nmillward.fsnet.co.uk

Ville Lieu de Fer — Manor House, Garden House, Artist's Studio
Le Gouray, Côtes-d'Armor

Luxurious living in the Manor House, the Garden House (the two linked by a central hallway) and the Studio; they flank three sides of a garden courtyard. All have been beautifully restored; even the barbecues are top of the range. In the Manor (below), a vast sitting/dining room with warm yellow walls, French windows, open fire and table for 12, and a super all-singing, all-dancing kitchen. Fine oak staircases lead to grand bedrooms: beds are king-size, the singles are 'Breton' (larger than usual) and there's fine French wallpaper. In the conservatory-living room of the Garden House: an African theme, pale washes, lots of light. A laundry has washing machines, driers and ironing boards in duplicate; a games room in the coach house is stocked with table tennis, darts, even plugs for Game Boys; the Studio, a loft apartment with a sunny balcony, is above. The pool, encircled by lawns and loungers, can be heated to 30 degrees. The setting is gorgeous, the village has both bakery and bar and medieval Lamballe, a 15-minute drive, has the rest.
Manor House & Garden House only rented together in July/August. B&B also.

sleeps	Manor House 4-6. Garden House 4. Artist's Studio 2.
price	Manor: £600. Garden: £400. Manor & Garden Jul/Aug: £2,000 p.w. Studio: £200.
rooms	Manor: 1 double, 1 twin, 1 twin on mezzanine, 1 bath, 1 shower, 1 separate wc. Garden: 1 double, 1 twin, 1 bath, 1 shower. Studio: 1 double, 1 shower.
closed	Never.

booking details

Mike & Gaile Richardson

tel	+33 (0)2 96 34 95 30
fax	+33 (0)2 96 34 95 30
e-mail	richardson.michael@wanadoo.fr

map 4   entry 62

Château de Bonabry

Hillion, Côtes-d'Armor

This little gem used to house the archives of the château (built by the Viscomte's ancestors in 1373): the family discovered piles of musty parchment documents when they restored it a few years ago. With the sea at the end of the drive, your own rose- and shrub-filled walled garden to spill out into in the summer, and two lively, loveable hosts who do B&B in the château, this is a wonderful place for a small family to stay. Furnishings are simple but adequate. Downstairs rooms have stone vaulted ceilings, crimson-washed walls and age-old terracotta floors, a new sofa, a stripey fauteuil. The kitchen is fitted white, with a round table and yellow chairs. In the twin, a stripped pine floor and pink *toile de Jouy*; more beams and lovely yellow fabric-clad walls in the double – an enthusastic redecoration by the Viscomtesse. If they are not out riding, your hosts will be on hand to help if you need them, and the Viscomte may bring offerings from his personal vegetable garden. Your 'English' garden is furnished with parasol, barbecue and plastic loungers – a pretty spot in which to unwind. *Bring own linen. B&B also.*

sleeps	4.
price	€460–€915.
rooms	2: 1 double, 1 twin, 1 shower room.
closed	Never.

booking details

	Vicomte & Vicomtesse du Fou de Kerdaniel
tel	+33 (0)2 96 32 21 06
fax	+33 (0)2 96 32 21 06
e-mail	bonabry@wanadoo.fr
web	www.bonabry.fr.st

L'Ancien Presbytère

Trégrom, Côtes-d'Armor

The scent of climbing roses and honeysuckle greets you as you arrive at this stunning 17th-century grey stone presbytery: Madame's passion is gardening, as you'll see from her colourful borders. You even have a large walled orchard all to yourselves. The house is a wing off the main house where B&B guests lodge, but you have complete privacy. Interior decoration is homely and personal – all Madame's handiwork – with plenty of painted wood in smokey hues. There's a small kitchen with blue-painted cupboards, waxed terracotta floor and sunny, yellow, wallpapered walls. Bedrooms, on the first and attic floors, are in old-fashioned pastels with matching floral curtains and bedspreads, unusual canework beds and antique painted wardrobes. Views are peaceful and of the garden. Buy your morning croissants at the organic baker's behind the house; for fruits, vegetables and cheeses there are local weekly markets. Charming Madame knows the area "like her pocket" and has itineraries for your deeper discovery of secret delights, as well as beaches and châteaux to visit. *B&B also.*

sleeps	5.
price	€560.
rooms	3: 2 twins, 1 single, 2 bathrooms.
closed	Never.

booking details

	Nicole de Morchoven
tel	+33 (0)2 96 47 94 15
fax	+33 (0)2 96 47 94 15

map 3　entry 64

41 rue de la Petite Corniche

Perros Guirec, Côtes-d'Armor

The ever-changing light of the great bay shimmers in through all your French windows. Sit in your armchair and gaze as the boats go by, or walk to the beautiful sands and waters of Trestriguel beach – it's 10 minutes away. (The village, too, is close.) Guy and Marie-Clo do B&B in the big house; they are attentive and generous and she has decorated your little white cottage in soft blues and lemons, enlivened by her patchworks and embroideries. On your single floor you have an open-plan sitting and dining room with a tiny, well-equipped kitchen to the back, and more radiant views from the little bedroom. Furniture is fresh and new and in keeping with the house; the bed is pine, the dining room chairs blue with painted birds. Outside, your own patch of garden with small terrace, barbecue and lawn. Head out for walks along the pink granite coast, make the most of the seafood restaurants, and be sure not to miss the Sept Iles archipelago – the most magnificent seabird colony in France. *Cot & highchair available. Use of washing machine in main house. B&B also.*

sleeps	2-4 + cot.
price	€450–€500.
rooms	1 double, 1 sofabed in sitting room, 1 shower room.
closed	December–January.

booking details

Marie-Clo & Guy Biarnès

tel	+33 (0)2 96 23 28 08
fax	+33 (0)2 96 23 28 23
e-mail	guy.biarnes@wanadoo.fr
web	perso.wanadoo.fr/corniche/

La Galerie
Huelgoat, Finistère

Breton style and charm is encapsulated in this wisteria-clad cottage. It was built in the late 1600s; its restoration by the artist owner is utterly authentic. Stone steps lead to a finely carved front door; oils, watercolours and *objets d'art* are scattered among a collection of period pieces; the whole place is an aesthetic delight. Floors are of slate, walls washed an earthy ochre, there are oak room dividers, a huge old fireplace and a Breton box bed (lovely for siestas). A stone spiral staircase rises to lofty bedrooms with oak timbers and magnificent quilt hangings; divided by half-walls, these rooms would be just right for a family. A steep, hayloft-type stair leads from the kitchen to an attic bedroom – exciting for older children. No en suite bathrooms here, but an ancient, high level loo; the kitchen is equally simple and atmospheric. There's an old well and a small private seating area out in front and, at the back, an almost secret garden you share with Tom; he is open, friendly, great with children and passionate about this place. There's a market in Huelgoat on Thursdays and a crêperie a mile away.

sleeps	4 + 2 children.
price	€ 425–€ 565.
rooms	3: 1 double, 1 twin, 1 twin for children, 3 shower rooms.
closed	Winter.

booking details

	Tom Hickman
tel	+33 (0)2 98 99 77 68
e-mail	jennybutlerjoseph@hotmail.com

map 3   entry 66

Le Manoir de Prevasy
Carhaix Plouguer, Finistère

You don't only get this stunningly renovated 16th-century manor, but all that encircles it: large barns and stables, high walls and a chapel. It is exceptional in every way. Inside, original stone-flagged floors, a 16th-century oak staircase (it creaks delightfully), white rendered walls, huge fireplaces, high ceilings, big beams. There's a sitting room carpeted with seagrass and rugs, an armoire for china, and blinds, not curtains, to show off ancient stone. In the cottage next door, a lovers' nest: you lie in bed under a painted blue sky, angels watching over you. Modern comforts include the fabulously equipped kitchen (with Smeg oven), powerful showers, central heating, and oak-framed conservatory. Off the lovely courtyard live the owners in yet another old building, happy to help and advise. A perfect place for families, with table tennis, badminton, boules and a decked, fenced pool. Through the old stone arch watch the cows from the nearby dairy farm wander up the lane – the only passing traffic. Carhaix Plouguer is two kilometres away so walk in or cycle – or take to the canal tow path and follow your nose. Magnificent.

sleeps	10-12.
price	£700-£1,500.
rooms	5: 2 doubles, 1 twin, 1 family room for 4, 4 bathrooms, 1 shower room. 1 double in separate cottage, 1 shower room.
closed	January-March.

booking details

	Peter & Clarissa Novak
tel	+33 (0)2 98 93 24 36
fax	+33 (0)2 98 93 24 36
e-mail	novak.prevasy@wanadoo.fr

Camezon

Locqueltas, Morbihan

An artist's touch has been at work in this dear little gîte so close to the Gulf of Morbihan – and what it lacks in space it makes up for in charm. Stone steps lead from the garden into the gentle colours and soft furnishings of the open-plan sitting/dining room. The floors are fresh-tiled, the ceilings old-beamed, and the pale pink kitchenette, tucked into a corner behind a wall, has pretty mosaics by the sink. Up the blue-painted wooden staircase to a large, airy bedroom with a huge window overlooking the garden and a high pitched roof… a room to dream in, awash with yellows, blues and greens and a *trompe l'oeil* on one wall. The shower room is off the living room downstairs – small but well-designed. The feeling of calm extends to the lawns surrounded by trees; sit out and listen to the birds. You have the best of both worlds in Locqueltas – countryside and coast – while the shops and restaurants are a short drive. The Gulf of Morbihan is a 20-minute drive, Carnac and Josselin just inland. Your delightful hosts do B&B next door and are there to greet you and give good advice. *B&B also.*

sleeps	2-3.
price	€ 220-€ 360.
rooms	1 double, extra bed available for living room, 1 shower room downstairs.
closed	Never.

booking details

	Guy Chevallier
tel	+33 (0)2 97 66 62 70
fax	+33 (0)2 97 66 63 66
e-mail	chambres-manoir@wanadoo.fr
web	gitemorbihan.free.fr

map 4   entry 68

Photography by Michael Busselle

western loire &
loire valley

Le Relais de la Rinière

Le Landreau, Loire-Atlantique

You're surrounded by vines: this is Muscadet country and the clay soils of the area produce some particularly ambitious wines. Indulge in some private tastings in the huge garden – a cocktail of wisteria, lawns and colourful surprises (with some excellent play equipment for children). Or pop off to one of the nearby *caves*. You'll enjoy your delightful hosts Françoise and Louis, who run a B&B in the imposing coaching inn next door – your cottage is one of the outhouses. He used to be a baker, she's a keen jam-maker, and they moved here from Normandy bringing some lovely antiques with them. A fine old dresser/armoire holds pretty crockery in a light and sunny living area with well-equipped kitchen, there's an old oak table for family gatherings, a sofa with a bright throw. Colour schemes are adventurous: ochre-sponged walls downstairs, and, in a bedroom for children, low ceiling beams painted blue. The downstairs bedroom has the old bread oven. Discover historic Nantes, with its splendid 18th-century houses and its château, or visit the slick wine museum at Le Pallet. There's great cycling, too. *B&B also.*

sleeps	5.
price	€220–€450.
rooms	2: 1 double, 1 triple, 1 shower room.
closed	Never.

booking details

Françoise & Louis Lebarillier

tel	+33 (0)2 40 06 41 44
fax	+33 (0)2 51 13 10 52
e-mail	riniere@netcourrier.com
web	www.riniere.com

Château la Paleine

Le Puy Notre Dame, Maine-et-Loire

The Wadoux give you a bag of walnuts with your welcome – a typical touch from these relaxed, lovely people who run B&B in the manor and a hotel in the old wine warehouse. Outbuildings are scattered in secluded corners, a hen house stores bikes; your 1890s gîte is more substantial, being once the house of the château's *gardien*. All has been freshly, brightly, newly done up: the little sitting room, with working fireplace and vine wood to burn, the bigger dining area with corner cupboard stocked with glass and crockery. The corner kitchen holds all you need. A downstairs bedroom leads into the garden, a larger room upstairs is under the eaves, spotless and charming and big enough to hold an extra bed for a child. With a safe, enclosed garden (with barbecue) this would make a great place for a family to stay; your hosts, with five children of their own, will anticipate your every need. You are on the edge of an interesting village with an auberge just down the road for supper, but do try dinner here: it's delicious, and you'll get to meet the other guests. Wine-tasting châteaux lie temptingly close by. *B&B also.*

sleeps	4-5 + cot.
price	€ 255–€ 385.
rooms	2: 1 double, 1 family room for 3, 1 bathroom.
closed	Never.

booking details

	Caroline & Philippe Wadoux
tel	+33 (0)2 41 38 28 25
fax	+33 (0)2 41 38 42 38
e-mail	p.wadoux@libertysurf.fr
web	www.france-bonjour.com/chateau-la-paleine/

map 10   entry 70

La Maison Aubelle – Tour, Gaudrez & Jardin

Montreuil Bellay, Maine-et-Loire

A 16th-century nobleman's house in an old country town. It stands in secluded gardens flanked by high stone walls, renovated by craftsmen, thoughtfully equipped by Peter and Sally. The original apartments are Tour, Jardin and Gaudrez. Tour – in the tower, as you'd expect – is one flight up a spiralling stone stair; it has a beamed living room/kitchen with trim red sofas and wraparound views (below). The garden apartment, with terrace, is as neat as a new pin; white-walled Gaudrez has a 16th-century window, discovered during restoration. The feel is airy, relaxing, comfortable; crisp linen, central heating and daily cleaning are included and the quality is superb. There's a terrace and games room for all and an appropriately large pool. If you can't face cooking, let the Smiths do it for you: they whisk up delicious meals five times a week, cheerfully served in the dining room in winter, on the terrace in summer. Peter and Sally are also on hand to advise, translate or leave you in peace. They run French courses, too. *Apartments rented separately or together. Children over 12 welcome. Shared laundry. Min. three nights.*

sleeps	Tour & Gaudrez: 4. Jardin: 2.
price	Tour & Gaudrez €775–€1,000. Jardin €675–€925.
rooms	Tour: 2 doubles, 2 shower rooms. Gaudrez: 2 doubles, 2 shower rooms. Jardin: 1 double, 1 bathroom, 1 separate wc.
closed	Rarely.

booking details

	Peter & Sally Smith
tel	+33 (0)2 41 52 36 39
fax	+33 (0)2 41 50 94 83
e-mail	maison.aubelle@aubelle.com
web	www.aubelle.com

La Maison Aubelle – Coach House & Stable
Montreuil Bellay, Maine-et-Loire

No sooner had the Smiths finished one renovation than they turned their hands to the old stables and coach house. And with aplomb: the impeccable exterior is matched by equally excellent interiors. Walls are whitewashed or exposed stone, some ceilings are sloped, there are lovely old beams and attractive new windows. In the old stable (below), the original hayrack survives in the sitting room. You'll find the odd country chest, good sofas, heating beneath terracotta tiled floors (winter warmth is guaranteed!). In summer, play chess in the garden, dine on the terrace, meet fellow guests round the pool. There's daily cleaning, the fitted kitchens are packed with mod cons and linen is provided; all you need do is turn up. Venture beyond the walls to discover the last remaining walled town in the region; the three-minute stroll to the château is rewarded by gorgeous watery views of the Thouet. Stretch out a little further and explore Fontevraud Abbey: Eleanor of Aquitaine and Richard the Lion Heart are buried here. *Properties interconnect for same-party bookings. Children over 12 welcome. Shared laundry. Min. three nights.*

sleeps	Coach house 4. Stable 2.
price	Coach house €775–€1,000. Stable €675–€925.
rooms	Coach house: 2 doubles, 2 shower rooms. Stable: 1 double, 1 bathroom, 1 separate wc.
closed	Rarely.

booking details

	Peter & Sally Smith
tel	+33 (0)2 41 52 36 39
fax	+33 (0)2 41 50 94 83
e-mail	maison.aubelle@aubelle.com
web	www.aubelle.com

map 10   entry 72

Le Manoir de Champfreau
Varennes sur Loire, Maine-et-Loire

In spite of imposing dimensions, there's a soft luminosity to this ancient place. It's a 15th-century fortified farmhouse – a home of huge character and style. History oozes from every crevice: family portraits and tapestries hang from thick limestone walls, solid antique furniture and coats-of-arms recall grand inhabitants. The kitchen, with its black tiles, pewter plates, dishwasher and every modern aid, is a dream; there are even 200 recipe books and Bruce, who has cooked professionally, is generous with advice – should you need it. (He and Steven live next door and are delightful yet discreet.) Bedrooms are smallish and sumptuous... a four-poster with velvet plum drapes, an antique claw-footed bath; the living room is baronial but cosy – deep sofas before a blazing fire, CDs, books and flowers; central heating, too. Views are of the three walled acres and the courtyard topiary. You are brilliantly placed for visiting some of the finest châteaux of the Loire, there's a fish pond and a brand new pool, bikes to borrow and cookery courses in the offing. A heavenly place. *Children over 14 welcome.*

sleeps	6.
price	€2,000.
rooms	3 doubles, 2 bathrooms.
closed	Rarely.

booking details

	Steven Guderian & Bruce Riedner
tel	+33 (0)2 41 38 40 41
fax	+33 (0)2 41 38 40 41
e-mail	stevenguderian@aol.com

La Chalopinière

Le Vieil Baugé, Maine-et-Loire

Michael and Jill live the country life. There are three horses, two children, a couple of cats and a guinea pig. Views stretch out over open country, and in the courtyard garden a towering willow weeps. On summer nights you can eat beneath its generous canopy; Jill has been known to bring out the candelabra. A very friendly place, where you are met with a cup of tea and a slice of homemade cake. Your apartment – a neat and cosy renovated grain store – has a private entrance up a steep outside staircase. Here are parquet floors, exposed beams and fresh white walls, and, in the huge living/dining room and kitchen all rolled into one, a woodburner and ceilings that open to the rafters. Bedrooms have light yellow walls, chests of drawers, good wardrobes and plenty of books. Jill does B&B in the main house and will happily help with advice. She'll also deliver bread and croissants in the morning, even an egg or two from the free-range hens. The market town of Baugé has restaurants and shops, while long walks start from the front door. Or head for the pretty forest of Chandelais. *B&B also.*

sleeps	4.
price	€ 320–€ 480.
rooms	2: 1 double, 1 twin, 1 bathroom.
closed	1 week in February, 1 week in July.

booking details

	Michael & Jill Coyle
tel	+33 (0)2 41 89 04 38
fax	+33 (0)2 41 89 04 38
e-mail	rigbycoyle@aol.com

map 5   entry 74

Le Four de Villeprouvé
Ruille Froid Fonds, Mayenne

Oodles of history, and a cranny-filled cottage as full of colourful stories and character as its delightful owners. It used to be the grain store for the monks who lived in the priory nearby, now it's a farm and B&B run by Christophe and Christine. Alongside raising cattle and children and caring for guests, they've miraculously found time to lavish care and attention on this exquisite stone house: she sewed pretty drapes for the antique four-poster bed; he crafted the new staircase within the old frame; both have carefully kept original features such as old beams, a bread oven and a *moru* chest, traditionally used to move a family's worldly belongings around the country. In the living room you'll even find an ancient settle against the wall, inside the seat of which free-range hens used to lay eggs which their owners would find in time for breakfast. It's charming and cosy and has all the mod cons. You can barbecue in the enclosed garden, or sample Christine's wholesome cooking if the B&B is not full – just ask in advance. Ducks paddle in the enchanting pond, cows graze in the fields, apples become cider – bucolic peace. *B&B also.*

sleeps	4-8.
price	€239–€367 (£150–£230).
rooms	4: 1 double, 1 double on mezzanine, 1 family room for 4, 2 bathrooms, 2 separate wcs.
closed	Never.

booking details

	Christine Davenel
tel	+33 (0)2 43 07 71 62
fax	+33 (0)2 43 07 71 62
e-mail	christ.davenel@wanadoo.fr
web	perso.wanadoo.fr/villeprouve/gite

Château de l'Hérissaudière

Pernay, Indre-et-Loire

Your pleasant quarters are in the long, low *longère*, once the tack room for the horses of the château (and the château was the hunting lodge of Diane de Poitiers). It's a one-storey building, one-room wide, airy and light. You have the bedrooms on your right and the living area on your left: a blue sofabed before a small open fire (boosted by central heating on chilly days), blue curtains, a tablecloth on a round table. Walls are white, beams dark and low, a rug adds warmth to tiles, country furniture adds personality. The kitchen, separated by a breakfast bar, is new and well-designed with matching blue and white crockery. The double bedroom is a good size, with a large painted wardrobe (blue, of course): crisp and cool; the twin is a lot smaller. Outside, the best of both worlds: the privacy of your own walled and fenced garden, with barbecue and games, and the lovely grounds, with tennis court to hire (the pool is for B&B guests only; a good public pool lies 10km away). A peaceful place for a family to stay – and a well-priced restaurant in nearby Semblançay, recommended by Madame. *B&B also.*

sleeps	4-6 + child.
price	€ 350–€ 600.
rooms	2: 1 double + child bed, 1 twin, 1 sofabed in sitting room, 2 shower rooms, 1 separate wc.
closed	Never.

booking details

	Claudine Detilleux
tel	+33 (0)2 47 55 95 28
fax	+33 (0)2 47 55 97 45
e-mail	lherissaudiere@aol.com
web	www.herissaudiere.com

map 10   entry 76

La Petite Giraudière

Villandry, Indre-et-Loire

An exceptional find, a luxurious working farm where you can eat the cheese that the owners produce. Béatrice has a herd of 40 goats and will show you round the milking parlour and the dairy. The place was inhabited by nuns until 1790, then it became a tithe farm to the château next door (the magnificent Villandry). The gîte is exhilarating, a 17th-century house conversion with a terracotta-tiled roof and old stone walls. At the back is a duck pond into which a weeping willow dips its branches; at the top an entirely private roof terrace that catches the sun. In between, you find dreamland. There are exposed stone walls, big beds and rich *toile de Jouy* fabrics. One bedroom is in a gallery above another – you climb a spiral staircase to get to it – and another has a chest of drawers that turns into a writing desk if you press the right button. The whole place swims in light, and there's a garden in which to seek silence. Béatrice is wonderful. She speaks fluent English and Spanish; her Italian isn't bad either. Her way is to provide the best of everything, which she does. There's a farm shop and a restaurant, too – prepare to indulge.

sleeps	4-6.
price	€800–€915.
rooms	3: 2 doubles, 1 twin on mezzanine, 1 bathroom, 1 separate wc.
closed	Never.

booking details

	Béatrice de Montferrier
tel	+33 (0)2 47 50 08 60
fax	+33 (0)2 47 50 06 60
e-mail	beatrice.de-montferrier@wanadoo.fr
web	www.letapegourmande.com

5 rue des Averries

Bourgueil, Indre-et-Loire

This elegant sweep of 19th-century stone started life as a *longère* (a long, low outhouse) and the dormer window in the small bedroom was the entrance to the hayloft. Michel, an interior designer and erstwhile antiques dealer, has a wonderful eye and has brought an uncluttered grace to the interior. In the sitting room, shiny stone walls are adorned with the odd oil, the terracotta-tiled floor is warmed by a bright rug and the beams have been scrubbed clean – neat, simple and easy on the eye. Low, slopey-ceilinged bedrooms are under the eaves; smallish, simple, delightful. One has a pretty 18th-century-style bed. You'll find antique bedside tables, good prints on the walls and fine linen. The largest room in lilac and green has a door that opens onto an outside stone staircase, and sweeps you down into the garden. Here are shade-giving trees, an unobtrusive pool and sun beds. The house stands in a residential neighbourhood of a small market town, but it is private nonetheless. Doors from the perfectly equipped kitchen open onto the terrace with wrought-iron tables and chairs.

sleeps	6.
price	€ 880–€ 1,200.
rooms	3 doubles, 1 bathroom, 1 shower room, 1 separate wc.
closed	Never.

booking details

	Michel Rondeau
tel	+33 (0)2 41 51 47 95
fax	+33 (0)2 41 51 74 86
e-mail	m.rondeau@wanadoo.fr

map 10 entry 78

Le Clos Saint André

Ingrandes de Touraine, Indre-et-Loire

A converted barn, a long, low stone building, typical of the region. The Pinçons have renovated with some style, keeping exposed stone walls and adding terracotta-tiled floors. The sitting room is huge, open to the rafters, flooded with light and swimming in space. Staircases at either end lead to bedrooms. The master suite is the pick of the bunch, with a low-slung bed that lies under a beamed roof and an antique dressing table in one corner. Elsewhere: good fabrics, patchwork quilts on children's beds, a traditional stone fireplace, wicker armchairs, cushioned sofas, an antique dresser and a small forest of flourishing greenery. The kitchen is immaculate and a delight to use, though on lazy days you may choose to spurn the allure of the eye-level oven and let Michèle rustle up something sublime. The Pinçons, kind and easy-going, live in the old, wine-grower's house opposite where they do B&B; you share the pool. Here time is measured in vintages, not hours; you are surrounded by vineyards, and Saumur, with its château, is close by. *B&B also.*

sleeps	8-10.
price	€ 600–€ 1,100.
rooms	4: 2 doubles, 1 twin, 1 family room for 4, 2 bathrooms, 1 shower room, 3 separate wcs.
closed	Never.

booking details

	Michèle & Michel Pinçon
tel	+33 (0)2 47 96 90 81
fax	+33 (0)2 47 96 90 81
e-mail	mmpincon@club-internet.fr

Le Pigeonnier

Chinon, Indre-et-Loire

No artificial pool here but a watery world where fish jump, coypu and the occasional beaver make nests and kingfishers, terns and herons fish. There are three gîtes in all; reached through lush water meadows, Le Pigeonnier is attached to the main house, with views up and downstream. Only the frogs disturb the perfect peace of the garden and riverside 'terrace' with barbecue. Inside: a clean, comfortable space for up to five. The main bedroom, up steep, wooden, open-tread stairs, is in the pigeon loft itself, complete with nesting holes. Across the landing, on the mezzanine, the second bedroom, curtained for privacy, has a lovely garden view. The bathroom is small, its bath tucked behind a beam. The ground floor is open plan, with a step up from the kitchen/dining area to the pleasant sitting section with three-piece suite. An excellent spot for châteaux lovers, cyclists, gourmets, bird-twitchers, or, of course, those wishing to mess about in boats – a punt, row boat and small sailing boat are all available. And you can swim in the river, but watch the sandbanks.

sleeps	4-5.
price	€ 295–€ 525.
rooms	2: 1 double, 1 twin on mezzanine, 1 sofabed, 1 bathroom.
closed	End October-March.

booking details

	Gordon Baker
tel	+44 (0)1440 702627
fax	+44 (0)1440 708790
e-mail	bookings@pigeonnier.co.uk
web	www.pigeonnier.co.uk

map 10   entry 80

The Well House

Anché, Indre-et-Loire

This 18th-century worker's cottage has a garden to beguile you. It faces south to soak up sun, has wild roses rambling on its stone walls and is bordered by an orchard... cypress trees and lavender, geraniums in pots and a carpet of colour in between. A fig tree grows against the wall and there's a covered terrace where you sit on cushioned stone benches. A great sense of peace envelops this pretty hillside village. David, who teaches in Alexandria, fell in love with the house when he was a student. He scraped the money together to buy, then spent his summers renovating. He also bought the 17th-century farmhouse next door and lives there for three months a year. The interior is a delightful mix of French and English. There's an open fireplace in the beamed sitting room, a big carved wardrobe in one of the bedrooms and a light and airy kitchen with French windows that open onto the terrace. Bedrooms are ample, with fine furniture and garden views. One looks onto the orchard; you can glimpse the church tower beyond. There are vineyards and châteaux nearby and a swimming hole in the river.

sleeps	4-6.
price	£380-£420.
rooms	2: 1 double, 1 triple, extra bed on landing, 1 bathroom.
closed	November-April.

booking details

	David Thomas
tel	+33 (0)2 41 51 47 95
e-mail	m.rondeau@wanadoo.fr

Hameau de la Saucraie

Lémeré, Indre-et-Loire

There are three houses here, snuggled round a sun-trapping courtyard. The property was a winery, while part of the gîte once housed a pig sty and chicken loft. Karl and Carol live in one of the houses for half the year, the rest in Florida. They have renovated with flair, imagination and determination, are lively and fun and love being part of local life. Carol trawls the flea markets for pretty things: an oak table, wicker chairs, an old panelled door for a bedstead, stained grey-blue... all bear testimony to a good eye. You are in a long, low, tiled barn of roughly-cut stone walls, a place with much rustic comfort. Expect a natural 'raw' look with original stonework and beamed ceilings, excellent bathrooms, a charming kitchen. The ground-floor bedroom has pine and soft-pink candlewick, and ceilings that rise to part of the old chicken loft. The main bedroom is lovely and large. French windows lead onto a terrace, courtyard lime trees offer shade, there's badminton in the field and a garden you can share. All around: gentle country and vineyards, and a glimpse of the nearby château and the steeple of the church.

sleeps	4-6 + child.
price	€ 620–€ 650.
rooms	2: 1 double with child bed, 1 twin, 1 sofabed in sitting room, 2 shower rooms.
closed	Mid-October-mid June.

booking details

	Carol & Karl Lindquist
tel	+33 (0)2 47 95 79 52
e-mail	islandfeverckl@aol.com

map 10   entry 82

The Cottage & The Farmhouse Loft

Le Grand Pressigny, Indre-et-Loire

Civray is a tiny hamlet hidden away in the countryside: it would be hard to find anywhere more tranquil. And if you tire of walking, cycling, fishing – or swimming in the silky waters of the river – there are vineyards to visit, *fermes auberges* to discover and all the attractions of the Loire châteaux. Lovely Jill is half Australian, passionate about rural France and has restored this little cluster of ancient stone buildings with the lightest of hands. The Cottage is compact but has all you need: a living area with little pine kitchen, woodburning stove, sofabed, play equipment in the garden. Upstairs, under magnificent curving beams, a large double bedroom, simply and attractively furnished. It has its own rustic balcony overlooking farmland – there's not a building in sight. Wooden stairs wind down to the gardens, which have a haphazard charm; fresh home-grown vegetables and home-laid eggs are often available. Jill has also converted The Farmhouse Loft, a heavily timbered and imaginative space with three bedrooms and a big, jolly kitchen/living area, easy for families. *Bring own linen.*

sleeps	Cottage: 2-3 + cot. Farmhouse Loft: 5 + cot. Can be rented together.
price	Cottage: £150-£250. Farmhouse Loft: £170-£305.
rooms	Cottage: 1 double, 1 single sofabed, 1 shower room, 1 bathroom. Farmhouse Loft: 2 doubles, 1 single, 1 bathroom.
closed	Winter.

booking details

	Jill Christie
tel	+33 (0)2 47 94 92 02
fax	+33 (0)2 47 94 92 02

La Davière

Manthelan, Indre-et-Loire

A 17th-century vigneron's house that has been elegantly restored, bringing out the natural grace of the original wood and stone. Irène, an artist, has immersed herself in the project and there is much to elate. The terrace is enclosed by a living arbour made from growing willow, climbing roses adorn stone walls and the swimming pool is flanked on one side by trees. A relaxing country feel fills the interior. There are natural colours and a wooden staircase that leads up to a pretty bedroom under the eaves. Through the windows the local countryside unravels; you are in a small hamlet surrounded by fields. Downstairs, in the open-plan kitchen/living/dining room, there's a large fireplace (cosy in winter), a big round table and baskets hanging from the beams. Irène's work hangs from the walls, mostly abstracts. She works every day in her studio and will happily show you round. She and Alain lived in England and they both speak the language well. The medieval city of Loches is 12km away and its market is a joy. *Babysitting available. B&B also.*

sleeps	4-6.
price	€ 527-€ 1,183.
rooms	2 triples, 1 bathroom, 1 shower room.
closed	Never.

booking details

	Irène & Alain Gourjon
tel	+33 (0)2 47 92 26 52
e-mail	alain.gourjon@wanadoo.fr
web	perso.wanadoo.fr/clos.de.la.daviere

map 10   entry 84

La Maison Rose

Loché sur Indrois, Indre-et-Loire

Slip through the little blue door in the wall and you could be in Hodgson Burnett's *The Secret Garden*. With its gorgeous pink roses and creeper-clad stone walls, the private courtyard garden in which this 18th-century farm cottage stands is magical. Sit out among the lavender bushes and absorb the deep peace of this pretty village on the poplar-lined banks of the Indrois river. Inside the house is no less bewitching, its delightful furnishings and old oak beams exuding warmth and well-being. James, the English owner, teaches art and design (he runs courses here for adults and children) and whitewashed walls are hung with his colourful paintings. One double is reached via the twin; both have poplar-tree views. Artists will celebrate the famous Touraine light, children will enjoy exploring the fields and woods beyond the house. You'll love Loches with its medieval citadel and blue slate roofs, and there are great walks along the river valley. On the well-established cookery weekends you're met at Tours, taken to the wonderful market at Loches, then back to cook and eat together. *Shared pool for those on courses only. B&B also.*

sleeps	6.
price	€422–€677 (£295–£495).
rooms	3: 2 doubles, 1 twin, 1 bathroom, 1 shower room.
closed	Never.

booking details

	Flora & James Cockburn
tel	+44 (0)1732 357022 or +33 (0)2 47 92 61 79 (school holidays)
e-mail	mrsfscockburn@aol.com
web	www.lamaisonrose.com

Oysters

Villeloin Coulangé, Indre-et-Loire

Tranquillity is yours in this Loire hamlet, so small there are no streets, and houses are numbered one to twenty. To shop you have the treat of going to Montrésor: a veritable treasure, as its name suggests, with its lovely château dominating a jumble of medieval houses. Visit the *boulangerie*, whose bread is justly famous. The 200-year-old stone farmhouse, which can be rented as one house or as two self-contained cottages – ideal for a family with grandparents – has been attractively refurbished by its lively and friendly owners, Janet and Edo, who live across the central courtyard. Spotless interiors are a feast of patterned rugs, high-quality furniture, old oak beams and wood-burning stoves. The smaller cottage is decorated in sunny yellows with a red sofa and matching armchairs while the larger house has a beige, red and gold colour scheme; the carpeted bedroom is under the eaves and has a window that starts from the floor. Each cottage has its little piece of private garden, with barbecue. Art courses are on offer in Montrésor, and there's everything you need, weekly market included, in medieval Loches.

sleeps	Maison A: 2-3. Maison B: 4-5.
price	A: €295-€440. B: €390-€535.
rooms	Maison A: 1 twin/double, 1 shower room.
	Maison B: 1 double, 1 twin, 1 shower room.
	Camp beds on request for both.
closed	Never.

booking details

Janet & Edo de Vries

tel	+33 (0)2 47 92 64 05
fax	+33 (0)2 47 92 64 97
e-mail	info@stayatoysters.com
web	www.stayatoysters.com

map 10   entry 86

Moulin de la Follaine

Azay sur Indre, Indre-et-Loire

A tranquil place that feels as old as the hills. The servants who worked in the medieval mill opposite lived in this house, and Danie will show you the old Azay flour sacks if you wish. Your young and friendly hosts run a B&B in the millhouse, but you have your own patio, barbecue and garden too, so there's perfect privacy and peace. Your kitchen/living room is pleasingly decorated with a comfortable mix of modern and antique country furniture and a stone fireplace (stacked with logs for out-of-season stays). Bedrooms are similarly uncluttered, with white walls and friezes that give an original touch, and the kitchen has every mod con. There's masses to do on the spot, from cycling to ping-pong to fishing, with tackle supplied – or simply enjoy the colourful gardens, rushing waterways and the lake adorned with ornamental ducks and geese. Don't miss the weekly markets in Azay and Loches (worth visiting for its castle and dungeon, too) and if you prefer not to cook there's an auberge a stroll away that specialises in traditional regional cooking. *Unguarded water makes the house unsuitable for young children. B&B also.*

sleeps	4-6.
price	€375–€488.
rooms	2 family rooms for 3, 1 bathroom, 1 separate wc.
closed	Never.

booking details

	Danie Lignelet
tel	+33 (0)2 47 92 57 91
fax	+33 (0)2 47 92 57 91
e-mail	moulindelafollaine@wanadoo.fr
web	www.multimania.com/moulindefollaine

Les Petites Ouldes
Francueil, Indre-et-Loire

A short stroll from the Loire's glittering prize, the Château de Chenonceau, this ground-floor flat in the wing of a manor house exudes elegance and good living. Its large light rooms and orangery-style French windows give a mediterranean feel, enhanced by charming furniture, sunny fabrics and terracotta floors. The house has been restored over three decades by the equally elegant owner, Valerie. She treats guests as friends but is more than aware of the privacy that most guests desire, and leaves a light meal and a bottle of crisp Sauvignon in your fridge for your arrival (and a Cabernet for those who prefer red wine). She will also happily cook you a delicious gourmet dinner using organic produce from her garden wherever possible. In the lovely sunny bedroom, crisp cotton and vases of flowers await. A private walled terrace leading from the gîte is yours to sun-soak in, and you have sole use of the pool until 6pm. The landscaped six acres are resplendent with topiary and lawns and you are encouraged to wander. The village, with shops, is a walk away. *Changeover day Wednesday.*

sleeps	2.
price	€ 600–€ 700.
rooms	1 double, 1 bathroom.
closed	Never.

booking details

Valerie Faccini

tel	+33 (0)2 47 23 95 07
fax	+33 (0)2 47 23 95 07 (on request)
e-mail	faccini@freesurf.fr
web	lespetitesouldes.free.fr

map 10   entry 88

La Cornillière

Tours, Indre-et-Loire

What once rambled is now trim and clipped and ever so neat. Monsieur, an antique dealer and interior designer, is originally from the Charente. He studied art in Tours 40 years ago, met Madame and that was that. In the grounds of their elegant house, this dear little 18th-century cottage has been decorated with restraint, in a traditional and pleasing style. Luckily for Madame, Monsieur is also a passionate gardener and happily digs and delves, bringing peace and a little serenity to the outside as well. Inside, all is as neat, charming and relaxing as your hosts. The furniture is country antique, the walls are plain, the tiles are polished old and spotless. The sitting room is small, with an open fireplace, a sofa and armchairs, an un-rugged, tiled floor. There is antique crockery in the kitchen/dining room, antique garden furniture and deckchairs in the garden. Beyond the stone walls of the grounds are gardens, festivals, markets, the Loire valley with its vineyards, châteaux and the elegant city of Tours, with its opera house and gourmet restaurants. Auberges for simpler dining lie nearby.

sleeps	5.
price	€ 540–€ 770.
rooms	3: 1 double, 1 twin, 1 single, 3 shower rooms, 3 separate wcs.
closed	Never.

booking details

Catherine Espinassou

tel	+33 (0)2 47 51 12 69
fax	+33 (0)2 47 66 90 20
e-mail	catherine@lacornilliere.com.fr
web	www.lacornilliere.com.fr

La Taille Rouge

Viglain, Loiret

One misty morning you may catch a glimpse of a doe and fawn deep in the woods. La Taille Rouge's 120 tranquil acres are heaven to explore and the house, with its steep, tiled roof and silver-brown beams, is lovely, too. A long, pretty living/dining room, full of books and country antiques, takes up much of the ground floor. Big comfortable sofas and chairs are grouped around the stone fireplace at one end; at the other, a fine old table with wrought-iron chairs. On both sides are windows looking out to the woods or the heated pool (soon to be fenced, say the owners). The ultra well-equipped kitchen has a veranda – a pleasant place to breakfast – and a laundry room. Upstairs are four charmingly individual bedrooms, each with an old, carved door and a gorgeous bathroom. They're furnished with a few choice antiques and extra-wide double beds which can be transformed into twins. A fifth room over the garage is more casual but clean and pretty, with five narrow single beds. Out in the summer house are many bicycles – early risers can be dispatched two miles to the village bakery in Viglain for fresh breakfast rolls.

sleeps	10-13.
price	€ 835–€ 1,520.
rooms	5: 4 twins/doubles, 1 dormitory with 5 singles, 1 bathroom, 2 shower rooms.
closed	Never.

booking details

Thierry & Nicole Hiltzer

tel	+33 (0)3 25 41 83 52
fax	+33 (0)3 25 41 91 33
e-mail	taille.rouge@laposte.net

map 6   entry 90

Le Grand Ajoux – Lavande

Chalais, Indre

One family comes here every year to watch the dragonflies hatch on the estate's two lakes. On the southern edge of the Brenne National Park – famous for its thousand lakes – and in 53 hectares of private parkland, the place is a paradise for birdwatchers and nature lovers. Lavande is one of two stables (see opposite) which have been elegantly converted by the equally elegant and energetic Madame Jonquière-Aymé, who runs a B&B in the handsome manor house next door. At opposite ends of the lavender-fringed pool, each cottage has a private patio for sunbathing or dining. Inside, cheerful sky-blue chairs and soft furnishings contrast sympathetically with the exposed stone walls, stripped ceiling beams and lovely terracotta tile floor, with old and new pieces of furniture sitting happily side by side. Watch the family's horses and donkeys grazing the paddocks from your pretty little downstairs bedroom. There are plenty of walks from the house, and Georges Sand fans can drive to the Vallée Noire, where she lived, and visit the museum at La Châtre. *B&B also.*

sleeps	2-4.
price	€275-€535.
rooms	2: 1 double, 1 sofabed in living room, 1 shower room.
closed	Never.

booking details

Aude de la Jonquière-Aymé

tel	+33 (0)2 54 37 72 92
fax	+33 (0)2 54 37 56 60
e-mail	grandajoux@aol.com
web	grandajoux.tripod.com

Le Grand Ajoux – Amande
Chalais, Indre

Fifty-three hectares of parkland are yours to roam, and, if you're interested, Madame will whisk you off on deer and wild boar spotting trips. Alternatively, fish in the private lake (bring your own rod), or simply unwind by the pool – it's a few steps from your pretty blue bedroom door. Elegantly cosy, this tiny 300-year-old converted stable has been imaginatively restored while keeping original stone walls and tiled floors. There's one bedroom on the ground floor, and steep pine stairs that lead to the small mezzanine twin bedroom for children. Settle down in front of the stone fireplace, cosy on cool evenings, and plan the next day's activities. There's the Abbey of St-Savin with its 13th-century frescoes of the hermit Saint Savinus to visit, and the Loire châteaux, a 90-minute drive. And there are wines to taste, if you're an *aficionado*: try Vouvray and Chinon from the Touraine… film buffs may prefer the Cuvée Cyrano, produced by the Château of Tigné, owned by actor Gérard Dépardieu. At the end of the day you'll want to rush back to blissful seclusion and let the owls hoot you to sleep. *B&B also.*

sleeps	2-4.
price	€ 245–€ 535.
rooms	2: 1 double, 1 twin on mezzanine, 1 shower room, 1 separate wc.
closed	Never.

booking details

Aude de la Jonquière–Aymé
tel	+33 (0)2 54 37 72 92
fax	+33 (0)2 54 37 56 60
e-mail	grandajoux@aol.com
web	grandajoux.tripod.com

map 10   entry 92

Les Genêts

Nozières, Cher

Compact, stylish and tranquil: this charming stone farm cottage looks like something out of *Alice in Wonderland*. Roses decorate the pale stone front, a great vine drapes over the pergola and in the fields all around Charolais cows gently munch. The house is far larger than it looks from the outside: rooms are light and airy, and are furnished simply but with French flair. Marie-Claude, the charming, dynamic, elegant owner who lives in the farmhouse – and runs B&B – a kilometre away, has thought through every detail, from moon and star cut-outs in the bedroom shutters to tartan bows on the picture hooks. Downstairs, tiled floors and whitewashed walls give a homely, country feel. The living room has inviting sofas with tartan throws and you can still see the old bread oven in the dining room fireplace. The two bedrooms have pine floorboards, antique beds and pretty fabrics. The kitchen leads into the grassy garden and you can eat on the patio in the front. There's good cycling all around and a Saturday market in Saint Amand. A real gem. *Phone number is booking agency. B&B also.*

sleeps	6–10.
price	€ 300–€ 365.
rooms	3: 2 family rooms for 3, 1 family room for 4, 1 shower room downstairs, 1 separate wc.
closed	Never.

booking details

	Marie-Claude Dussert
tel	+33 (0)2 48 48 00 18
fax	+33 (0)2 48 48 00 28

xplanations

Abbreviated address

ot to be used for correspondence.

Italics

entions other relevant details e.g.
B also, or when changeover day for
lf-catering is not Saturday.

sleeps

he lower number indicates how
any adults can comfortably sleep
re. The higher is the maximum
umber of people that can be
commodated.

price

he price shown is per week
d the range covers low season
high season, unless we say
herwise.

rooms

e give total numbers of each type
bedroom e.g. double, triple, and
tal numbers of bathrooms. We give
c details only when they are separate
om bathrooms.

closed

'hen given in months, this means for
e whole of the named months and
e time in between.

map & entry numbers

ap page number; entry number.

symbols

ee the last page of the book for
xplanation.

sample entry

WESTERN LOIRE

La Maison Aubelle - Tour, Gaudrez & Jardin
Montreuil Bellay, Maine-et-Loire

A 16th-century nobleman's house in an old country town. It stands in secluded gardens flanked by high stone walls, renovated by craftsmen, thoughtfully equipped by Peter and Sally. The original apartments are Tour, Jardin and Gaudrez. Tour – in the tower, as you'd expect – is one flight up a spiralling stone stair; it has a beamed living room/kitchen with trim red sofas and wraparound views (below). The garden apartment, with terrace, is as neat as a new pin; white walled Gaudrez has a 16th century window, discovered during restoration. The feel is airy, relaxing, comfortable; crisp linen, central heating and daily cleaning are included and the quality is superb. There's a terrace and games room for all and an appropriately large pool. If you can't face cooking, let the Smiths do it for you: they whisk up delicious meals five times a week, cheerfully served in the dining room in winter, on the terrace in summer. Peter and Sally are also on hand to advise, translate or leave you in peace. They run French courses, too. *Apartments rented separately or together. Children over 12 welcome. Shared laundry. Min. three nights.*

sleeps	Tour & Gaudrez: 4. Jardin: 2.
price	Tour & Gaudrez €775-€1,000; Jardin €675-€925.
rooms	Tour: 2 doubles, 2 shower rooms. Gaudrez: 2 doubles, 2 shower rooms. Jardin: 1 double, 1 bathroom, 1 separate wc.
closed	Rarely.

booking details

Peter & Sally Smith
tel	+33 (0)2 41 52 36 39
fax	+33 (0)2 41 50 94 83
e-mail	maison.aubelle@aubelle.com
web	www.aubelle.com

entry 71   map 7

Photography by Michael Busselle

poitou-charentes limousin & auvergne

La Grande Métairie – The Cottage
Leugny, Vienne

The stuff of dreams! Rose was bewitched by La Grande Métairie which she thought looked like an illustration by Arthur Rackham. Ten years and 200 rose bushes on, this ancient farm with views over the Creuse valley keeps its enchantment. The stone farm buildings with their unusually sloping roofs surround a courtyard, shaded by fruit trees; under one stands a life-size effigy of your opera singer host Richard. This fun and cultured couple do B&B next door and are often there to help if you need them. The inside of the cottage will cast its spell over you too: friendly old armchairs around a woodburner in the cool kitchen/living room, wonderful gnarled beams. Upstairs there are ancient iron bedsteads (with modern mattresses) and gabled beamed ceilings. Dine out on a private terrace in the large dreamy garden, jump into the (shared) pool surrounded by roses, or treat yourself to tennis – there's a private court. Rose even runs rose-pruning days, in season. *Let with studio and owners' house, sleeping total of 16, for six weeks from mid-July. B&B also. See studio on next page.*

sleeps	4–5.
price	€538–€918 (£340–£580).
rooms	3: 1 double, 1 twin, 1 single on landing, 2 bathrooms.
closed	Never.

booking details

Richard & Rose Angas

tel	+44 (0)20 8743 1745
fax	+44 (0)20 8743 1745
e-mail	angas@freeuk.com

La Grande Métairie – The Studio
Leugny, Vienne

There's wood everywhere in this little jewel-among-the-rafters in the old farm stables. Stripped age-worn beams carry the sloping ceilings and there are hefty old boards on the floor. A large iron-framed double bed is screened from the living/kitchen area by pretty Indian-print curtains; similar fabrics cover a sofabed. You look onto the grassy courtyard on one side and onto the Creuse valley and the tennis court (shared with the owners and their B&B guests) on the other. Stone steps lead down to a private terrace and garden. Come here to relax in the company – out of season – of your interesting hosts, Rose and Richard, and to discover this unspoiled area of France. Once you've explored the property's three acres of gardens, woodland and pool, there are châteaux to visit, restaurants and wines to sample, and pleasant walks and cycle rides. A baker delivers daily, and you can buy fresh eggs, goats' cheese and honey from the local farm. *Let with cottage & owners' house for six weeks from mid-July. Babysitting available. B&B also. See cottage on previous page.*

sleeps	2-3.
price	€319-€415 (£200-£260).
rooms	1 double, 1 single sofabed, 1 shower room.
closed	Never.

booking details

Richard & Rose Angas

tel	+44 (0)20 8743 1745
fax	+44 (0)20 8743 1745
e-mail	angas@freeuk.com

map 10   entry 95

Rue de la Cour – Les Écuries

Mandegault, Deux Sèvres

Enjoy a glass of chilled pineau de Charentes, the wickedly delicious local aperitif, under the wisteria-clad pergola of these sweet stone stables. Alison and Francis, both artists and ex-teachers of art and technology, have put their talents to wonderful use, carefully furnishing and decorating the ground-floor cottage; the result is pure rustic charm. As in the old bakery next door (see opposite), natural colours and fabrics predominate and rooms have exposed honey-coloured stone walls and oak beams. Spotless bedrooms are small and simple yet elegant, with scrubbed wooden floorboards and iron or polished wooden beds. Pick herbs from your garden and sprinkle them over the fresh organic vegetables the Hudsons supply; they also serve a delicious four-course dinner. Your garden is private and pretty, with fig trees, lawn and teak loungers – and can interconnect with the one next door if two families rent the cottages together. There's a large paddling pool for children to share, and bikes to hire. Chef Boutonne, the nearest town, has a fairytale château, fascinating ancient *lavoirs* (washhouses) and a lively Saturday market.

sleeps	4.
price	€305–€530.
rooms	2: 1 double, 1 twin, 1 shower room.
closed	Never.

booking details

	Francis & Alison Hudson
tel	+33 (0)5 49 29 65 31
e-mail	mandegault@aol.com

Rue de la Cour – Le Four de Boulanger

Mandegault, Deux Sèvres

With its sunflower fields, honey stone walls and carthorses, the tiny village of Mandegault reminds one how rural France used to be. Life slows to a tranquil trot, a pace which English owners Alison and Francis have been delighted to adopt at their 18th-century farmstead. Hens and ducks potter in the courtyard (children are invited to help collect the eggs at feeding time), sheep graze in the fields, and the wonderfully fertile soil produces everything from cherries to the famous Charentais melons. The couple have been equally respectful of local styles and materials in the conversion of the bakery and the stables, both rented out as cottages. In the bakery, the original vaulted stone bread oven and authentic diamond-shaped *œil de boeuf* windows have been kept, while natural fabrics, pale colours, oak beams and walls of creamy stone create a mood of soothing elegance. There's pretty red stencilling on the floorboards in the main bedroom, and curtains give a dash of colour to the splendid carved wooden bed and wardrobe, both painted cream. The owners are lovely and do an excellent *table d'hôtes*.

sleeps	4-6.
price	€ 335-€ 600.
rooms	2: 1 double, 1 twin, 1 sofabed in living room, 1 bathroom downstairs.
closed	Never.

booking details

	Francis & Alison Hudson
tel	+33 (0)5 49 29 65 31
e-mail	mandegault@aol.com

map 10 entry 97

4 chemin du Moulin

Mauzé sur le Mignon, Deux Sèvres

A small 19th-century miller's house (though the mill is much older) right in the middle of the village. The river Mignon flows by, hence the collection of grasses in the garden; in summer it dries up completely and vegetation bursts from the river bed. This is a tranquil, pretty place; windows are shuttered, roses cling to the wall, kingfishers visit the lush garden. Inside is a quietly artistic world. Benjamin and Blott are creative souls – she, an *artiste en coquillage*, is known for her artistry with shells – and the interior reflects their love of shape and design. It is original, sophisticated, fun. There are slatted blinds, a roll-top bath, lime-washed walls, linen throws over armchairs, books and magazines, games and toys – nothing precious, just a creative family feel. The ceiling of the children's room is multi-coloured, the kitchen has a painted wooden floor, and there are fine views to the river and the surrounding potagers. Venture beyond and you'll come to La Rochelle, the enchanting Ile de Ré, Roman churches and market towns. You can even go canoeing on the water-maze of the Marais Poitevin. A wonderful place to stay.

sleeps	6.
price	€ 500–€ 700.
rooms	3: 2 doubles, 1 twin, 1 bathroom, 2 shower rooms, 2 separate wcs.
closed	Halloween-Easter.

booking details

	Benjamin Krebs & Blott Kerr-Wilson
tel	+33 (0)5 49 35 22 56
fax	+33 (0)5 49 35 22 56
e-mail	benomoulin@aol.com

9 clos des Gouverneurs

Ile de Ré, Charente-Maritime

Spot film stars and celebrities strolling the streets of this pretty fishing port whose whitewashed houses cluster around the stone quays of a well-protected harbour. The Ile de Ré, with its 30km of sandy beaches, pine forests, stylish restaurants and shops, is a place people return to again and again – with good reason. This old green-shuttered ground-floor apartment in a quiet side street is a great spot from which to explore St Martin's narrow cobbled streets, relax in harbourside cafés, and watch flat-bottomed oyster boats arriving with their catch. You can investigate the island by bike (a cycleway goes all the way round) and there's birdwatching in the salt marshes. The apartment has been superbly restored by its (absent) English owners. In the light, open-plan living room/kitchen, beautiful terracotta tiles and a couple of antique pieces contrast with the pure white ceiling and clean exposed stone walls. Bedrooms have a modern feel, and there are two tiny patios, one with an old well, where you can eat. A delicious retreat, wonderful for families.

sleeps	4.
price	€ 407–€ 574 (£275–£395).
rooms	2: 1 double, 1 room with bunkbeds, 1 bathroom.
closed	Rarely.

booking details

	Elspeth Charlton & Graham D'Albert
tel	+33 (0)5 46 33 60 88

map 9   entry 99

Blacksmith's Cottage

Romazières, Charente-Maritime

Another pretty stone cottage, this one the former home of the blacksmith. His forge is next door and Elspeth and Graham have breathed new life into old stones. The dapper exterior hides a snug interior and the full architectural works: beamed ceilings, stonework walls, smart wooden floors – the latter courtesy of an artisan carpenter who excelled himself. The style is clutter-free, authentic and easy on the eye. The downstairs bedroom has French windows that open onto the garden where a walnut tree looms; the kitchen/sitting/dining room has plastered walls, stone-flagged floors and a wooden staircase that spirals up to the other rooms (one of which has a low ceiling and is for small children only). The kitchen holds all you need. A pretty walled garden offers lawn, parasols, a barbecue and shade-giving trees. There is also a wild fruit and vegetable garden from which you are free to harvest whatever is in season; the nearest shops are at Néré, three miles away. The shared pool is beautifully private in its walled and gated garden between the cottage and the owners' house. *Extra room for two available close by.*

sleeps	4 + 2 children.
price	£275-£395.
rooms	3: 1 double, 1 children's room, 1 twin with wc downstairs, 1 bathroom.
closed	Rarely.

booking details

Elspeth Charlton
& Graham D'Albert

tel   +33 (0)5 46 33 60 88

Le Clos du Plantis – Le Goulet

Sonnac, Charente-Maritime

Le Clos du Plantis is wrapped up in two private acres. Beyond its walls the hamlet of Le Goulet paddles in undiscovered country... this is a charming pocket of France, full of romanesque delights. And here, a warm, inviting place to stay, with delightful hosts who do B&B in the main house. Meet the other guests round the large pool; and fish, in season, in the trout stream that runs through. You will feel nicely private in your stone-walled barn, beautifully renovated in Charentaise style. Smartly painted shuttered windows come in sage green, one ceiling is beamed, walls are colour-washed plaster or stone. The interior is simply furnished with a hotchpotch of pieces; white cotton throws on old sofas, pretty white drapes. Bedrooms have pale carpets, rough plaster walls, voile curtains – a neat contemporary feel. The kitchen has all (new) mod cons, French windows open onto a terrace, and your own garden (watch young children as the gate does not shut!) has country views. There's boules and table tennis and Madame is an enthusiastic gardener who grows organic veg. A lush and lazy paradise. *B&B also.*

sleeps	4-6.
price	€ 450-€ 1,050.
rooms	2: 1 double, 1 twin, 1 sofabed in sitting room, 1 bathroom, 1 separate wc.
closed	Rarely.

booking details

	Frédérique Thill-Toussaint
tel	+33 (0)5 46 25 07 91
fax	+33 (0)5 46 25 07 91
e-mail	auplantis@wanadoo.fr
web	www.auplantis.com

map 10   entry 101

Manoir Souhait – Le Verger

Gourvillette, Charente-Maritime

You can still see the stone oven in the dining room in which the house's former inhabitants cooked their pigeons. The birds, a delicacy reserved for the gentry, were reared in the pigeonnier, just outside the gates. In the tiny village of Gourvillette, the house stands in the grounds of the 17th-century manoir which is also rented out by British owners Liz and Will (see next page). Camaraderie between the two houses is encouraged: guests at both are invited to an aperitif on the day they arrive, and you'll get to know each other by the pool (heated, with a section for children). Or make friends over snooker, badminton, table tennis... The interior is light and clean and the furniture mostly modern pine, although ancient roof beams have been kept. Le Verger used to house farmworkers who made cognac, and in the pretty village of the same name (a 20-minute drive) you can go on tours of the distilleries of Remy Martin, Hennessy and Courvoisier. Try the area's other tipple too, pineau de Charentes, a sweet aperitif. If you feel active, bikes can be hired locally and there are lovely rides and walks. *B&B also.*

sleeps	4-5.
price	€ 490-€ 1,050. (£350-£750).
rooms	2: 1 double plus single, 1 twin, 1 bathroom.
closed	Rarely.

booking details

	Will & Liz Weeks
tel	+33 (0)5 46 26 18 41
fax	+33 (0)5 46 24 64 68
e-mail	willweeks@aol.com
web	www.manoirsouhait.com

Manoir Souhait – Le Manoir

Gourvillette, Charente-Maritime

The name means 'wish' and you might well make one to come here. The majestic arched Charentais porchway promises something grand, and you won't be disappointed: a stunning 17th-century manor house in an enclosed garden, its old *lavoir* (washhouse) and pigeonnier intact. Liz and Will, a young and energetic British couple who live next door, have researched the manor's origins meticulously and will be happy to show you the coats of arms of the Merveilleux family, who built the house in 1620. There's a homely kitchen with a terracotta-tiled floor and a massive table; in summer you spill onto the patio. An amazing period staircase takes you to bedrooms decorated with a successful mix of antique and modern furniture. This is ideal walking and cycling terrain, the coast and La Rochelle are only an hour's drive, and you can visit the distilleries in nearby Cognac. Or stay here and relax by the L-shaped heated pool (with a section for children), shared with guests from the neighbouring cottage (see previous page). For large family gatherings it's perfect. *B&B also.*

sleeps	14 + 1 cot.
price	€ 1,190–€ 3,080 (£850–£2,200).
rooms	7: 3 doubles, 4 twins, 2 bathrooms, 1 shower room.
closed	Rarely.

booking details

Will & Liz Weeks

tel	+33 (0)5 46 26 18 41
fax	+33 (0)5 46 24 64 68
e-mail	willweeks@aol.com
web	www.manoirsouhait.com

map 10   entry 103

Château Mouillepied – La Maison du Vivier

Port d'Envaux, Charente-Maritime

Big French windows overlook the water-lily-strewn fishpond which gives the house its name. It was once the château's summer house and stands at the edge of the gardens: a graceful, 18th-century cottage, built of creamy stone and covered with vines. Inside, all is airy and open plan, with unobtrusive, modern furniture and a cool, understated feel. The whole of the first floor is taken up by one big family room where whitewashed walls, exposed beams and a new pine floor give an effect of freshness and simplicity. There are three single beds, two in the middle and one at the end, hidden behind heavy linen curtains. The big sunny living room has an open fireplace and a well-equipped kitchen area. (Martine and Pierre are lovely and will, on request, deliver croissants to your door.) You have your own, unfenced garden *and* the beautiful grounds, which hold a fine pigeonnier and various intriguing outhouses, including one with the huge decorated *lessiveuses* – the 18th-century precursors of the washing machine. All this in pretty countryside close to the Charente; stroll the banks, pick up a fishing licence from the local bakery. *B&B also.*

sleeps	3-4.
price	€ 240–€ 398.
rooms	2: 1 triple, 1 single, 1 bathroom, 1 separate wc.
closed	Never.

booking details

Pierre & Martine Clément

tel	+33 (0)5 46 90 49 88
fax	+33 (0)5 46 90 36 91
e-mail	chateau-mouillepied@voila.fr
web	www.chateaumouillepied.com

Le Moulin des Agrilles

Lorignac, Charente-Maritime

A gracious, friendly house, outside and in, and a marvellous place for a family party or group of friends. Formerly a *maison de maître*, built in the 17th century, it has seven acres of land, semi-wild in places, and views on all sides. (From one point you can see as far as the Gironde estuary.) The pretty, formal front faces the garden and there's a real feeling of seclusion. Even the lovely pool lies discreetly away behind some trees. Josette and Rodney have done wonders indoors, too, and have created a fresh, pretty elegance. The pale yellow country kitchen with its Charentaise fireplace and huge farmhouse table is splendidly equipped. There are two very attractive sitting rooms, one designed for the adults of the party, the other has TV, music and games for all ages. From the tiled hall, a graceful stone staircase curves its way up to the first and second floors, where bedrooms are big and delightful. Josette and Rodney do all they can to make things easy for you; they'll send you a grocery list so you can pre-order supplies, and Josette can sometimes be prevailed upon to cook. *B&B also.*

sleeps	15 + cot.
price	€ 2,050–€ 3,050 (£1,600–£3,000).
rooms	8: 4 doubles, 3 twins, 1 single, 5 bathrooms, 1 separate wc.
closed	Occasionally in winter.

booking details

	Josette Cooke
tel	+44 (0)1939 250258 or +33 (0)5 46 48 17 09
fax	+44 (0)1939 250278
e-mail	josettecooke@aol.com

map 9   entry 105

Moreau

Cercoux, Charente-Maritime

Understated elegance and homeliness are skilfully combined in this 18th-century farmhouse; its mood of tranquillity and sophistication beguiles and soothes. Plain yet luxurious, it is decorated throughout with antiques; no surprise to learn that the English owner Marian, who lives next door, is an antiques dealer. The house used to be a wealthy farm where the aperitif pineau was made; the chestnut beamed ceilings and stone fireplace have been superbly preserved. The spectacular kitchen – the old distillery – has a huge vaulted ceiling, a woodburning range, and dazzling white walls and floors which set off a sensational display of navy and white china. Enjoy the dreamy views over the fields from the carpeted double bedroom, with its fabulous antique bed under huge beams. Outside, a small garden with splash pool for children. Stock up in Cercoux, or shop at the twice-weekly market at pretty Coutras, a 20-minute drive. Nearby medieval Montguyon holds a folklore festival in July and August; there's also a lake for swimming and a beach area, with a little café. Marian is delightful, available yet unobtrusive.

sleeps	4-8.
price	€350–€630 (£250–£450).
rooms	3: 2 family rooms for 3, 1 sofabed, 1 bathroom, 1 shower room.
closed	November–March. Winter lets by arrangement.

booking details

Marian Sanders

tel	+33 (0)5 46 04 01 66
fax	+33 (0)5 46 04 01 66
e-mail	marianatmoreau@hotmail.com
web	www.holidayatmoreau.com

Les Galards

Montlieu la Garde, Charente-Maritime

The wonderful 17th-century *maison de maître* has never left the family and it fell to Monsieur Menanteau to renovate and revive. The attached one-storey building is your gîte. The kitchen is wonderful – the hub of the house – with an original sink carved from stone, three black cooking pots hung on stonewashed walls and the finest of mod cons. There's central heating, too. French doors open to a terrace with barbecue and a young garden with trees, swings and sandbox. Soft yellow bedrooms are equally minimalist and pleasing. Expect high beams, terracotta or stripped floors, an ancient stone fireplace, a Louis Philippe chest of drawers, a delightful small-pebble floor. Bathrooms are excellent: yellow-tiled, beamed, spotless. The salon has upright antique wooden settees, an exquisite grandfather clock and simple chandelier – and there's delicious, local cognac in the cupboards for you to buy. Outside are unbroken views of rolling countryside, a private wood and a small lake where you can swim, fish or get pedalo-fit. For things watery, head to Lac Baron; for a perfect meal, to Chepniers, two miles up the road.

sleeps	8 + 1 cot.
price	€ 445–€ 690.
rooms	4: 2 doubles, 2 twins, 1 bathroom, 2 shower rooms, 2 separate wcs.
closed	Never.

booking details

	Pascal Menanteau
tel	+33 (0)5 46 04 53 62
fax	+33 (0)5 46 04 32 33
e-mail	menanteau.pascal@free.fr

map 10 entry 107

Buffetaud

Passirac, Charente

Remote and peaceful – a hamlet of two houses! This 18th-century scrubbed-stone farmhouse has a fenced pool, a big garden and is encircled by farmland. Inside, a large hall bisects the house. Terracotta runs throughout the ground floor, graced by the odd Persian rug, while space has been created by removing the double doors from dining and sitting rooms. White walls soak up light. Bedrooms are excellent and the downstairs doubles huge; one has a lovely fireplace, the other, double doors that open to the terrace. Both are uncluttered, light and airy, and furnished with the odd antique. Upstairs rooms have exposed beams; compact bathrooms come with shining white tiles and plush towels. The feel is not grand but handsome and homely, with stone fireplaces, comfy sofas and armchairs, lots of space. The kitchen has new appliances and absolutely all you need; in summer you can eat on the terrace by the pool. There's also a good restaurant nearby. A great place for one huge family or three small ones. Don't miss the Charente, one of France's best kept secrets, or the town of Cognac, within striking distance.

sleeps	11.
price	€1,200–€1,800.
rooms	6: 2 doubles, 3 twins, 1 single, 2 bathrooms, 2 shower rooms, 2 separate wcs.
closed	Never.

booking details

	Florence Descoqs
tel	+33 (0)1 39 53 50 02
fax	+33 (0)1 39 02 78 34
e-mail	albert.descoqs@wanadoo.fr

Haute Claire
St Séverin, Charente

An exceptional house that dates to 1860 and which sits in two acres of private land with long views over sun-drenched fields. An ideal place for two families, with loads to keep the children happy (table tennis, table football, DVD), space enough for the adults to find some peace, and a brand-new, lagoon-like pool in a courtyard… or, to be exact, within the walls of an old stone barn that has lost its roof. The main salon is in elegant country-house style (fine sofas, exquisite mirrors, paintings old and new, brass chandelier), the kitchen in relaxed farmhouse style, the dining room somewhere between the two. Bedrooms are large, with wooden floors, brass beds and patchwork quilts; for the children, three twins, simply furnished with new pine beds and white walls. The house swims in light and style; every window has a green view. The whole 1.5 acres are fenced and gated, there are books and satellite TV, boules and barbecue and badminton on the lawn. In winter you're as warm as toast. Aubeterre – one of the prettiest villages in France – is five kilometres up the road: its Sunday market is a must.

sleeps	10.
price	€ 700–€ 2,100.
rooms	5: 2 doubles, 3 twins, 1 bathroom, 2 shower rooms.
closed	Never.

booking details

Michael & Jutta Wrobel
tel   +44 (0)1892 783822
e-mail michael.wrobel@ukgateway.net

L'Abbaye du Palais – Moines
Bourganeuf, Creuse

Another graceful restoration by Dutch owners in rural France. Embraced by five hectares of forest, meadow and orchard: a Cistercian abbey, chapel, outbuildings and ruins. Your delightful hosts have three children and a background in hotel management; since 2001 they have poured hearts and talents into this special place. They live in the 12th-century abbey, do luxury B&B, and have converted the old bakery into a gîte for six. A tangle of greenery envelops this generous, two-storey cottage, with its terracotta floors, open-stone walls, cream drapes, antiques and open fire. The bread oven – still intact – is medieval, the kitchen brand new. A U-shaped bar separates it from the dining area, there are French windows to a west-facing patio (with wooden loungers and barbecue), serenity and light. Children love the whole place: they have an attic above the stables full of games, a treehouse, swings, farm animals, tractor rides, from time to time, with the owners' children, and early meals for early bed. Martijn is a passionate cook and produces three-course dinners: a treat for gîte guests as well as B&B-ers. *B&B also.*

sleeps	6.
price	€ 400–€ 750.
rooms	3: 1 double, 2 twins, 1 bathroom.
closed	Never

booking details

	Martijn & Saskia Zandvliet-Breteler
tel	+33 (0)5 55 64 02 64
fax	+33 (0)5 55 64 02 63
e-mail	info@abbayedupalais.com
web	www.abbayedupalais.com

L'Abbaye du Palais – Templiers & Pellerins

Bourganeuf, Creuse

Attached to Moines (previous entry), the old stable block: a low-slung building with an ancient-stoned terrace and a washed-terracotta roof. One-storey Pellerins is a new house built near the main gates away from the rest, and custommade for wheelchairs. Both have open-plan kitchens, country furniture, an open fire or woodburning stove, plenty of space. Terraces are furnished with wooden loungers and barbecues. The whole domaine (abbey, outbuildings, treehouse) has been beautifully renovated by the Dutch owners, who, with offspring of their own, have made the place family-friendly *par excellence*. Not only is there a play area and games room but also, in their house, a library, billiards and a piano, tuned to play (and people do). These several private acres lie in a richly conifered area of oaks, chestnuts and lakes, bordered by the river Thavrion; no wonder they call it Little Canada. Fish, canoe, ride and swim – or visit the spectacular Gorges du Thavrion. Saskia collects baguettes for your breakfast and prepares picnic baskets; Martijn promises wonderful dinners – just book in advance. *B&B also.*

sleeps	6.
price	€ 400–€ 750.
rooms	3: 1 double, 2 twins, 1 bathroom.
closed	Never

booking details

	Martijn & Saskia Zandvliet-Breteler
tel	+33 (0)5 55 64 02 64
fax	+33 (0)5 55 64 02 63
e-mail	info@abbayedupalais.com
web	www.abbayedupalais.com

map 11   entry 111

Au Nom de la Rose

Turenne, Corrèze

Not the prettiest house in the book, but the views are breathtaking from every window and the house floods with light. Meadows and woods roll away down the valley: a mighty sight. The sitting room is simply furnished; one wall is mostly glass, and double doors open onto a small balcony – lovely for meals. Bathrooms are spotless, bedrooms have polished wooden floors and white bedspreads, and the kitchen is well-equipped, with an electric kettle "for the English" and a dishwasher. An exterior facelift is in the offing, in the form of a pergola with lots of lovely climbing plants. There is also a big, enclosed, orchard-filled garden that falls down the hill, and a barbecue. The stunning village of Turenne climbs a steep, rocky hill, on top of which stands a medieval castle. Monsieur and Madame Cheyroux also own La Maison des Chanoines, the local hotel. It has been in the family for generations and you can book in here for dinner; the food has won awards. Take your pick from canoeing, walking, prehistoric caves, lakes for swimming – and five, characterful Villages de France.

sleeps	6.
price	€ 535–€ 650.
rooms	3: 1 double, 2 twins, 1 bathroom, 1 shower room, 2 separate wcs.
closed	Never.

booking details

Chantal Cheyroux

tel	+33 (0)5 55 85 93 43
fax	+33 (0)5 55 85 93 43
e-mail	maisondeschanoines@wanadoo.fr
web	maison-des-chanoines.com

L'Étable, Le Roux

St Bonnet Elvert, Corrèze

The Carvers' love of the place is infectious. The barn, which they have renovated themselves, pleases everybody. The gîte, forming one half of the ground floor – the former cowshed – has its own entrance, great views and a large covered and seated barbecue area. In the L-shaped kitchen/dining and living room, the predominant feeling is of serenity and space. Floors are pale tiled, walls are white or exposed stone, colours are muted; the kitchen is delightful. More exposed beams and stonework in the bathroom, cheerful with spotlights and yellow towels. In the large, carpeted and centrally heated bedroom the old manger has been converted into a window seat, and the king-size bed is dressed in white and Wedgewood blue. With five acres of wooded walks, a beautifully tended garden with interesting nooks and crannies and a pool with stunning views (shared with Sue's B&B guests) you won't be tempted to linger for long indoors. Pets are welcome and the resident three dogs – and pony – do not encroach. Mobile shops serve the village regularly for stay-at-homes – or it's 15 minutes to Argentat and all the action. *B&B also.*

sleeps	2.
price	€ 290–€ 425.
rooms	1 double, 1 bathroom.
closed	Never.

booking details

Sue Carver
tel +33 (0)5 55 28 38 36
e-mail ceavia@aol.com

map 11 entry 113

Fleuret – Main House
Curemonte, Corrèze

The setting of this 17th-century farmhouse is breathtaking: views of hills and woodland flood in from every window. Although close to the busy Dordogne river, Fleuret, once a hamlet of 12 families, stands in its own secret valley. Your multi-roomed home has been sensitively restored by Gilly and architect/photographer Tim, whose photographs dot the walls; ask about his courses on landscape photography. These young, easy-going owners live with their two children in another part of the house, but walls are thick and space is plentiful. The welcoming kitchen/dining room has warm wooden flooring, a woodburner in the huge ancient hearth, a wonderful table for family feasts; the sitting room has terracotta-washed walls, exposed stone, sofas to lounge in. One double is downstairs, the other bedrooms are in the attic with gabled ceilings and fabulous views. There are books, games, a video library – and a shared pool and games room to keep everyone happy. The medieval hilltop village of Curemonte is three kilometres away, its market opens in summer, and there are masses of castles and caves to discover.

sleeps	9-10.
price	€ 1,250–€ 2,050.
rooms	5: 2 doubles, 1 twin, 1 triple, 1 single, 1 bathroom, 1 shower room.
closed	Never.

booking details

Tim & Gilly Mannakee
tel	+33 (0)5 55 84 06 47
fax	+33 (0)5 55 84 05 73
e-mail	info@fleuretholidays.com
web	www.fleuretholidays.com

Fleuret – The Cottage

Curemonte, Corrèze

You can still see the 200-year-old bread oven in the kitchen, its brick surround charred by the ages. It was excavated by owners Tim and Gilly, who have restored this red sandstone farm cottage with imagination and sensitivity. Stonework and ancient roof beams have been carefully preserved and terracotta floors and pine cupboards added; strings of garlic, cookery books and games add a personal feel. Bedrooms are cosy and carpeted, and the twin has a bedside table made from the bread oven chimney-breast. French doors lead from the airy sitting/dining room to an outdoor dining and barbecue area where you can eat in privacy and enjoy wonderful views of fields, woods and rolling hills and the 11th-century village of Curemonte. There's a huge pool, shared with your delightful young British hosts next door, and an amazing barn with a vast oak floor which you are free to use for whatever you like: ping-pong, billiards, dancing, grand piano – you can even hire it for weddings. A perfect home for a family in search of peace and space. *With Main House (see previous entry) sleeps 14.*

sleeps	4.
price	€550–€990.
rooms	2: 1 double, 1 twin, 1 bathroom.
closed	Never.

booking details

Tim & Gilly Mannakee
tel	+33 (0)5 55 84 06 47
fax	+33 (0)5 55 84 05 73
e-mail	info@fleuretholidays.com
web	www.fleuretholidays.com

map 11 entry 115

La Farge

Monceaux-sur-Dordogne, Corrèze

As ideal a hideaway today as it was for refugees during the war, this large Correzian barn overlooks the pastures of the plateau above the Dordogne. The English owners, who do B&B up the lane, have a wealth of local knowledge. Helen also gives guests a big welcome; her kind neighbour may offer eggs. This is a proper working farm – mostly sheep and dairy – and yes, the chanticleer crows! Inside: a fresh feel to the big, terracotta-floored living room, amply furnished with chunky chairs in flowery covers, usefully stocked with books, games and CDs. The kitchen is equally well-equipped. There's a large white bathroom upstairs, and a cool, blue bedroom with new pine beds, blue-painted furniture and round blue rug; a dehumidifier, too. Big blue pots of geraniums surround the barn in summer, and 'Le Parc', as it is known by the locals – a large, enclosed area of lawns and trees, with comfortable garden furniture and a barbecue – is all yours. There's central heating for winter, a shared pool for summer. This would be a perfect spot for those who love quintessential rural France. *Washing machine in B&B.*

sleeps	2.
price	€275–€390 without pool; €315–€435 with pool.
rooms	1 twin, 1 bathroom.
closed	Never.

booking details

Helen & Keith Archibald
tel +33 (0)5 55 28 54 52
e-mail archi-at-lafarge@wanadoo.fr

La Vieille Auberge
St Julien aux Bois, Corrèze

The quintessential character-steeped holiday home – a former coaching inn (early 1800s) with a tangle of exposed oak beams, original wooden floors, hand-blown glass in the oldest windows and a minstrel gallery. The owners have restored the house taking care not to spoil the charm. A fireplace separates the inner sanctum of lounge, kitchen and dining area… then up dark wooden stairs to a horseshoe mezzanine in the eaves, off which the bedrooms lie. Amazing – like being in Shakespeare's Globe Theatre. There's a medley of furniture, some old: an enormous dining table with bench seating, church pew and armoire, a medieval-style chandelier, new wicker armchairs and comfortable Russian-style sleigh and Alhambra beds. Mod cons include central heating. Outside, a little garden in which to barbecue or relax with a glass of wine. You get your provisions in nearby St Privat, and there's also a baker who drives by each day in his van. Argentat, filled with art galleries and restaurants, is a 20-minute drive. The area is packed with things to do, from swimming to golf, and is sheer heaven for nature lovers.

sleeps	6-7+.
price	£350-£475.
rooms	3 doubles, 1 single four poster in sitting room, z-bed, 2 bathrooms, 1 shower room.
closed	Never.

booking details

	Anita & Roy Bell
tel	+44 (0)1342 836127
fax	+44 (0)1342 833674
e-mail	exfrt@aol.com
web	www.labellmaison.com

map 11   entry 117

Longevialle
St Paul de Salers, Cantal

Pack your hiking boots. Bang in the heart of the dramatic Parc des Volcans d'Auvergne, this newly converted barn will delight walkers and anyone who wants a glimpse of an area of rural France which has changed little in centuries. Nearby medieval (if touristy) Salers with its cobbled streets, gateways and turreted mansions crafted from the dark Auvergnat volcanic rock is another treat. Don't miss the weekly market where farmers sell delicious Cantal and other cheeses for which the area's lush pastures are famous. Although in the hamlet, the house feels totally private, and has south-facing views over a pleasant garden for al fresco dining. The downstairs is open plan, with new pine floors and panelled walls which give a roomy, airy feel. The kitchen has one of the original stone walls, and the (absent) French owner thoughtfully leaves a selection of recipes for you. Spotless pine-clad bedrooms, one a mezzanine, have fabulous views. Walk from the door onto the GR400 Tour du Cantal footpath which takes in Puy Violent and Puy Mary. There's cross-country skiing in winter.

sleeps	6-8.
price	€300–€545.
rooms	3 twins, 1 sofabed in living room, 2 shower rooms, 1 separate wc.
closed	Never.

booking details

Marie-Geneviève Bauchant

tel	+33 (0)2 47 29 50 70
e-mail	mg.bauchant@wanadoo.fr
web	membres.lycos.fr/longevialle

Raymond
Aurillac, Cantal

Walk straight out of this traditional Auvergnat house with its steely slate roofs into stupendous countryside. You can hear a gurgling stream from your bed and all around are breathtaking views of the cone-shaped *puys*. The 200-year-old house used to be two cottages. One half retains the living room where once the family lived, ate and slept: it still has the original wooden beams, long table and fireplace with seats where you can toast your toes and wind down after a day in the mountains. The other half, a ruin when the Haines found it, has a more modern feel, and extra windows give a light and airy feel. Bedrooms too are a blend: ancient, crannied and characterful or well-lit modern; one leads to a terrace. Visit local cheesemakers to sample Cantal for which the area is famous, shower under the waterfall in the river, or visit the market in Aurillac. You can buy fresh milk, yogurt and goat's cheese from the farmer next door, and a travelling shop drives to the house three times a week – listen out for his horn. There are guided mountain walks and adventure sports all summer long, and mushroom-picking in autumn.

sleeps	6.
price	€ 450–€ 500.
rooms	3: 2 doubles, 1 twin/double, 2 shower rooms, 1 separate wc.
closed	December-Easter

booking details

	Ann & Stephen Haine
tel	+44 (0)20 7267 8936
fax	+44 (0)20 7813 5573
e-mail	annhaine@blueyonder.co.uk

map 11 entry 119

Sweet Little House

Condat, Cantal

Tiny, south-facing and built into the rock, this stone house is described by its owners as "doll's house pretty". Di and her farmer husband Peter moved here from Devon in search of solitude; they live nearby and hope you'll drop in for a chat and a glass of wine. The little house was built a century ago for the haymaker, and its slate roof (steeply sloped to fend off snow) is typical of the Auvergne. Materials are basic – there's lots of pale pine – but Di has given it style through careful selection of furniture and furnishings. A set of antique copper pans decorates the compact but beautifully equipped kitchen; in the bedrooms upstairs are a fine wrought-iron bed and country antiques. Rooms are uncluttered and immaculately clean, creating a feeling of light and space. The living room has parquet floors and a Godin woodburner; the walls are decorated with the farm implements used by the original haymaker. There's a tiny patio where you can eat out; your gardens are the narcissi-filled meadows, your backdrop, the mountains of the national park. Birdwatchers and walkers will be in heaven.

sleeps	4.
price	£265–£530.
rooms	2: 1 double with wc, 1 twin, 1 bathroom.
closed	Never.

booking details

	Di Scott
tel	+33 (0)4 71 78 63 57
fax	+33 (0)4 71 78 50 33
e-mail	di.scott@wanadoo.fr
web	www.auvergnehols.co.uk

Laquairie

Condat, Cantal

Neat, stylish and endearingly crooked, this lovely little one-storey house, perched at 1,000m in the tiny hamlet of Laquairie (permanent population three families), is a find. Di and Peter, who live 10 minutes' drive away, have restored the Auvergnat house immaculately, keeping original beams and fireplaces and adding comfy, elegant furniture and many mod cons, including dishwasher and phone. They also give you a massive folder of local info on arrival – and a meal, if requested beforehand. The living room has a wonderful sloping wooden floor, and books, maps and games. There's a pretty single bedroom with a white iron bedstead and the wonkiest walls you've ever seen, and a double with cream walls and *toile de Jouy* bedcover. (Its en suite shower room is shared by the single.) Metre-thick walls keep the house cool in the summer; central heating keeps you snug in winter. It's hard to beat if you like walking: you're deep in the Auvergne and have breathtaking views of the Rhue valley and the pointed, volcanic Sancy mountains in the distance. The peace is a balm. *Changeover day Sunday.*

sleeps	3.
price	£285–£530.
rooms	2: 1 double, 1 single, 1 shower room.
closed	Never.

booking details

Di Scott

tel	+33 (0)4 71 78 63 57
fax	+33 (0)4 71 78 50 33
e-mail	di.scott@wanadoo.fr
web	www.auvergnehols.co.uk

map 11 entry 121

Les Frênes

St Nectaire, Puy-de-Dôme

Perched on the rugged central spine of France known as the Massif Central, surrounded by the black protuberances of extinct volcanoes or *puys*, the cottage has unbeatable views. There are snow-capped peaks in the distance, endless forest and mountain, lush pastures all around, a romanesque church. And, on your doorstep, the lovely village (popular in summer) of Saint Nectaire, famous for its church and creamy cheese. The 18th-century, three-storey house is typical of the Auvergne: built of volcanic stone with little windows and thick walls, it faces east to protect it from prevailing winds. Rooms are small and furnishings simple and functional. There's a low-ceilinged double bedroom on the first floor, and an attractive triple with vaulted ceilings on the second. In summer you can spill out into the rose-decked private garden, and there's another bigger one in which you may meet the B&B guests who lodge in the house next door. Monique, kind and enthusiastic, can advise on anything and everything, from where to buy local cheese to the best walks in this glorious, little-known region. *B&B also.*

sleeps	4-5.
price	€275–€380.
rooms	2: 1 double, 1 triple, 1 bathroom.
closed	Rarely.

booking details

Monique Deforge
tel +33 (0)4 73 88 40 08
e-mail daniel.deforge@wanadoo.fr

Demeure d'Hauterive

La Ferté Hauterive, Allier

Sandwiched neatly between the Lefebvres' imposing *maison de maître* and the half-timbered tower of a medieval priory, an exquisite 19th-century guard's house. Step out of the kitchen's French windows into three hectares of walled lawns and parkland; stroll into the village; make yourself at home. The cottage and the big house next door where Annick and Jérôme run B&B had both been empty for 30 years when the couple fell in love with them. They've restored with taste and style, creating spotless, welcoming rooms furnished with delightful family antiques – a grandfather clock, an oak dresser – and paintings by artist members of the family. Old terracotta floors and beamed ceilings have been beautifully preserved as has the great stone fireplace; an open-tread oak stair leads to bedrooms with delicately printed wallpapers and immaculately dressed beds. You want for nothing, with dishwasher, woodburner, central heating, new pool. Be sure to eat at Les Muriers, the local restaurant – and to visit some of the Allier's glorious châteaux: there are almost as many here as in the Loire. *B&B also.*

sleeps	8-9 + 1 cot.
price	€ 460-€ 530.
rooms	4: 2 doubles, 1 twin, 1 bunkbed for 3, cot in corridor, 1 shower room, 1 separate wc.
closed	Never.

booking details

Annick & Jérôme Lefebvre

tel	+33 (0)4 70 43 04 85
fax	+33 (0)4 70 43 00 62
e-mail	j.lefebvre@demeure-hauterive.com
web	www.demeure-hauterive.com

map 11   entry 123

Photography by Michael Busselle

aquitaine

La Grange de Belle Fontaine
Bellefond, Gironde

This is claret country, and those who like their wine 'red and French' will be in heaven. The immaculately renovated 17th-century barn opposite the *mairie* was once part of Madame's family farm; views uphill take in the village and its ancient church, those down stretch across field, orchard and vineyard. The spotless interior is a mix of 'uncluttered contemporary' and classical French. A floating, light-wood staircase slinks up the wall, French windows in the salon rise to the top of the house and most walls are cream-washed rough plaster – simple and striking. Furniture is painted in light pastel colours, much by Madame, a talented artist. Floors are pale-tiled, underfloor-heated and graced with the odd rug, the open-plan kitchen/dining room is wonderfully light and brilliantly equipped. Bedrooms are exceptional: painted brass beds, sloping ceilings, delicate fabrics, elegant swags. There's a balcony, a terrace for evening drinks and a small secluded garden. The village dates from the 11th century, St Émilion is four miles away, Bordeaux is close. *Swimming pool spring 2004. Children over eight welcome. B&B also.*

sleeps	6.
price	€ 1,100-€ 1,400.
rooms	3 doubles, 1 bathroom, 2 shower rooms.
closed	Never.

booking details

France Prat
tel +33 (0)5 57 47 13 74
e-mail france.prat@wanadoo.fr
web www.gite-bellefontaine.fr.st

La Gouraude
Rimons, Gironde

Your only neighbours are the owls in the woods that surround this 300-year old farmhouse and its gardens; the nearest humans live a mile away. Stroll down the stone path which meanders across the lawns to the pool, floodlit at night; eat out on the wisteria-draped veranda. You even have your own stream, reached through a tunnel in the woods... children will also love the big games room in the barn opposite, and the Wendy house. Marginally less grand than Christopher and Louisa's other houses, La Gouraude has nevertheless been decorated to the same high standard, with antiques, colourful rugs and high quality fabrics. Original features like the old stone basin built into the sitting room wall and the great oak beams have been carefully kept. One bedroom, on the ground floor, feels nicely self-contained; the rest are upstairs, where the granary once was. White walls are hung with pretty china plates and paintings, the beds are antique and gorgeous – there's a mellow feel. Visit the Cathar stronghold of Montségur and its evocative château, from where you can take the dramatic four-hour walk to the Têt valley over the Montagne de la Frau.

sleeps	12.
price	€ 1,427–€ 3,069 (£750–£2,100) for up to 12; € 1,036–€ 1,873 (£650–£1,175) for up to 5.
rooms	6: 2 doubles, 4 twins, 1 bathroom, 2 shower rooms.
closed	Rarely. Long winter lets available.

booking details

Christopher & Louisa Taylor

tel	+33 (0)5 53 20 88 03
fax	+33 (0)5 53 83 61 79
e-mail	taylor.christophe@wanadoo.fr
web	www.frenchmanoirs.net

map 15   entry 125

Manoir du Gaboria – St Émilion, Medoc, Entre-Deux-Mers
Ste Gemme, Gironde

Willy has his own vineyard, produces a good drop, and visits can be arranged. He and Mieke run cookery courses, too. They are a delightful couple – warm, human – and keen to promote the quiet, rambling country that surrounds you and which teems with bastides, vineyards, medieval villages, walking paths, cycling tracks, and fast-flowing rivers. They do B&B – their 18th-century manor house is immaculate – and have three gîtes, but the gardens and lawns are so extensive and the mood so relaxed that no one seems to mind and peace and quiet prevail. There are low stone walls, wandering roses, a well in the courtyard and a sense of rightful permanence. You are high on the hill – views stretch over fields and vineyards (the competition's) and you can gaze out from the smart terrace that encircles the pool. All gîtes have a private terrace, too. Expect a contemporary style, white walls, coir matting, pretty views and lots of space. Furniture is simple, clean and neat. You might have a high-ceilinged room in yellow, a vast kitchen/dining/sitting room or an old original terracotta-tiled floor. Wonderful. *B&B also.*

sleeps	St Émilion: 6. Médoc: 4-5. Entre-deux-mers: 2.
price	St Émilion: €525-€1050. Médoc: €375-€750. Entre-deux-mers: €420-€650.
rooms	St Émilion 3: 2 doubles, 1 twin, 2 baths. Médoc 2: 1 double, 1 triple, 1 bath. Entre-deux-mers: 1 double, 1 bath.
closed	Rarely.

booking details

Mieke & Willy Borremans

tel	+33 (0)5 56 71 99 57
fax	+33 (0)5 56 71 99 58
e-mail	manoir@gaboria.com
web	www.gaboria.com

Les Quatre Vents – Le Clos I & II

Cauneille, Landes

Swiss-born Denise and Arnold did B&B, happily, for years; now they live in these secluded 20 acres, caring for their gîte guests and their few donkeys and sheep. They live 100 yards away, on this hilltop hideaway with magnificent views, and are there when you need them, full of advice and happy for you to share their pool. Clos I and Clos II fill two floors of a chalet-style house: one on the ground floor, with French windows to the terrace, the other above, reached via an outside stair. They are not the last word in contemporary chic but are comfortable, carpeted and newly equipped; there's pine on the walls, patterned duvets on the beds and the odd wool rug and framed poster. Kitchen/sitting rooms are open plan, and your terraces are well-furnished. Sally forth to discover this off-the-beaten-track part of Gascony, dubbed 'the new Dordogne'. The wooded hills are glorious, golf courses abound, Biarritz isn't far, nor Dax, famous for its waters that steam at a steady 64 degrees. It's surrounded by a romanesque wall and is worth visiting not just for its restorative mud baths but also its bustling Saturday market. *Children over 12 welcome.*

sleeps	2 apts for 4–6.
price	€ 500.
rooms	2: 1 double, 1 twin, 1 sofabed in sitting room, 1 bathroom.
closed	Never.

booking details

	Denise & Arnold Brun
tel	+33 (0)5 58 73 25 57
fax	+33 (0)5 58 73 70 60
e-mail	arnold.brun@wanadoo.fr

map 14 entry 127

Résidence Lilinita

Biarritz, Pyrénées-Atlantiques

Watch the rolling waves of the Atlantic from both French windows. Perched on the cliffs above Biarritz's Côte des Basques – a surfers' paradise – this luxury turret, built by a Polish countess in 1905, has staggering views. And if you tire of watching the surfers, gaze at the distant peaks of the Spanish Pyrenees along the coast to the south. Don't be deceived by the apartment's turn-of-the-century exterior: inside all is modern and ultra cool. There's a state-of-the-art kitchen, a large dining/living room with polished floors, and a futuristic central staircase that leads to bedrooms with immaculate white bedcovers and lovely antiques. There's are books, videos, music and oodles of towels. Choose between the two south-facing balconies to dine, and watch the sun set over the sea. You're brilliantly placed to taste the delights of this resort, made fashionable by Victorian ladies in search of winter sun. Boutiques and restaurants are a five-minute walk, as is the Casino Municipal, restored to its 1930s grandeur. *No children under 15. Rates for two, or for longer stays, on request. Flexible changeover day. Minimum three nights.*

sleeps	4.
price	€850–€1,960.
rooms	2 twins/doubles, 1 bathroom, 1 shower room.
closed	Never.

booking details

Sue & Bill Barr

tel	+33 (0)5 59 34 34 14
fax	+33 (0)5 59 34 35 44
e-mail	barr.bill@online.fr
web	www.summerflat.com

Les Collines Iduki – Apartments

La Bastide Clairence, Pyrénées-Atlantiques

A surprisingly attractive holiday complex (there are 22 gîtes in total, in a choice of two styles) that overlooks one of the prettiest bastide villages of France. A dreamy river sweeps round at the foot of the hill, 100-year-old oak trees and fields surround you. The 'village' was designed in Basque-style by the architect that built Les Halles in Bayonne, and fits its landscape perfectly. Whitewashed apartments have private terraces with teak furniture and parasols, brightly painted shutters and pretty interiors. Small bedrooms are dressed in modern fabrics, in Basque reds and greens, in checks and stripes, bathrooms are white, kitchens contain all you need. Sitting rooms have stencilled walls, tiled floors, old wooden furniture nicely painted. All is comfortable and gently stylish. There's a shared pool, a play area and a games room: this is a sociable place, brilliant for families. The Haramboures run the restaurant by the river and meet you on arrival. The village is a four-minute walk; come in the last week of July for the fête and three days of carousing in the square. *Shared laundry.*

sleeps	Apartment A: 2-4.
	Apartment B: 4-6.
price	Apartment A € 237-€ 900.
	Apartment B € 319-€ 1,145.
rooms	Apartment A: 1 double, 1 sofabed in
	lounge, 1 bathroom.
	Apartment B: 1 double, 1 twin,
	1 sofabed in lounge, 1 shower room,
	1 bathroom.
closed	Never.

booking details

	Marie–Joelle Haramboure
tel	+33 (0)5 59 70 20 81
fax	+33 (0)5 59 70 20 25
e-mail	iduki@iduki.net
web	www.iduki.net

map 14   entry 129

Château d'Agnos – Agnos 1, 2 & 3

Agnos, Pyrénées-Atlantiques

The hallmarks of stately style are here in abundance: a huge stone archway, iron gates, a fountain in the rose garden. The château paddles with one toe in the village, the other in open country, and on clear days the view across the fields stretches as far as the Pyrenees. The gîtes themselves are simple – good value for money, not overly plush – and will suit those in search of a simple base from which to explore. The single-storey wing was once a dormitory for the nuns who lived here when the château was a convent; bedrooms are lightly furnished – white walls, wicker chairs, pine beds, colourful linen – and windows open to a communal terrace that runs along the front and flanks the garden. Each open-plan kitchen/sitting/dining room comes with sofas and armchairs, garden chairs around the dining table and a few books. There are trim carpets, good plain bathrooms and all is spotlessly clean. Heather and Desmond do B&B and are not short of ideas for an active holiday: white-water rafting, mountain fishing, paragliding, horse riding, hiking, cycling, skiing – and hot-air balloon flights from the château. *B&B also.*

sleeps	Agnos 1: 6. Agnos 2 & 3: each 4.
price	Agnos 1: £350–£480. Agnos 2 & 3: £250–£380 each.
rooms	Agnos 1: 2 doubles, 1 twin, 1 bathroom. Agnos 2 & 3: each 1 double, 1 twin, 1 bathroom.
closed	Occasionally.

booking details

Heather & Desmond Nears-Crouch
tel	+33 (0)5 59 36 12 52
fax	+33 (0)5 59 36 13 69
e-mail	chateaudagnos@wanadoo.fr

Maison Jas du Pic

Lasseube, Pyrénées-Atlantiques

The house facing the mountain is actually a copy of the Browne family house in South Africa – though its exterior reflects the Bearnaise style. Only fields and forests separate you from the peaks of the Pyrenees and every room leads onto a pretty terrace or the garden, filled with 25 varieties of rose. This is a special place to stay, delightful in every detail, from the ornate garden chairs to the handmade oak stair. Down four steps from the arched doorway, the large living room has checked sofas round an open fire; then through an arch to the dining/kitchen room with a walk-in pantry and fine crockery. Floors are tiled, covered with an exotic mix of rugs big and small; underfloor heating switches seamlessly to a cooling system during summer. Generous drapes of fabric cover the walls to form bedheads in the serene bedrooms with their built-in wardrobes, French windows and views. Each has its own immaculate bathroom, except for one: dormitory style if needed, perfect for children, with a TV room a step away. There's a pool to share and birdsong to serenade you. *Weekly lets preferred. B&B also.*

sleeps	8.
price	€ 2,100.
rooms	4: 3 doubles, 1 twin, 2 bathrooms, 1 shower room, 1 separate wc.
closed	Rarely.

booking details

Simon Browne

tel	+33 (0)5 59 04 26 37
fax	+33 (0)5 59 04 26 37
e-mail	missbrowne@wanadoo.fr
web	www.missbrowne.com

map 14 entry 131

Manoir Coutenson

Grezet Cavagnan, Lot-et-Garonne

The electronically controlled gates and the sweeping gravel drive – floodlit at night – signal grandness and luxury. This 17-century manoir does not disappoint: a large heated pool in a four-acre garden, French antiques, a cellar stocked with 250 bottles. As if that weren't enough, a stone tower – a perfect little guest nest for two – and a full-time gardener are included. This and the neighbouring farmhouse were discovered a few years ago by Louisa, who's French, and her husband, Christopher, who used to run an architectural salvage business. Downstairs rooms have terracotta tiled floors and lovely twisted oak beamed ceilings; the lounge has two fireplaces; the kitchen is oak-fitted. China plates on the walls and artfully arranged pots of dried flowers make the Manoir feel like home. Carpeted bedrooms are reached via two separate staircases leading to landings so comfortably furnished you'll want to go no further; one has a polished floor and an antique desk and chair. Eat on the veranda by the swimming pool, play pool or table tennis in the games room in the grounds.

sleeps	16.
price	€2,390–€4,261 (£1,500–£2,895) for up to 16; €1,585–€2,390 (£995–£1,500) for up to 7 people.
rooms	8: 6 doubles, 2 twins, 7 bathrooms.
closed	Rarely. Long winter lets available.

booking details

	Christopher & Louisa Taylor
tel	+33 (0)5 53 20 88 03
fax	+33 (0)5 53 83 61 79
e-mail	taylor.christophe@wanadoo.fr
web	www.frenchmanoirs.net

Manoir Desiderata

Grezet Cavagnan, Lot-et-Garonne

Sip a gin and tonic by the floodlit pool as you watch the sun set over the distant hills and woods… Desiderata, spotless and newly restored, demands that you unwind. No effort has been spared by Louisa and Christopher in adapting its 300-year-old stones to contemporary tastes and needs; if you like oak beams and period furniture, you'll love it here. The layout is unusual, with most rooms leading off a vast terracotta-floored sitting room; a balustraded walkway runs its entire length leading to four mezzanine-level bedrooms above. A further three bedrooms are downstairs. The large tower bedroom, pretty with sandy exposed stone walls and floral bedcovers, has peaceful views of woods and the 12th-century church. Visit the bastide town of Casteljaloux, on the edge of the pine forest of Les Landes, with its old timber-framed houses with projecting storeys; there's fine walking, too. With table tennis, billiards, darts, exercise machines *and* a big garden this is a great place for two or three families to stay. The Taylors go out of their way to make sure you have all you need.

sleeps	14.
price	€2,390-€3,744 (£1,250-£2,595) for up to 14; €1,585-€2,390 (£995-£1,500) for up to 5 people.
rooms	7: 4 doubles, 3 twins, 7 shower rooms.
closed	Rarely. Long winter lets available.

booking details

	Christopher & Louisa Taylor
tel	+33 (0)5 53 20 88 03
fax	+33 (0)5 53 83 61 79
e-mail	taylor.christophe@wanadoo.fr
web	www.frenchmanoirs.net

map 15   entry 133

La Gare de Sos
Ste Maure de Peyriac, Lot-et-Garonne

Once your wake-up call would have been the hoot of the 06h27 from Sos to Nérac, and the platforms, so peaceful now, would have bustled. This railway station, which finally ground to a halt in 1970, has been delightfully converted by its English owner David, who gave up a City career in London for life at the end of the line. He lives in the village and is happy to make meals on occasion, even to act as tour guide. The former waiting-room and parcels office are your living and dining room, where 1900s advertising posters, a 1924 timetable and some of the original clocks adorn the walls. The old wooden benches on which passengers waited have been swapped for jolly red sofas, good terracotta tiles have replaced workaday boards, and there's a woodburner, piano and books. It's a happy place. The ticket office makes a superb kitchen and pantry; the original oak staircase leads up to bedrooms in the former station master's apartment. For children: a fabulous attic, with four beds, an outdoor pool, and a model railway, of course. Unmissable. *B&B also.*

sleeps	8-10.
price	£385-£1,450.
rooms	4: 2 doubles, 1 twin, 1 quadruple, 1 bathroom, 1 shower room.
closed	Never.

booking details

	David Heath
tel	+33 (0)5 53 97 09 93
fax	+33 (0)5 53 97 09 93
e-mail	adavidheath@aol.com
web	www.garedesos.com

Château de Rodié

Courbiac de Tournon, Lot-et-Garonne

It's more fortress than château, complete with canon loopholes, drop toilets and tower... you are welcome to wander. The story of how Pippa and Paul have breathed new life into these old stones is inspiring: Paul had a serious accident, they bought the 13th-century hillside ruin and its 135 acres (now with nature reserve) and began the triumphant restoration. Your quarters are in what were the old bakery and stables, across the arched, flowered courtyard from where the owners live. The old smokery is one of the bathrooms; the kitchen, delightfully modern, has two of the old bread ovens. A beautiful stone stair (made by Paul) leads to sleigh beds under the eaves; rich rugs sit on tiled floors; there's underfloor heating in winter. Walls are white or pointed stone, windows are small and low. Paul and Pippa farm sheep and run a B&B: Pippa cooks her guests sumptuous organic dinners using much of their own produce. You may join them, by arrangement. There's a terrace off your living room, your own back garden, a shared pool, swings for the children, wild countryside. A deeply authentic place, with special hosts. *B&B also.*

sleeps	7-9.
price	€572–€1,145.
rooms	3: 2 twins, 1 triple, 2 single beds on request, 3 bathrooms.
closed	Rarely.

booking details

	Paul & Pippa Hecquet
tel	+33 (0)5 53 40 89 24
fax	+33 (0)5 53 40 89 25
e-mail	chateau.rodie@wanadoo.fr

map 15   entry 135

La Gabertie

Thézac, Lot-et-Garonne

Monsieur Faffa is as charming as his name suggests. This rabbit warren of stone cottages perches on the plateau that runs above the vineyard-chequered valley, and has outrageously beautiful sunset views from the long, tiled veranda. It is wonderfully old and informal, though the interior has been recently – and beautifully – decked out. Bedrooms hide up worn stone steps and the whole place is far bigger inside than you would think – you may still be unearthing rooms at the end of your stay. Children are well catered for with table football, billiards, ping-pong, board games and a pool, yet there are myriad hidden corners and a large scrub garden into which the more sedate may retreat. The decoration is unfussy – stone walls, clean stretches of wooden flooring, dark wooden shutters, an antique armoire – and offers cool respite from the summer heat. Geared towards large groups, the kitchen has a vast cooker, an industrial-sized fridge and cooking pots reminiscent of school canteens. Open-air dinners for 28 are wild fun – especially after a day's canoeing on the river Lot. *Gîte for 6-10 also available.*

sleeps	20-28.
price	€950–€4,450.
rooms	10: 3 doubles, 5 twins, 1 quadruple, 1 annexe with 4 sets of bunks, 1 bathroom, 5 shower rooms, 7 separate wcs.
closed	Never.

booking details

	Jean Claude Faffa
tel	+33 (0)5 53 40 74 36
fax	+33 (0)5 53 40 23 20
e-mail	faffa@wanadoo.fr
web	www.agades.com/faffa

Manoir de Soubeyrac

Le Laussou, Lot-et-Garonne

Up the tiny winding road to the *gardien's* house, hiding behind its gates in a garden of trees. It sits across the lane from the manor where Monsieur does sumptuous B&B. Pale old stones and sun-bleached tiles; inside, a surprising mix of humble and grand. Monsieur Rocca has thought it all through with great care: the lavender-blue paintwork, the lush fabrics, the bedroom fans. Exposed brickwork and terracotta floors are a plain foil for lavish taste in the bedroom on the ground floor, replete with its apricot-satin-swagged bed. Up the steepish stair to the cottagey triple, where beds line up in a row – a light room with valley views, under the eaves, perfect for children. The living/dining room too is inviting: a clothed table with painted country chairs, patterned rugs, a good sofa, an antique mirror. The little kitchen has an old dresser and bags of charm; the bathroom cossets with aromatic oils. Outside, one of those amazing swimming pools that looks as if it spills over the edge of the hill – all yours. Dine at the manor: you'll eat well; or pick a restaurant in hilltop Monflanquin. *B&B also.*

sleeps	4-5.
price	€ 300-€ 1,300.
rooms	2: 1 double, 1 triple, 1 bathroom.
closed	Never.

booking details

	Claude Rocca
tel	+33 (0)5 53 36 51 34
fax	+33 (0)5 53 36 35 20

map 15   entry 137

As Bernis

Beaugas, Lot-et-Garonne

You're in deep prune country; plums used to be dried in the three brick-clad ovens in the living room wall. This 18th-century stone building was once a farmhouse, and it took Pierre and Annick 18 years to convert it into the gorgeous home it has become. They've teased out the building's original character by recycling old materials wherever possible: old wood has become new banisters, ancient stones ledges and steps. You also have your own bar – picked up by Pierre from an antique dealer – where you can serve yourself a tipple and sip it at a bistro-style metal table. The huge sitting/dining room has beautiful country antiques, a stone fireplace and a stunning original quarry-tile-and-wood floor; the kitchen is small but contains all you need. Bedrooms are large and simple, with old-fashioned wallpapers and big views of the lawn and woods beyond. A garden spring feeds two small ponds, there's table tennis and a court for volley ball, four terraces and a pool just for you. Buy your prunes in Villeneuve sur Lot, your hazelnuts in hilltop Cancon and your provisions in the wonderful cobbled market squares of Monflanquin.

sleeps	10-12 + cot.
price	€ 1,100–€ 2,440.
rooms	5: 4 doubles, 1 quadruple with cot, 1 bathroom, 2 shower rooms, 2 separate wcs.
closed	Never.

booking details

	Pierre & Annick Durin
tel	+33 (0)5 53 01 76 83
e-mail	asbernis@libertysurf.fr
web	perso.libertysurf.fr/as_bernis

Chalet des Rigals
Castillonnès, Lot-et-Garonne

The cherry-tree-lined drive is sensational, so are the 38 wooded acres with trails. Come for carpets of wild orchids in spring, for deer and red squirrels, sunsets and views. Your 150-year-old cottage was once home to the guardian of the manor next door, where the Babers now live. All is delightful and homely: a kitchen/dining room fresh with check curtains, rugs on tiles, round table and wheel-back chairs; a sitting room with good old-fashioned sofas and cosy woodburning stove. There's heating in every room, fans for summer, and a kitchen with all you need. Flowery bedrooms are comfortable and light: a twin downstairs leading to an en suite double, both with French windows, one with a sofa, and a big dormitory under the eaves, brilliant for kids. Young ones will love the pool too (it has a shallow section), shared with the Babers and their B&B guests. There's badminton, tennis and a lake with a boat (do fish), fruit from the orchard, eggs from the hens. Restaurants, shops and a weekly market are a two-minute drive, and the Babers – great gardeners, kind hosts – may have fresh vegetables for you, too. *B&B also.*

sleeps	6-8.
price	£600-£1,225.
rooms	3: 1 double, 1 twin, 1 attic room with 4 singles, 1 bathroom, 1 shower room, 1 separate wc.
closed	Never.

booking details

David & Patricia Baber
tel	+33 (0)5 53 41 24 21
fax	+33 (0)5 53 41 24 79
e-mail	babersrigals@wanadoo.fr

map 15   entry 139

L'Héritier, Parranquet
Villeréal, Lot-et-Garonne

You'll not want to leave this tranquil farmstead in the rolling Quercian countryside. Read, eat or snooze in the blissfully private, shaded courtyard in front of the house, enclosed by stone barns, or cool off in the pool (lit for night-time swims) with views of fields and a pigeonnier. Birdwatchers and nature lovers will be in their element: look out for hoopoes and bee orchids. Homely, well-loved and informal in feel, the house is perfect for one or two families with children. You have a beautifully equipped kitchen, and a bakery in the village. Barbecue in summer or on cool evenings, eat round the cherrywood refectory table in the beamed living room, warmed by the woodburning stove. Attractive English and French country furniture, chestnut floors, well-used rugs and a fireside settle create a cosy atmosphere; simply furnished bedrooms, in two separate sets, have the air of a provincial country hotel. Some will find nostalgia in the naively floral wallpapers, and the master bedroom has a lovely antique bed and polished wooden floor. There's a games room to entertain you, tennis a walk away. *Babysitting available.*

sleeps	6-9.
price	€ 798-€ 1,516 (£500-£950).
rooms	4: 2 doubles, 1 connected to twin, 1 triple, 1 bathroom.
closed	Never.

booking details

Jane Quincey
tel +44 (0)1503 240599
fax +44 (0)1503 240599
e-mail jquincey@mistral.co.uk
web www.farmhouseinfrance.com

Le Branchat – The Cottage, Casa Luisa & Villa Clara
Sagelat, Dordogne

Richard is half-Spanish, Isabelle is French; both ensure your stay will be a happy one. The highlight is the garden – seven hectares of it – which combines fruit and nut orchards with forests, fields grazed by the family ponies, donkey, hens and ducks, and a huge pool. Share your adventures over dinner with the family and their B&B guests. The Cottage, with clean modern lines and pure white walls, has been decorated in a straightforward style using much pine (below); the kitchen/dining room has polished floors and furniture handmade by a family friend; bedrooms under the gables are in sunny yellows and creams. The newer gîtes are bigger, and more luxurious, dishwashers and electric coffee-makers de rigeur. Each has a large, shady terrace off the living room, a private, hazel-nut-treed garden and its own 4mx8m heated pool. One is furnished in Perigourdian style, the other in a mix of contemporary pieces and exotic finds Richard and Isabelle have picked up on their travels. A wonderful place to rest awhile, where you, your children – and even your horse! – can be as private or as sociable as you please. *B&B also.*

sleeps	Cottage: 4-5. Casa Luisa: 6-8. Villa Clara: 6-8.
price	€ 305–€ 610.
rooms	Cottage 2: 1 double, 1 triple, 1 shower room. Casa Luisa & Villa Clara: each with 2 doubles, 1 family room for 4, 1 bathroom, 1 shower room.
closed	Never.

booking details

Richard & Isabelle Ginioux

tel	+33 (0)5 53 28 98 80
fax	+33 (0)5 53 28 90 82
e-mail	info@lebranchat.com
web	www.lebranchat.com

map 15   entry 141

Lavande
Cénac et St Julien, Dordogne

Brigitte and Christophe spotted this 18th-century farmhouse and its wooded acres while on holiday. It was love at first sight – a *coup de cœur*; several busy years on they run an enchanting B&B and have converted the stone stables into two self-catering cottages. Lavande, with its serene views over wooded hills, is the largest and, despite the proximity of the other buildings, is peaceful and private. The inside has been thoroughly restored and, despite the old beams and exposed walls, has a newish feel. In the living room: sumptuous black leather armchairs and a sofa on an immaculately polished wooden floor; in the dining room: an antique trestle table and chairs. The pièce de resistance, however, is the beamed white and blue bedroom which looks like a piece of Delft china. Gourmets will make a beeline for the restaurant L'Esplanade in Domme – you can glimpse the splendid hilltop town from here. You share the delightful park – and pool – with other guests; if you like good home cooking, you may share meals, too. And do buy Brigitte's delicious homemade pâtés for your picnic baguettes. *B&B also.*

sleeps	6.
price	€ 576–€ 1,050.
rooms	3: 2 doubles, 1 attic twin, 1 bathroom, 1 shower room, 1 separate wc.
closed	2 November–1 April.

booking details

	Brigitte & Christophe Demassougne
tel	+33 (0)5 53 29 91 97
fax	+33 (0)5 53 30 23 89
e-mail	contact@la-gueriniere-dordogne.com
web	www.la-gueriniere-dordogne.com

Le Petit Tilleul
Domme, Dordogne

The Dordogne laps 150 yards from the door (great for summer swims) and busy, beautiful Domme is up the hill. Here you have privacy and peace. The compact stone cottage was built around 1650 as a hay barn, and later converted into the baker's house. Friendly owners Mary and Alan live in another building along the lane: they do B&B and Mary holds painting classes from May to September (booked in advance). She was an art teacher and Alan taught woodwork and design; see his handiwork in this simple, successful conversion. Old beams and stone walls are all intact and there's a woodburner in the beautiful stone fireplace in the living room. The well-lit kitchen has white formica worktops and French windows onto the terrace and garden – perfect for eating out. Bedrooms are simple, with wooden shutters and open hanging space. The double has views of Domme and fields, the twin is furnished in pine. Your problem will be to decide what to do first: there's fishing and canoeing on the spot, the GR64A footpath runs past the door, there's a riding school four miles away, and medieval Sarlat is a delight. *B&B also.*

sleeps	4.
price	€375–€675.
rooms	2: 1 double, 1 twin, 1 shower room.
closed	November–March.

booking details

	Alan & Mary Johnson
tel	+33 (0)5 53 29 39 96
fax	+33 (0)5 53 29 39 96
e-mail	montillou@hotmail.com

map 10   entry 143

La Treille Haute
Castelnaud la Chapelle, Dordogne

The setting smacks of a fairytale and five of the Perigord's most spectacular châteaux, clinging to the craggy cliffs of the River Dordogne, are a short drive from your beautiful converted stone barn. You can even see the floodlit Château de Beynac, awesome and grand, from the comfort of your bed. By day, buy some local foie gras and picnic in the rich fields and wooded hills or stroll among the warm stone houses of steep riverside villages – enchanting examples of ancient rustic architecture. English owner Felicity lives in the house at right angles to the barn but metre-thick walls between the two buildings mean total privacy and you have your own adorable garden with amazing views. You may also use a large pool in the neighbouring château. Furnishings are modest yet the kitchenette has dishwasher and washing machine. Exposed stone walls and (in the bedroom) old oak beams speak of the days when the building sheltered pilgrims of the Knights Templar. The exquisite village has a shop with fresh produce and an excellent charcuterie. *Babies and children over four welcome: garden unsuitable for toddlers. B&B also.*

sleeps	4-6 + cot.
price	€290-€490.
rooms	2: 1 twin, 1 family room for 3 with cot, 1 shower room. Folding bed on request.
closed	Never.

booking details

Felicity Martindale

tel	+33 (0)5 53 29 95 65
fax	+33 (0)5 53 29 95 65
e-mail	martindale@free.fr
web	martindale.free.fr

La Grande Marque – Cottage & Studio
Marnac St Cyprien, Dordogne

The views are liberating from this hilltop haven overlooking the river Dordogne. Twelve acres of private parkland surround you, dotted with walnut groves and fruit trees. Jenny and Michael are friendly, open hosts and have put much thought and energy into La Grande Marque – the four gîtes, the B&B, the tennis, gym, sauna, play area, restaurant and pool. There's a roomy stone cottage on three floors with a big old fireplace (below), a vine-draped pergola and divine views from the kitchen sink, and a studio with a tiny kitchen, an open-plan living area on the mezzanine and a quiet, shady garden. (There are also two cheerful, light and airy homes in the barn where they once dried tobacco, their terraces side by side – ideal for young families together.) Furniture is a mix of styles, beds are extremely comfortable and floors are wooden or blue-carpeted. There are music systems and TVs and maybe books and games; all bar the studio have long valley views. There's something to keep everyone happy here, even cookery classes with ex-hotelier Jenny, who's a talented cook – if your children are eight or over they, too, may learn to chop and stir. *B&B also.*

sleeps	Cottage 8. Studio 2-5.
price	Cottage € 480–€ 1,600. Studio € 320–€ 720.
rooms	Cottage: 2 doubles, 1 room with bunkbeds, 1 twin, 1 bathroom, 1 shower room, 2 separate wcs. Studio: 1 twin/double, 1 sofabed & single in living room, 1 shower room.
closed	Rarely.

booking details

Jennifer Cockcroft
tel +33 (0)5 53 31 61 63
e-mail grandemarque@perigord.com
web www.lgmfrance.com

map 10 entry 145

Château de Cazenac – La Maison

Coux et Bigaroque, Dordogne

A divine 16th-century Perigord farmhouse, the sort of place you expect to see within the pages of a magazine. Windows frame sublime views of valley and forest, while beautiful rooms mix contemporary minimalism, classical design and a kaleidoscope of colour. Vast bedrooms (the one on the ground floor has an original fireplace) are lime-rendered and terracotta-floored, and have vaulted ceilings and exposed beams. Bathrooms have a Moroccan touch. The open-plan sitting/dining room has sliding glass doors that open to a terrace and, beyond, the pool; the kitchen is top-notch. You'll find pretty dressers, rugs to soften tiled floors, the odd chandelier. There's a vine-shaded terrace under which you can barbecue, a delightful garden in which to fall asleep to the sounds of the valley. The house stands high on a steep hill whence dreamy views over the river... you're in the middle of nowhere, beyond the call of the outside world. Perfect for all things Dordogne: the château trail, prehistoric rock art, medieval cities, fishing, golf, canoeing, good food. Or stay and discover the 27 hectares of private château grounds. *B&B also.*

sleeps	6-8.
price	€1,800–€2,500.
rooms	3: 2 doubles, 1 twin, 2 extra beds available, 3 shower rooms, 3 separate wcs.
closed	Never.

booking details

Philippe & Armelle Constant

tel	+33 (0)5 53 31 69 31
fax	+33 (0)5 53 28 91 43
e-mail	info@cazenac.fr
web	www.cazenac.fr

Domaine de Leygue – Cottages
Bourniquel, Dordogne

This is a pretty pocket of France, peaceful and pleasing on the eye: six acres of grounds insulate you from all but wildlife. There are four little cottages, two near the courtyard and barn where the owners live, two (more modern) the far side of a pretty grove of walnut trees. All are utterly private. There are even two pools; the sun loungers remain by the cottages, so you will have plenty of private swims. And more: an excellent tennis court, boules, croquet, even bikes for those who wish to pedal round paradise. Peter and Geraldine have thought of everything. Leygue was once a small farm; two of the gîtes are conversions, two newly built; all have stone walls and a private terrace. Bedrooms are on the ground floor, except in Tower Cottage, whose views stretch over woods and farmland. All is spotless, light, immaculate. Checked sofas in one, new cherrywood in another, chestnut beams, good linen, Villeroy & Boch china. There's central heating for cool days, fans for warm nights and no TV to spoil the peace. The Dordogne, its river, markets, vineyards and prehistoric caves await.

sleeps	4 cottages for 2.
price	€ 625–€ 960 (£410–£630).
rooms	3 cottages with 1 double, 1 shower room; 1 cottage with 1 double, 1 bathroom.
closed	November–April.

booking details

	Peter & Geraldine Jones
tel	+33 (0)5 53 73 83 12
fax	+33 (0)5 53 73 83 20
e-mail	leygue@shieling.com
web	www.shieling.com/leygue

map 10   entry 147

Domaine des Blanches Colombes – Monet & Renoir

Grand Castang, Dordogne

The doves are still here. Only their cooing disturbs the calm – and the hum of a tractor. Domaine des Blanches Colombes is a 17th-century manor in a hilltop hamlet, built of golden stone, encircled by high walls. It belongs to Clare and Steven, a delightful, friendly, enthusiastic couple. Steven organises rock concerts in Poland, Clare runs cookery evenings and B&B. Two of their cottages stand side by side in the west wing but still manage to feel private. Renoir is creeper-covered, Monet (above) has an array of hanging baskets. They are engaging, comfortable, homely: wooden or tiled floors, open-plan living rooms, blue and white crockery, gay gingham. The furnishings are a mix of old-fashioned and funky modern and the kitchens are brilliantly equipped. If there's an evening when you don't feel like cooking or going out, Clare and Steven will rustle up boeuf bourguignon and fresh fruit pavlova (for example), deliver it to your table, then clear up afterwards. They can arrange for bread and croissants to be delivered each morning, too. With a games room and pool, it's ideal for families. *Babysitting available. B&B also.*

sleeps	Monet: 4. Renoir: 6.
price	Monet €375–€1,200.
	Renoir €570–€1,400.
rooms	Monet: 1 double, 1 twin,
	2 bathrooms.
	Renoir: 1 double, 2 twins,
	1 bathroom, 1 shower room.
closed	Never.

booking details

	Clare Todd
tel	+33 (0)5 53 57 30 38
e-mail	clare.todd@quality-gites.co.uk
web	www.quality-gites.com

Domaine des Blanches Colombes – Degas & Matisse
Grand Castang, Dordogne

Through a large gate over the road are Clare and Steven's other two gîtes, converted from an old village house. They're relaxing, friendly, comfortable places to stay, each with its own private terrace and brand new kitchen. Degas (above) is diminutive and cosy – ideal for a couple – with a painted double bed and views over rooftops to the rolling hills; its little yellow and terracotta bathroom is downstairs. Matisse is larger and full of character, with a wooden staircase that winds up to two attractive, big bedrooms (below). Both cottages share the delights of the domaine. The L-shaped pool, sheltering in the angle of two barns, surrounded by palm trees and shrubs, is fabulous; one barn has been converted into a games room. If the pool table, darts and table tennis don't keep the young happy, every cottage has a DVD player (you can hire titles from Steven's vast collection) and there are board games available – just ask. Six miles off is Lalinde, a pretty village with a spectacular market on Thursdays. Bergerac is close by, and there are the caves of Lascaux and an abundance of fascinating places to visit. *Babysitting available. B&B also.*

sleeps	Degas: 2. Matisse: 4.
price	Degas: € 280–€ 400. Matisse: € 375–€ 900.
rooms	Degas: 1 double, 1 bathroom. Matisse: 1 double, 1 twin, 1 bathroom.
closed	Never.

booking details

	Clare Todd
tel	+33 (0)5 53 57 30 38
e-mail	clare.todd@quality-gites.co.uk
web	www.quality-gites.com

map 10   entry 149

La Font Trémolasse – La Grange

Ste Alvère, Dordogne

Once you'd have heard the ruminating of cows in this house. As its name suggests, this was a barn and a cowshed, and the old chestnut cowstalls divide the kitchen and living room still: the headholes form perfect hatches. The cottage is the ground floor of a wing of a vast 19th-century Perigord farmhouse, restored and lived in by hardworking British owners Victoria and Julius and their three children. He's a landscape gardener and will supply herbs if you need them; she used to cook professionally and will lay on dinner – using their own produce – if you book. There's a sunny modern kitchen with hardwood work surfaces and terracotta tiled floor, and a rather more old-fashioned, pleasantly genteel, living cum dining room. The bedroom, with wooden floors and cheerful red curtains, has tranquil views of the garden and fields of the 45-acre estate. Eat outside on your private south-facing terrace, swim, fish or sail (dinghy provided) in the lake, or visit the many prehistoric caves in the area. Sainte Alvère, the nearest village, is famous for its truffles.

sleeps	2.
price	€350–€458 (£195–£300).
rooms	1 twin/double, 1 bathroom.
closed	Never.

booking details

Victoria White

tel	+33 (0)5 53 23 94 33
fax	+33 (0)5 53 23 94 87
e-mail	vjwhite@club-internet.fr

Bourdil Blanc

St Sauveur de Bergerac, Dordogne

All this could be yours: a fine 18th-century manor with a long, tree-lined avenue, views down to the lake and a super big pool. When you're finished lazing in the huge grounds or being sporty around tennis or croquet balls, retreat to the sitting room, with its lovely old wooden floors, open fire, comfortable sofas. The dining room seats 14 on upholstered chairs – magnificent with William Morris-type fabrics, mirrored fireplace and polished floors. Upstairs, a long, light passage leads to the roomy bedrooms, every one en suite, and a loft dormitory for eight – brilliant for kids. The sunny kitchen and the bathrooms are more functional than fabulous, and there's central heating so you're as warm as toast in winter. The Wing is less grand than the main house but has an open fire, tiled floors, warm kilim rugs, some good antiques and a fitted kitchen; the Pigeonnier is charming, with fine furnishings, stunning stone fireplace and private walled garden. So much space indoors and out to gather and disband, and stacks to do in the area. *Cooking & babysitting. Riding & wine-tasting. Rent House &Wing together in July &August.*

sleeps	House 8-12+. Wing 2-4+. Pigeonnier 4.
price	House €1,800–€2,850. Wing & Pigeonnier €800–€960 each. July-August: House & Wing €6,000 (with Pigeonnier €6,800).
rooms	House: 2 doubles, 2 twins, 1 dorm, 2 sofa, 5 baths. Wing: 1 double, 2 sofa, 1 bath. Pigeonnier: 1 double, 1 twin, 1 bath.
closed	Never.

booking details

	Jane Hanslip
tel	+44 (0)7768 747610
fax	+44 (0)20 7221 6909
e-mail	jhanslip@aol.com
web	www.dordognerental.com

map 10 entry 151

La Martigne

Lamonzie Montastruc, Dordogne

This glorious stone *chartreuse* could be nowhere else but France. Utterly French, it's a pleasing mix of simple and luxurious, unadorned yet ornate. Splendidly isolated, with magnificent views of the Perigord Noir, the house has been beautifully restored by its French owners, who have lived here for generations. They occasionally use the grounds, but otherwise the cascading terraced lawns, the private park and the pool are all yours. The house is furnished with dark antiques and pretty checked fauteuils to harmonise with the simple bare stone, the soft painted walls and the aqua-blue-painted doors with their porcelain handles. The two living rooms have polished wooden floors, comfy sofas and elegant blue and white upholstered Regency chairs; next door is a formal dining room with rich red wallpaper and attractive rugs. There are several open fireplaces, one in one of the bedrooms – huge and light, these open onto the south-facing terrace with the loveliest views. The kitchen is as well kitted out as you'd expect, bathrooms are super. *Security deposit of £400 payable when booking.*

sleeps	8-9.
price	€ 1,400–€ 2,300.
rooms	4: 1 double, 2 twins, 1 family room for 3, 1 bathroom, 2 shower rooms, 2 separate wcs.
closed	Never.

booking details

Jane Hanslip

tel	+44 (0)7768 747610
fax	+44 (0)20 7221 6909
e-mail	jhanslip@aol.com
web	www.dordognerental.com

Les Bigayres

Liorac sur Louyre, Dordogne

You'll not forget the bedrooms of this elegant converted pigeonnier: one has old gnarled beams that grow like trees through the tall pointed ceiling, another has an amazing *Princess and the Pea* bed with the highest mattress you have ever seen. Teenagers will approve of the third – a sunny bunk bedroom with its own poolside entrance. In 30 acres of grounds belonging to a lovely 17th-century manor, and with its own private drive and terrace, this beautifully furnished cottage is quite a find. You share the pool with the French owners, but they use it infrequently so you are likely to have it all to yourself. The open-plan kitchen, living and dining area is pure, light and roomy, with white or exposed stone walls, grey-green beams supported by unusual stone columns, and prettily-patterned red and green curtains. Fine, hexagonally-laid tiles run through the ground floor, there are wooden boards upstairs. Wallow in the luxurious sofas by the stone fireplace, stroll out of the French doors to the lawn with its long wooded views. You have everything you need, from dishwasher to barbecue, and charming Bergerac is no distance at all.

sleeps	6-8.
price	€ 800-€ 1,700.
rooms	4: 2 doubles, 1 room with bunkbeds, 1 sofabed, 1 bathroom, 1 separate wc.
closed	November–February.

booking details

Jane Hanslip

tel	+44 (0)7768 747610
fax	+44 (0)20 7221 6909
e-mail	jhanslip@aol.com
web	www.dordognerental.com

map 10   entry 153

Domaine de Foncaudière – Gros Dondon & Ange Gardien
Maurens, Dordogne

Hard to believe you're minutes from Bergerac town. A winding driveway takes you through woodland and suddenly, in a clearing, voilà! – the manoir, built 250 years ago on the foundations of a medieval castle. Beyond: the tiny estate hamlet – a scattering of extraordinarily pretty cottages which Marcel and his partner have restored with tender care. Each honey-coloured stone building has oak beams, stone and timbered walls, wood or terracotta floors. Each is charmingly furnished – antiques, new sofas and armchairs, perfect kitchens and bathrooms. One-storey Gros Dondon (above) was the baker's house (the great stone ovens are still in place); Ange Gardien (below) the caretaker's. Both have their own gardens with lawns, fruit trees (figs, walnuts, cherries), barbecues, rustic furniture. Age-old paths criss-cross the meadows; the pool is down a sloping hill; views are wonderful. The estate covers 100 acres and takes its name from a hot spring. Farmers used to bring their animals to drink here when everywhere else was frozen. The sense of peace and history is profound. *Shared laundry. B&B.*

sleeps	Gros Dondon: 4. Ange Gardien: 6.
price	€ 1,100–€ 1,900.
rooms	Gros Dondon: 1 double, 1 room with bunkbeds, 1 bathroom. Ange Gardien: 1 double, 2 twins, 1 bathroom.
closed	Rarely.

booking details

Marcel Wils

tel	+33 (0)5 53 61 13 90
fax	+33 (0)5 53 61 03 24
e-mail	info@foncaudiere.com
web	www.foncaudiere.com

Domaine de Foncaudière – Fraise Soûle & Parfum de Rose
Maurens, Dordogne

Two more delightful cottages on the domaine; they share one roof but are otherwise independent. Fraise Soûle, with its large kitchen/dining room and separate sitting room, has three fine bedrooms; Parfum de Rose has two and is next to ancient stalls which once housed the estate's farm animals. (Is there an irony in the name?). Both cottages have been restored, then furnished with care. The jolly kitchens are a pleasure to cook in, the shower rooms gorgeous, the beds well-sprung. Apart from the pool there's a barn full of games to gladden children's hearts, a period library in the château, bikes for hire so you can pedal beyond. You could spend a whole week just exploring these 40 hectares; Marcel gives you a map – seek out Le Cave, where a medieval priest went into hiding during the Wars of Religion. There's a pond, too, inhabited by a 100-year-old carp, a beech walk, even a medieval potager. You can buy organically grown herbs and vegetables from the estate and your lovely hosts are happy to advise on markets, wine-tastings and regional specialities. Magical. *Shared laundry. B&B.*

sleeps	Fraise Soûle: 6. Parfum de Rose: 4.
price	€ 800–€ 1,650.
rooms	Fraise Soûle: 2 doubles, 1 twin, 1 shower room. Parfum de Rose: 1 double, 1 twin, 1 shower room.
closed	Rarely.

booking details

	Marcel Wils
tel	+33 (0)5 53 61 13 90
fax	+33 (0)5 53 61 03 24
e-mail	info@foncaudiere.com
web	www.foncaudiere.com

map 10   entry 155

Le Balet du Val – La Maison
Bertric Burée, Dordogne

Eric, Marie and their young child upped sticks from Brussels and bought a 300-year-old house in a Dordogne hamlet. They are designers and perfectionists and restored with meticulous attention to detail, then moved into the bigger house next door. They love this place: the two gîtes, the architect-office in the barn, the B&B for two. La Maison sleeps a big family or small group, has two ground floors because of its sloping site, two stairs, a garden with foliage lit magically at night, its own pool. Old charm and new simplicity are woven together within these thick stone walls: chestnut floors, open fire, halygon lights, stainless steel oven, glass wash basin, sunken bath. Doors slide open to the garden, scented with jasmine, roses and lavender. Bedrooms feed off the salon and a second stair leads to the mezzanine where two beds lie beneath a spectacular web of ancient beams. Breakfast under the tamarisk in sunshine, or lunch in dappled shade; you have the luxury of your own summer kitchen, with barbecue. Views sweep to little Lusignac with its romanesque church, flanked by the oldest tree in the Dordogne. *B&B also.*

sleeps	6-8.
price	€890–€1,677.
rooms	3: 2 doubles, 1 twin, 1 mezzanine with 2 single beds, 1 bathroom, 2 shower rooms.
closed	Never.

booking details

	Éric Borgers
tel	+33 (0)5 53 90 51 46/91 38 57
fax	+33 (0)5 53 91 38 58
e-mail	borgers.eric@wanadoo.fr
web	www.le-balet-du-val.com

Le Balet du Val – Gîte

Bertric Burée, Dordogne

Rustle up lunch in the summer kitchen of the *balet*, the covered terrace that gives the place its name. The apartment for four is on the ground floor of the farmhouse, facing south-west. Thick walls keep you cool in summer; shutters shade you from the sun. It is not as large or luxurious as the bigger maison, but the conversion has been perfectly done. Floors are newly tiled, beams are chunky, plain walls are adorned with Marie's fresh paintings. The whole place is finely proportioned with a contemporary feel. Furnishings are minimalist: a plant here, a white rug there, muslin drapes. You have two rooms, each with two single beds and built-in cupboard space; a kitchen with hob, microwave, fridge; an ultra-modern shower room. You share barbecue, garden and delicious, bamboo-fringed pool with Éric, Marie and daughter Josephine – but you're private here, with your own large terrace and sweeping views. There are two good restaurants where the locals eat, both five minutes by car. Ribérac is six miles, with shops, church and superb *marché au gras* on Fridays in winter: stock up on truffles, duck, delectable foie gras. *B&B also.*

sleeps	2-5.
price	€ 470-€ 837.
rooms	2: 1 family room for 3, 1 twin, 1 shower room, 1 separate wc.
closed	Never.

booking details

	Éric Borgers
tel	+33 (0)5 53 90 51 46/91 38 57
e-mail	borgers.eric@wanadoo.fr
web	www.le-balet-du-val.com

map 11   entry 157

La Geyrie – Le Pigeonnier

Verteillac, Dordogne

A pair of nesting barn owls has taken up residence in the tower of this charming 15th-century pigeonnier. You might spot short-toed eagles and roe deer in the fields and woods, too. Furnishings are basic and well-used, and though you are not steeped in *la grande luxe*, the simple pleasures of a small farmstead should more than compensate. Dogs, cats and hens stroll the courtyard, children will see goats being milked, and there's a Welsh pony. Louise, the down-to-earth and dedicated English owner, raises goats and grows organic produce; she and her family live in the attached farmhouse. Your little pigeonnier is pleasantly cool, with tiled floors downstairs, floor boards up, and everywhere, heavenly old rafters. The big bedroom has a fine armoire; the almost-as-big shower room a rustically paved floor. The nearest shops and market are a mile away, in La Tour Blanche, so take the bikes. Down the road, too, the wonderful Limousin-Perigord National Park, and rare orchids in the Limodore reserve nearby. Combined with the gîte for eight next door, two families could be very happy here. *Service wash available.*

sleeps	2 + 2 children.
price	£115–£290.
rooms	1 family room for 3, 1 single bed downstairs in kitchen/diner, 1 shower room.
closed	Never.

booking details

Louise & Peter Dunn

tel	+33 (0)5 53 91 15 15
fax	+33 (0)5 53 90 37 19
e-mail	peter.dunn@wanadoo.fr
web	perso.wanadoo.fr/gites.at.la.geyrie

Le Noyer

St Félix de Bourdeilles, Dordogne

The walnut tree which gave the farmhouse its name was blown down in a recent storm, but otherwise nothing has changed for centuries. Sheep graze lazily in the seven acres of fields and woods surrounding the house, and life continues much as it always has in the pretty village of Saint Félix across the valley. Bridget and Pete, both teachers, live nearby during British school holidays, and have restored with taste and skill. Wonderful warm beams, Shaker-style green-painted cupboards and a terracotta tile floor give a welcoming atmosphere to the kitchen/dining room, prettily decorated with English china, country antiques and ceramic sink tiles. Enjoy the serene views from the windows, or eat out on the terrace. Bedrooms have high vaulted ceilings with white painted beams, pine-boarded floors and small floor-level windows; bathrooms are carpeted. Walking and cycling are good around here, you can canoe on the Dronne and take in some prehistoric wonders at the Grottes de Villars. Brantôme is famous for its ancient belltower and wonderful Friday market. An excellent place for families with young children.

sleeps	6.
price	€ 479–€ 797 (£300–£500).
rooms	3: 2 doubles, 1 room with bunkbeds, 2 bathrooms.
closed	Never.

booking details

	Bridget & Pete Jones
tel	+44 (0)1491 682834
e-mail	bridget@rcol.org.uk

map 10   entry 159

La Brugère

Nantheuil de Thiviers, Dordogne

A treasure trove of surprises lies behind the sober facade of this 19th-century house, once a paper mill. Tapestries and curtains glow in the dining room off a wood-panelled entrance hall, the drawing room is elegant in cream and gold, with a stone fireplace, sofas and antiques. Vast French windows open onto two sides of the terrace. There's a panelled library with TV and a fabulous kitchen: two fridges, a large gas and electric oven, silver for the dining room and cutlery for the terrace. Two of the double bedrooms have four-posters with luscious curtains, chandeliers and polished wood floors. The master bedroom is reached by its own staircase; the *trompe l'oeil* in its bathroom is fantastic. The twin room has antique sleigh beds. The decoration and comfort is lavish, even breathtaking, right down to the parasols round the pool and the delicious towels. But the house is first and foremost a home – children will love it, there's badminton and table tennis and three acres of parkland to explore, and swimming and fishing in the river Isle. The owners' daughter lives nearby, full of friendly advice. A magnificent place.

sleeps	12.
price	£1,200-£2,600.
rooms	6: 5 doubles, 1 twin, 5 bathrooms.
closed	Never.

booking details

	Lisa Grist
tel	+44 (0)1992 632612
fax	+44 (0)1992 630038
e-mail	pgrist@tractionseabert.com
web	www.labrugere.com

Domaine d'Essendieras

St Médard d'Excideuil, Dordogne

You could walk for three hours and still not reach the estate's border – the domaine spreads for thousands of acres. This is a super place for busy families: a play area in the woods with a tree hut and platform, mountain bikes for teenagers, a 'beach' for tinies, fishing on one lake, swimming and pedaloeing on another. B&B in the château, camp in the orchards, self-cater in the chalets – or in the white, shuttered, 1819 farmhouse. It has recently been renovated from top to toe, so all is new and everything works – beautifully. Downstairs, an L-shaped living area with black leather furniture, a refectory table and a corner kitchen, marvellously equipped; up an open-tread stair to carpeted floors and big comfortable beds. There are spectacular apple-orchard views – though not from your garden – and space for everyone. Hardworking Mrs Bakker juggles the running of it all with a young family, jumping in the jeep several times a day to check everyone's happy. You can rent a jeep, too, and take yourselves off for an hour or a day. *Sauna available. B&B also.*

sleeps	6–8.
price	€300–€840.
rooms	3: 1 double, 2 triples, 1 bath/shower room, 1 bathroom & separate wc downstairs.
closed	Never.

booking details

	Ellen & Jeroen Bakker
tel	+33 (0)5 53 52 81 51
fax	+33 (0)5 53 52 89 22
e-mail	info@essendieras.fr
web	www.essendieras.fr

map 10   entry 161

Photography by Michael Busselle

midi-pyrénées

Le Coin Fleuri

Carennac, Lot

It's like something out of *The Pied Piper of Hamlyn*, this quaint little Quercian house. Its position, on a bluff above the Dordogne river, takes your breath away, and the tiny village, with its steep-roofed stone houses clustered around a 10th-century priory, dates to Roman times; it is recognised as being one of the loveliest in France. Climb the wooden stairs to the front door and step into the living/dining room/kitchen – a good-sized space with whitewashed stone walls. It is modestly but comfortably furnished, with unusual knick-knacks giving it a homely feel; the new owners plan to repaint and update. What were once goat sheds are now little bedrooms, with yellow or pink painted stone walls, carpeted or lino floors, simple furniture. There's no garden but a balcony/terrace to the rear and a timbered veranda to the front: sit among the geraniums and watch the world drift by. Or stroll to the banks of the river, great for swimming and canoeing. Carennac has a couple of restaurants serving regional food, there's a *boulodrome* and a tennis court.

sleeps	4.
price	£250–£350.
rooms	2: 1 double, 1 twin, 1 bathroom, 1 shower room.
closed	Never.

booking details

Alison Gomm
tel +44 (0)1276 505101
e-mail a.gomm@ntlworld.com

Pouch

Rignac, Lot

The 1793 farmhouse is quaint and inviting with its steep roofs and light-coloured stone: the Bells' restoration has been a labour of love. The original character of beams, old floors and twisty corners has been preserved, furnishing is simple with cast-iron beds, good colours, original paintings, masses of books and, in the ancient stone kitchen, where baskets hang, a vast open hearth and a closed stove. Rooms are divided between the main house and the erstwhile goat shed, now an apartment; one of its bedrooms is tucked into the eaves and its French windows open to the fenced garden and small decked pool. The feel is comfortably bohemian, happily relaxed. Gavin, an artist and potter, and Lillian live nearby – lovely, humourous people who will look after you well. Gavin runs art courses for guests. The three-house hamlet is perched majestically on the top of a wooded hill, with views across a valley of walnut orchards… a deeply rural spot, the peace punctuated by the early crow of the cockerel (you may get eggs from next door's hens) and the night time hoot of the owl. Shops and simple restaurants are a mile off.

sleeps	7-8.
price	€925–€1,280.
rooms	4: 1 double, 1 twin, 1 shower room; 1 double, 1 single with extra bed, 1 shower room in separate apartment.
closed	Never.

booking details

Lillian Bell
tel	+33 (0)5 65 33 66 84
fax	+33 (0)5 65 33 66 84
e-mail	bellpouch@hotmail.com
web	www.bellfrance.com

map 11   entry 163

Le Barn
Bio, Lot

Here you have a chance to get a taste of French farming life: cows and sheep trundle past the gate twice a day and the butcher and grocer bring their vans to the village several times a week. This lovely barn conversion is the only foreign-owned house in the village so you'll have ample opportunity to perfect your French. The orchard, lawn and small pool behind are totally private and if you come in season you can feast on apples, walnuts, plums and grapes. Stone steps lead up to the hugely characterful living/kitchen room which runs the length of the house, with a pitched beamed roof and a woodburner against an exposed stone wall. The feel is pure, clean and contemporary with a hint of Scandinavia. Colours are blue and cream and there are comfy, modern, Ikea-style sofas to flop into. The bedrooms downstairs are functional without being austere, with old beams, modern furnishings, rough plastered walls and curtained-off hanging space. There's plenty to see in the area, from Neolithic caves and rock paintings to famous Rocamadour. The area is wonderful for walking and cycling too.

sleeps	4.
price	€ 455–€ 805.
rooms	2 twins, 1 shower room, 1 separate wc.
closed	Never.

booking details

Gavin & Lillian Bell

tel	+33 (0)5 65 33 66 84
fax	+33 (0)5 65 33 71 31
e-mail	lilianbel@aol.com
web	www.bellfrance.com

Le Couvent
Lauzès, Lot

An elegant village retreat that started life in 1837 as a convent school for girls: today's sunlit rooms were once classrooms and dormitories. Rosalie and Malcolm have renovated in abundant style: original wooden floors, Victorian wrought-iron beds, fluttering muslin at shuttered windows, a free-standing bath. There's a dreamy sense of country life … old floral linen cushions on a sofa in one bedroom, sunlight bouncing off colour-washed walls and a chandelier in the salon that was rescued from a barn. The medieval village of St Martin de Vers is 'protected': a beautiful collage of tiled roofs and mellow stone houses, it hunkers down quietly in a lush valley, encircled by the river Vers. The old well stands in the gorgeous garden which is on three levels leading up to woodland, so you can chase the sun or retreat to the shade. The dining room table is made from a neighbour's oak wine vat and there's a hungry woodburner in the beautifully equipped country kitchen. Rosalie and Malcolm are happy to organise painting tuition with a local artist for individuals or families and groups – bring your paints. *B&B also.*

sleeps	7.
price	£450–£550.
rooms	4: 2 doubles, 1 twin, 1 single, 1 bathroom, 1 separate wc.
closed	November–April.

booking details

	Rosalie Vicars–Harris
tel	+44 (0)20 7435 5900 or +33 (0)5 65 31 28 91
e-mail	rosalievh@yahoo.co.uk
web	www.lecouvent.pwp.blueyonder.co.uk

map 15 entry 165

Château de Couanac – Forge, Métairie, Mennier, Fournis

Varaire, Lot

Not *the* château but near the château. This one is 17th-century – a lovely, weatherbeaten pile in the oak forests of the Dordogne, with an 11th-century chapel. And the four gîtes, outside the quadrangle walls but still under the seigneurial eye, were once barns or estate workers' cottages. They are all quite close to each other so would be ideal for a group of families: there's a shared pool and plenty of space for children to rampage. Inside the low, rustic buildings: plaster or rough stone walls, beamed ceilings, stone floors to keep them cool. Small windows mean that the rooms are fairly dark, while furnishings are adequate rather than luxurious, with a medley of old, new and repro. There are some striking touches – huge copper bowls, a spinning wheel – and the small bedrooms have entertaining beds. For those who hanker after the splendours of the château, there's a restaurant in one of its great rooms, where the honey-coloured stone walls are covered with decorative plates and the cavernous fireplace could roast whole one of Monsieur d'Armagnac's 400 sheep. *Dishwasher only in La Forge.*

sleeps	Forge 8. Métairie 6–7. Mennier 6–7. Fournis 4.
price	€ 525–€ 1,365 for 8. € 455–€ 985 for 6. € 345–€ 665 for 4.
rooms	Forge: 2 doubles, 2 twins, 1 bath, 1 shower, 2 wcs. Métairie: 1 double, 1 family for 3, 2 singles, 1 shower, 1 wc. Mennier: 2 doubles, 1 family for 3, 1 shower. Fournis: 1 double, 1 twin, 1 shower, 1 wc.
closed	Rarely.

booking details

	Pierre d'Armagnac
tel	+33 (0)5 65 31 52 32
e-mail	chateau.de.couanac@free.fr
web	www.chateaudecouanac.fr.st

La Chave
Cézac, Lot

Lindy and Tony found a rare jewel here: a farmhouse untouched for over a century. Inhabited, when they bought it, by a bachelor French farmer who still cooked his stews over the open fire, the house has many of its original 1880s features. Working wells and an old bread oven still stand in the large garden, and in the outbuildings you'll spot the wires where leaves of tobacco were hung to dry. Lindy, who also runs a (Sawday) B&B in the UK, clearly has a flair for decoration and has produced a stunning result: rooms are painted in soothing greens and creams, furnished with period country pieces – a French walnut armoire, an English antique quilt – and have sanded floors with colourful kilims. There's a beautiful, friendly, well-equipped kitchen, and a comfy sitting room with a woodburner that makes the house just as snug in autumn and spring. Bedrooms are divided between the first floor and the attic, cosy for children; a small group would be as happy here as a big one. Across the courtyard, where the old kitchen garden once was, a lovely, large saltwater pool. *Children over five welcome.*

sleeps	10.
price	£700–£1,350.
rooms	5: 3 doubles, 2 twins, 2 bathrooms, 2 shower rooms.
closed	November–April.

booking details

	Lindy & Tony Ball
tel	+44 (0)1725 518768
fax	+44 (0)1725 518380

map 15   entry 167

Domaine de Roubignol

Luzech, Lot

The approach is an adventure in itself, along the high winding road above the vineyards of the Lot valley. This place – a 17th-18th-century winemaster's house – is breathtaking in its scale, space and architectural peculiarities. You have ancient stone floors, creaking floorboards, hidden alcoves and a beam to duck... three eating places inside, four terraces out and, cut into the steep side of the valley below, an infinity pool, underwater-lit at night. There's even an old bell to summon people (frolicking in the pool, playing ping-pong in the barn) to lunch. There are five bedrooms in the main house, from the tiny single in the pigeonnier to the vast Romeo and Juliet bedroom with its balcony and canopied bed. There's a further double in the tower; it has the additional luxury of central heating and a sofabed in its sitting room on the top floor. Furniture is a happy mix of French antique and modern and the L-shaped sitting room is big enough to waltz in. You are five minutes from the shops and market at Luzech (25 on foot down the valley path) surrounded by wine-tastings and gastronomic opportunity. The views sweep and soar... A heavenly place.

sleeps	9-13.
price	Main house €650-€1,950. Tower alone €290-€430, not available July-August.
rooms	5 + 1: 2 doubles, 2 twins, 1 single, 2 bathrooms, 1 shower room; Tower: 1 double, 1 sofabed in sitting room, 1 bathroom.
closed	Main house: November-March. Tower: never.

booking details

	Roger & Jill Bichard
tel	+44 (0)1225 862789 or +44 (0)1380 828677 (evening)
e-mail	info@moxhams-antiques.demon.co.uk

Pagel

Catus, Lot

Pagel is a wonderland for children in high summer, with every conceivable dream catered for. Yet in low season it transforms into a haven for those who seek silence and rustic comfort: May, September and October are perfect for tranquil poolside siestas. There are five gîtes, neatly fitted into the walls of the old stone granary. The feel of each is open plan, airy and light; there are brass beds, tiled floors, glazed-pine ceilings, squishy sofas. Downstairs gîtes have their own little patios with plastic furniture, barbecue and parasol, upstairs ones a raised terrace each. Some have exposed beams, one has long views to local hills, another basks in morning sun. Swimming pools come in two sizes: large and 'toddler'. Beyond, an oak copse and a small fruit orchard stand, while the large well-designed garden is full of private nooks and crannies. Butcher, baker and *brocante* lie a mile off in the village of Catus; market day is Tuesday – and is not to be missed. Head off to Le Lac Vert where you can fish, swim and picnic… or to the spectacular prehistoric art at Lascaux. Your young hosts are lovely and will tell you all you need to know.

sleeps	4 apartments sleep 5 each. Studio: 3.
price	€ 231–€ 1,036.
rooms	Apartments: each 1 double, 1 twin, 1 single, 1 bathroom. Studio: 1 double, 1 single, 1 bathroom.
closed	November–March.

booking details

Lara & Mark Bishop

tel	+33 (0)5 65 21 69 19
e-mail	mark@pagel-france.com
web	www.pagel-france.com

map 15 entry 169

Cubertou

St Martin le Redon, Lot

Both place and setting are completely delightful. Warm, golden stone, shuttered windows, cascades of vines and wisteria… crickets hum, buzzards wheel, there are acres of meadow and woodland in which to escape. The farmhouse and barns, round a grassy courtyard, were turned into a summer art school in the 1960s by an eccentric painter and his ballerina wife. Their love of colour is still in evidence, particularly in the striking, peacock-blue salon with its Provençal cushions. Taken as a whole, Cubertou sleeps up to 23 but you can rent the main house alone and still have the place to yourself. The bedrooms are simple and interesting – two are in the pigeon tower – and the bathrooms adequate; views are to the valley. Cooking for large numbers is no problem in the brilliantly designed kitchen, or on the barbecue on the terrace. The huge open games barn at the far end of the courtyard also makes a marvellous place for candlelit suppers. Generous owners, friendly locals, a housekeeper, cook and babysitter on request, and various lively weekly village markets where you can buy melons, strawberries, goat's cheese, foie gras… Bliss.

sleeps	23.
price	€800–€2,100.
rooms	13: 1 double, 6 twins, 5 singles, 1 family room, 1 bathroom, 3 shower rooms, 5 wcs.
closed	November-March except Christmas & New Year.

booking details

	Claire & John Norton
tel	+33 (0)5 63 95 82 34
fax	+33 (0)5 63 95 82 42
e-mail	claire@cubertou.com
web	www.cubertou.com

Maison Castera
Puy l'Évêque, Lot

The setting is magical. You are in one of the prettiest villages in the Lot valley, where every view sweeps down to the river past those grand, gracious, honey-stone houses... and the castle of the bishops of Cahors at the top. Your little family house, thick-walled and terracotta-roofed, is attached to the Arnetts' and borders their garden, which you share. Enter via the kitchen, practical and well-equipped, on the ground floor. Then up to the living room, sandwiched by bedrooms on either side (a good layout ensuring privacy) and onto the window-boxed terrace, inviting with parasol and plastic table and chairs. The views are marvellous – what a place to eat out in summer! The rooms are light and a good size, the furnishings fairly workaday: a blue sofa with yellow cushions, rugs on a wooden floor, two bookshelves, some old framed photographs of the town. Your hosts are lovely and give you drinks when you arrive; they like to keep gîte and B&B separate, and make sure that for much of the day you have the garden and pool to yourselves. There's masses to do on the river, and riding, cycle hire and tennis are close by. *B&B also.*

sleeps	5-7.
price	€ 690–€ 820.
rooms	3: 1 double, 1 twin, 1 single, 1 sofabed in sitting room, 1 bathroom, 1 shower room.
closed	Never.

booking details

	Bill & Ann Arnett
tel	+33 (0)5 65 36 59 39
fax	+33 (0)5 65 36 59 39
e-mail	williamarnett@hotmail.com
web	www.puyleveque.com

map 15   entry 171

Lagardelle

Ste Croix, Montcuq, Lot

Much of Europe was like this half a century ago – few cars, many species of birds and flowers, lots of space. This line from the brochure gives you a taste of what to expect when you arrive at this stunning 17th-century stone barn surrounded by fields of lavender and sunflowers. It gives you an idea, too, of the infectious enthusiasm of its nature-loving, knowledgeable owners, Ben and Susanna, who do B&B next door. If you want to walk, you're in the best hands, as Ben runs walking holidays and knows the Quercy Blanc intimately. The couple have converted the barn with religious respect for original materials and structures (resisting the temptation to enlarge the small upstairs windows) and have aimed for a mood of calm and simplicity. There are clean wooden floors, white and stone walls, a welcoming woodburner for cooler evenings. Engravings in the sitting room depict the various ports Ben (ex-Navy) has sailed into. Visit medieval Montcuy to stock up at its vibrant Sunday morning market… then back to cool off in the pool. Simply heaven. *B&B also*

sleeps	5.
price	£200-£725.
rooms	3: 1 double, 1 twin, 1 single, 1 bathroom, 1 separate wc.
closed	Never.

booking details

	Ben & Susanna Hawkins
tel	+33 (0)5 65 31 96 72
fax	+33 (0)5 65 31 81 27
e-mail	hawkinsben@aol.com

Domaine Lapèze

Montcuq, Lot

Domaine Lapèze, once a resting place for pilgrims on their way to Santiago de Compostela, is a place to linger. Those who come find much to recharge city-drained batteries: pool, vineyards, plum orchards, peace. This starkly beautiful collection of old stone buildings is wrapped up in 12 acres of blissful rolling country and you can gaze across to an 11th-century tower in the village of Montcuq (busy with two markets, three bars, four restaurants, shops with all you need). Caroline and Knud have renovated magnificently in both cottage and studio – expect rich, warm colours and oodles of style. Terracotta tiles keep you cool, white walls soak up the sun. In the cottage, an open-plan living area with yellow sofa and armchairs, big fireplace and beautifully equipped kitchen, a red and orange bedroom, a fresh and summery feel. The kitchen in the studio is simpler; the double bed has a pale pink and white quilt. Both gîtes have private patios. There's a gorgeous pool (floodlit at night) which you share with B&B guests, bikes to rent, horses to ride, lakes to swim in, wine to taste and romanesque churches to visit. *B&B also.*

sleeps	Cottage & Studio: each 4.
price	Cottage € 600–€ 900. Studio € 500–€ 800.
rooms	Cottage: 1 double, 1 twin, 1 bathroom, 1 separate wc. Studio: 1 double, 1 twin, 2 bathrooms.
closed	Rarely.

booking details

Caroline & Knud Kristoffersen

tel	+33 (0)5 65 24 91 97
fax	+33 (0)5 65 24 91 98
e-mail	lapeze@libertysurf.fr
web	www.domainelapeze.com

map 15 entry 173

Le Mas

Roquecor, Tarn-et-Garonne

There's a relaxed, dishevelled charm about Le Mas. Creepers rampage over rough, luminous Quercy stone walls and the little, tousled garden is full of herbs and roses. (It has its own swimming pool, too, and a tiny shaded terrace for outdoor meals.) Inside the ancient barn, Ann and JJ have created an appealing, uncluttered place to stay. Bright, clear fabrics are vivid against white walls and the golden wood of ceilings and floors. The long living space, with shower room off, has a stone fireplace and central heating for winter; the bedroom has French windows onto the garden. It's all very private and rural: the barn is in a hamlet, standing with its back to the main house where Ann and JJ live with their two small daughters. They're a charming, friendly couple, who welcome children. Ann gives painting lessons – her oils decorate the walls – and JJ is an Irish accountant turned acupuncturist. Visit the pretty town of Roquecor, so full of restaurants that you may never get round to using your own little perfectly equipped kitchen. There's a truly excellent market, especially on Sundays, and a lake nearby with a sandy beach.

sleeps	4.
price	€375–€985.
rooms	2: 1 double, 1 twin, 1 bathroom.
closed	Never.

booking details

Ann & JJ O'Brien

tel	+33 (0)5 63 95 26 31
e-mail	jjobrien@wanadoo.fr

Las Bourdolles – Le Pigeonnier

Tréjouls, Tarn-et-Garonne

Deep in rural France, a square, creamy-grey stone tower topped by a pointed roof. Its deep-set windows look out over 20 acres of woods and fields belonging to the 17th-century farmhouse owned and run by Erica and Linda. Having restored the main house and established a B&B, they have now turned the little pigeon house into a delightful gîte. Flights of ladder-like stairs link each rough-walled room to the one above. At ground level are a small, newly fitted kitchen, dining area and shower room, then up to the first floor to a simple, attractive bedroom with painted screens and a handmade oak bed. (A roll-top bath stands in front of the window, so you can gaze at the countryside as you soak.) Up another stair to the comfortable sitting room with a sofabed and a gloriously beamed ceiling. You have your own tiny courtyard, too, but may wander at will in Las Bourdolles' grounds, and use the saltwater pool. There's central heating and an open fire to keep you snug in winter, and if you tire of self-catering, you can always dine at the farmhouse: Linda and Erica are fabulous cooks. *Flexible changeover day. B&B.*

sleeps	2-4.
price	€ 250–€ 450.
rooms	1 double, 1 sofabed, 1 bathroom, 1 shower room.
closed	Never.

booking details

Linda Hilton & Erica Lewis
tel +33 (0)5 63 95 80 83
e-mail erica.lewis@wanadoo.fr
web www.frenchbedbreakfast.com

map 15 entry 175

Le Petite Grange & La Petite Maison
Tréjouls, Tarn-et-Garonne

Two diminutive gîtes in a delicious setting outside the hamlet of Tréjouls. They stand with their backs to the hillside at different levels in the Nortons' seven-acre garden. Thick stone walls keep you cool and the rooms are pleasantly furnished, with splashes of colour from cushion and poster. Petite Grange, reached by a flight of steps, is a multi-stable conversion, its several doors opening onto the lawn: a comfortable, one-storey home with an L-shaped living room/kitchen. Lavender and morning glory edge the patio. The other end of the barn is open-sided, providing shade for hot-weather meals near the pretty, shared pool. Petite Maison is smaller, with an overhanging roof and long, south-facing terrace. Its bedsitting room has an antique bed and spectacular views, but you have to go onto the terrace to reach the shower and wc. John and Claire are a charming couple with two teenage children, and two friendly cats, certain to come and visit. You may prefer the greater comfort of La Petite Grange in winter, with its central heating, dishwasher and own washing-machine.

sleeps	Grange: 2. Maison: 2
price	Grange € 270–€ 440. Maison € 200–€ 350.
rooms	Grange: 1 double, 1 bathroom. Maison: 1 double, 1 shower room.
closed	Never.

booking details

	Claire & John Norton
tel	+33 (0)5 63 95 82 34
fax	+33 (0)5 63 95 82 42
e-mail	claire@cubertou.com
web	www.cubertou.com/petite

Les Sapins

Varen, Tarn-et-Garonne

It's at the end of a little road high above a valley, the dapper stone house with its perfect blue shutters. A small *maison de maître*, it is encircled by its own seven acres and fabulous views. Jacqueline and Darryl are a friendly, civilised couple who do B&B and enjoy having people to stay. Your stylish gîte is attached to the house, your privacy assured in these two rooms with a little piece of garden and terrace. The main bedroom has a balcony and a softly-dressed bed; the second bedroom, long and narrow, doubles as a sitting room if you are two. Furniture is country style, colours are serene; central heating means you're as warm as toast in winter. The kitchen, beautifully equipped, is big enough to fit a table and chairs; a door leads to the terrace with barbecue and furniture. The views are so lovely you could spend all morning here, under the parasol, then slip off to the shared pool, out of sight (just) of the house. A shop selling bread, wine and all you need is a short walk, there's a good restaurant in Varen, a Sunday market in St Antonin, and your hosts do fine *table d'hôtes* – Indian or French. *B&B also.*

sleeps	4.
price	€ 230–€ 760.
rooms	2 doubles, 1 shower room.
closed	Never.

booking details

Jacqueline & Darryl Vaz

tel	+33 (0)5 63 26 45 56
fax	+33 (0)5 63 26 45 56
e-mail	les_sapins@hotmail.com

map 16 entry 177

Fénéyrols – Country Cottage

St Antonin Noble Val, Tarn-et-Garonne

Just a short drive away is historic Saint Antonin Noble Val, a medieval town that clings to the banks of the Aveyron beneath towering white cliffs. The town's prosperity from manufacturing cloth and leather has left a stunning heritage of ancient houses which fan out from the lovely Place de la Halle, and the weekly market is unmissable... take advantage of the guided walks. Surrounded by pasture and woodland, and Brezou's acre of garden, this old stone farmhouse is a tranquil, comfortable retreat. Drink in the serene views from the blue and white bedrooms up the open spiral stair, charming with colourful rugs on wooden floors. The fabulous double bedroom downstairs, furnished with antiques and luxurious linen, has wooden doors leading to a terrace; the delightful living room/kitchen has beams and exposed stone walls, old pine and mod cons. Be serenaded by birdsong from the large, fenced pool in front of the house, or explore this ruggedly beautiful area on foot – GR footpaths abound. There's canoeing, too, through the Aveyron Gorge. Wonderful for families in early or late summer. *Not available July or August.*

sleeps	6.
price	€518–€836 (£350–£560).
rooms	3: 2 doubles, 1 twin, 1 shower room, 1 bathroom.
closed	December–March & July–August.

booking details

Jayne & Rod Millard

tel	+33 (0)5 63 30 68 89
fax	+33 (0)5 63 30 68 97
e-mail	rod@brezou.com
web	www.brezou.com

Fénéyrols – Brezou Main House

St Antonin Noble Val, Tarn-et-Garonne

Follow in the steps of the stars: many have stayed here, which gives you some idea of the luxurious style of this gorgeous 1901 manor house. Owners Rod and Jayne and their young daughter Nicole live here most of the year so it feels like an exceedingly smart home rather than a rented property. With spectacular views, an acre of mature garden, an inviting, fenced pool, and sumptuous furnishings, you'll want for nothing. If you are two or three families holidaying together, feast in the vast but welcoming open-plan kitchen/dining room with great oak beams and a long antique dining table and benches. The kitchen area, with soft yellow walls and pretty check curtains, is immaculately equipped, with plenty of beech work surfaces on which to prepare the treats you've bought from the market (the Sunday one in Saint Antonin is a must). There's a comfortable sitting room and a well-stocked formal terracotta and white library, too. *Only available July & August, let with Lodge House (see next page) as six-bedroom house.*

sleeps	12 (with Lodge House).
price	£1,875-£2,400.
rooms	4: 3 doubles, 1 twin, 3 bathrooms.
closed	September-June.

booking details

	Jayne & Rod Millard
tel	+33 (0)5 63 30 68 89
fax	+33 (0)5 63 30 68 97
e-mail	rod@brezou.com
web	www.brezou.com

map 16   entry 179

Fénéyrols – Lodge House

St Antonin Noble Val, Tarn-et-Garonne

With its pretty blue shutters and soothing views, this hilltop gatehouse has been attractively restored by Rod and Jayne who moved here several years ago to live the rural dream. They live in the main house across the courtyard (except in July and August, when the two houses are rented together) and will be more than happy to put themselves out for you and your children; they also understand the need for privacy. Sand-coloured walls, enlivened with interesting pictures, and terracotta-tiled floors create a warm, cosy atmosphere in the open-plan kitchen/dining/living room, which has huge oak beams and a wood-burning stove. Stroll out into your small south-facing private garden where you can eat *en plein air* – or simply sit back and enjoy the peace of this beautiful place. The long, narrow twin bedroom downstairs has pretty antiques, while the double upstairs has a navy and white colour scheme. Children will love the large (shared) gardens and pool, and the fenced play area with a climbing frame and paddling pool. The excitement of pony and donkey trekking lie a short drive away.

sleeps	4.
price	€446–€558 (£290–£390).
rooms	2: 1 double, 1 twin, 1 bathroom.
closed	Never, but only available with Main House July–August.

booking details

	Jayne & Rod Millard
tel	+33 (0)5 63 30 68 89
fax	+33 (0)5 63 30 68 97
e-mail	rod@brezou.com
web	www.brezou.com

Barrau

Esparsac, Tarn-et-Garonne

This is something special: terrifically earthy and wonderful for those who long to lose themselves in the hills and leave creature comforts behind. The main house, where Jennifer lives, is 30 yards away; she'll provide breakfast if you ask in advance. Otherwise you are alone – on a 15-acre hillside estate with two eating-out areas, one filled with lavender and figs. And trees, long views and wildlife. Deer and badgers live on the land, 42 species of butterflies have been identified, nightingales sing, the odd salamander scampers by and beehives dot the landscape. Your retreat is a former house for the pigs and hens (it dates to 1890) and has been renovated simply. This is like camping but without the tent. You have a pine-floored, rugged room with a laminate table, a cupboard, a radio/cassette player, two beds and two easy chairs, a tiny creamy-brick shower room, a corridor kitchen. Jennifer has a telescope and will let you borrow it; the night skies are pollution-free. She is also an expert on the churches and brocante fairs in the area. Expect the tree frogs to sing you to sleep. *Extra charge for heating. B&B also.*

sleeps	1-2.
price	€ 160–€ 300.
rooms	1 twin, 1 shower room.
closed	Rarely.

booking details

	Jennifer Boncey
tel	+33 (0)5 63 26 12 72
e-mail	boncey@wanadoo.fr
web	www.haumont.com

map 15 entry 181

Domaine de Peyloubère – Les Rosiers

Pavie, Gers

Peyloubère is a dreamlike grouping of 350-year-old buildings around a rose garden in acres of private parkland. There's a river, waterfall, lake and long, long walks across the fields; a swimming pool, table tennis, badminton, even a spa (in the former pig shed!) for all to share; and a manoir that was hand-painted and inhabited by Italian 20th-century artist Mario Cavaglieri. Les Rosiers is on the ground floor of the old manor itself and the Martins' sensitive refurbishment goes perfectly with its piece of "genuine Cavaglieri": the vibrantly colourful ceiling of the brass-bedded double bedroom, originally the family dining room. The other feature is the monumental inglenook fireplace in the living room, large and light with white painted beams and walls washed with Strassevil chalk paint. Tall French windows lead out to the shady garden which includes the original well house, still in working order but safely secured. Inside are books, games, videos, music, excellent beds and central heating for winter. Children will love the secret summer house in the woods, and the magical waterfall. *B&B also.*

sleeps	4.
price	€ 600–€ 1,200.
rooms	2: 1 double, 1 room with bunkbeds, 1 shower room.
closed	Never.

booking details

Theresa & Ian Martin
tel	+33 (0)5 62 05 74 97
fax	+33 (0)5 62 05 75 39
e-mail	martin@peyloubere.com
web	www.peyloubere.com

Domaine de Peyloubère – Fermier

Pavie, Gers

Look out for hoopoes by the waterfall. It's fed by the river Gers that flows through the breathtakingly beautiful estate of the 17th-century manor. With 35 acres of lawns, Italian gardens (the legacy of Italian artist Mario Cavaglieri who lived here) and ancient woods, there's space to roam. You'll scarcely be aware of the guests in the other cottages, or the English owners, Theresa and Ian. Peyloubère used to be a working farm and Fermier was the farmer's cottage: its original beamed inglenook fireplace still warms and welcomes in the living room. Today there's central heating, too. Furnishings are crisp and new, with attractive modern beech furniture, deep-blue sofas and full-length curtains. The state-of-the-art kitchen is painted grey-green and sunflower, with a Saint Hubert dresser and steps to a sunny downstairs double bedroom. French doors lead out to the patio and a large pool shared with the gîte guests, and the garden beyond. Gaze over the fields, listen to the birds, pick wild flowers, fish in lake and river, then treat yourself to armagnac after supper, the dry golden brandy for which the area is famous. *B&B also.*

sleeps	8.
price	€ 800–€ 1,600.
rooms	4: 2 doubles, 2 twins, 1 bathroom, 1 shower room, 2 separate wcs.
closed	Never.

booking details

Theresa & Ian Martin

tel	+33 (0)5 62 05 74 97
fax	+33 (0)5 62 05 75 39
e-mail	martin@peyloubere.com
web	www.peyloubere.com

map 15   entry 183

Setzères – Petit Setzères
Marciac, Gers

The house is the converted stables of a fine manor set on the soft slopes of this unspoilt part of rural France. Petit Setzères has a big, well-furnished ground-floor living area where you can snuggle down in front of a log fire in winter (there's central heating, too). In summer, take lunch into the lush garden and picnic on the terrace under a high old barn roof; the Pyrenees look down on you with a different face every day. Above the living room are three pretty bedrooms with good beds, functional storage, lots of books, glorious views. One bathroom upstairs, a shower room downstairs and an excellent, fully-fitted kitchen complete the picture. You feel perfectly secluded and have your own garden space beside the lily pond, yet are free to share the pool and main garden with other guests and the attentive, civilised Furneys. It is a quiet and beautiful spot, and there's badminton and tennis (and, in May, French cookery classes) to keep you busy. You could even set off for a day's skiing in the Pyrenees; leave at 8am and you'll be there by 10. *Long winter lets available at £600 per month. B&B also.*

sleeps	7.
price	€ 545–€ 1,710 (£350–£1,120).
rooms	4: 1 double, 1 twin, 1 room with bunkbeds, 1 tiny single, 1 bathroom, 1 shower room.
closed	Never.

booking details

	Christine Furney
tel	+33 (0)5 62 08 21 45
fax	+33 (0)5 62 08 21 45
e-mail	setzeres32@aol.com
web	www.setzeres.com

Setzères – Le Grenier

Marciac, Gers

In the same stupendous surroundings of fine old buildings, green garden and stunning views, the smaller of the Setzères cottages is in the old grain loft and a rustic outside staircase leads to its new yet typically gabled front door. The Furneys have done another excellent conversion here. There's a lovely warm feel (enhanced by central heating in winter), with four characterful old armchairs on an oriental carpet, a round table with Windsor chairs and a window like a lens homing in on a slice of green country topped by snowy Pyrenean peaks beyond. This is a roomy, one-storied space for four. The neat, sky-lit kitchen, a mix of natural wood and blue tiles, gives onto this end of the room; the bedrooms are off either side. The yellow and pink double is smallish but has its own basin and the pink-tinged twin room is larger; both are well lit, have good storage and share the neat white bathroom. A terrace area and a good patch of garden are yours alone, but you can also share the wonderful grounds and pool with other guests. White-water rafting is a two-hour drive. *Long winter lets available at £400 per month. B&B also.*

sleeps	4.
price	€390–€930 (£250–£610).
rooms	2: 1 double, 1 twin, 1 bathroom.
closed	Never.

booking details

Christine Furney

tel	+33 (0)5 62 08 21 45
fax	+33 (0)5 62 08 21 45
e-mail	setzeres32@aol.com
web	www.members.aol.com/setzeres32

map 15   entry 185

Larriberau

Gers

Come for the sound of silence – though if you bring the children you must expect some frolicking in the pool. (It's perfect even for the youngest, being gently stepped at one end.) This is an old Napoleonic farmhouse, built in 1811, with loads of character and an elevated position: countryside rolls out on every side and on a clear day you can see the Pyrenees. There's an easy, relaxed feel: squashy floral sofas in front of a big fire (which roars in winter), a large kitchen with beautiful Gascon fireplace, and several bedrooms, some of which are in the next-door barn, heaven for children. The double bedrooms in the house have a casual, faded charm: big flowers on old-fashioned wallpaper, a four-poster, a quaint sofa – indisputably French. Fans keep you cool in summer. There's masses of space out as well as in – a big, safe garden bordered by ancient oaks, a cavernous barn with ping-pong and a table to feed 20 (you can eat in the house, too). Couples and parties would be equally happy here. The salon doubles as a library and TV/video room, there's a barbecue for meals under the stars, a dishwasher for all the plates.

sleeps	Main house: 5; Wing 9; + 2 cots.
price	£450-£1,875.
rooms	6: 2 doubles, 2 triples, 1 single, 1 family room for 3, 2 cots, 4 bathrooms, 1 shower room.
closed	Never.

booking details

Hugh & Nony Buchanan

tel	+44 (0)1367 870497
fax	+44 (0)1367 870497
e-mail	huggymummy@hotmail.com

Domaine de Hongrie – Gauloise Dorée

Lupiac, Gers

Even today Domaine de Hongrie merits its name. Translated from the 11th-century Basque, it means 'place of rest'; there's a real feeling of peace and remoteness here. You approach along country lanes deep in the Gers, before turning up a long, long drive. On either side are arid fields but you arrive at the domaine to be confronted by trees and flowering shrubs – a miracle of greenness. At the core of the main house is a tower which is thought to have sheltered pilgrims on the route to Santiago. (The chapel in the village is dedicated to St Jacques.) The domaine belonged Claudia's parents; she and Regis have taken it over and are in the process of transforming it. Young, friendly and energetic, they've achieved a great deal and their two gîtes promise to be simply but smartly, stylishly furnished. Set apart from the main house – and each other – they are surrounded by trees, shrubs and lawns. The larger has a big first-floor balcony and a terrace, the smaller is ideal for a couple. You can swim in the lake a mile away, and shop in Aignen – with its little market and three restaurants, it's a five-minute drive. *B&B also.*

sleeps	2-6 + 2 children.
price	€ 800.
rooms	For 2: 1 double, 1 bathroom, 1 shower room. For 6 + 2 children: 3 doubles, 2 childrens beds in sitting room, 3 bathrooms, 1 shower room.
closed	Rarely.

booking details

Claudia & Regis Meyer

tel	+33 (0)5 62 06 59 58
fax	+33 (0)5 62 64 47 55
e-mail	domaine-de-hongrie@wanadoo.fr
web	www.domaine-de-hongrie.com

map 15   entry 187

Maison Puech Malou – The Cottage
Teillet, Tarn

Sharing the same park-like garden as the house, the prettiest gîte. You step straight into a whitewashed, pine-floored, open-plan living room with woodburning stove, cheerful red sofa, books and easy chairs. The galley kitchen has sun-yellow tiles, dishwasher and hob (no oven). The bedroom is cosy and cool – white walls, antique pine, bed linen and towels to match, and a shower room en suite. You have your own terrace, with barbecue, to the rear, and, off the lovely courtyard, reached via an outside stair, an extra bedroom you can rent with the gîte – perfect for grandparents, older children or anyone wanting some independence. Monique is charming, bakes her own bread (which she's happy to sell), keeps her own hens. There's nothing she likes better than to prepare dinner for a big friendly crowd: enjoy *table d'hôtes* in the garden, washed down by Harry's good wines. You're high on a sunny hill (Puech means 'hilltop' in the regional dialect, Malou is a type of apple) in a garden lush with lavender, hibiscus, shady corners and pool. Teillet for simple shops is a five-minute drive, Albi and Toulouse are under an hour. *B&B also.*

sleeps	2-4 + 2 children (12-14 with Farmhouse).
price	€ 400.
rooms	1 double, 1 sofabed for children in sitting room, 1 shower room, extra double & shower room available with outside entrance.
closed	Never.

booking details

Monique Moors

tel	+33 (0)5 63 55 79 04
fax	+33 (0)5 63 55 79 88
e-mail	info@maisonpuechmalou.com
web	www.maisonpuechmalou.com

Maison Puech Malou – The Farmhouse

Teillet, Tarn

A beautiful restoration that manages to be both immaculate and rustic. You arrive via a very pretty back road through wooded country, then wash up at this creeper-clad 19th-century farmhouse. Inside, a graceful, calming home full of antiques, swimming in crisp light. Walls are exposed stone or whitewashed, the floors are terracotta-tiled, ceilings are beamed in heavy oak. The master suite has a huge double bed and hessian cloth on the walls, a couple of bedrooms come with stripped pine floorboards, another is entered by a wooden staircase that rises from the covered courtyard, where terracotta pots spill with colour. The sitting room has a huge open fireplace, the dining room an appropriately rustic dining table and you eat under beams. The open kitchen is delightfully designed. Attractive teak garden furniture stands on the terrace and the lawn runs down to the pool; there is also a vegetable garden and guests are free to harvest from it. A marked walk leads out from the garden into the hills that surround you. Dutch Monique and Harry are very friendly and on hand to help. A gorgeous place. *B&B also.*

sleeps	10 (12-14 with Cottage).
price	€ 1,350-€ 2,400.
rooms	5: 2 doubles, 3 twins, 3 bathrooms, 1 shower room, 1 separate wc.
closed	Never.

booking details

Monique Moors

tel	+33 (0)5 63 55 79 04
fax	+33 (0)5 63 55 79 88
e-mail	info@maisonpuechmalou.com
web	www.maisonpuechmalou.com

map 16   entry 189

Château de Garrevaques

Garrevaques, Tarn

Here you have all the advantages of the hotel (two restaurants, two pools, bar, spa, gardens and the gentle attention of the staff) yet you are wonderfully private. Your two-storey house next to the orangery – once the estate manager's quarters – is quarry-tiled, rustically furnished (the odd piece on loan from the château), comfortable, roomy… perfect for families. There's a dishwasher in the kitchen, two rooms with satellite TV (one for the children, one for you), an office for workaholics, a terrace with a barbecue, central heating, an open fire. The grounds, too, are a good place to be, studded with old trees as grand as the château, and big shrubs for hide and seek. There's an easy mood here, in spite of the brand-new pool and spa – it's the sort of place where children leave their bikes lying around and no one will worry. There's a Wendy house, swings, slides and an old tennis court, too. Marie-Christine loves having people around and is unstoppable; she organises cookery courses, itineraries, even flying lessons next door. You are in good hands. *Babysitting available. B&B also.*

sleeps	9-12.
price	€ 1,150–€ 2,300.
rooms	5: 1 double, 1 twin, 1 single, 1 family room for 3, 1 family room for 2-4, 2 bathrooms, 1 shower room, 2 separate wcs.
closed	Rarely.

booking details

	Marie-Christine Combes
tel	+33 (0)5 63 75 04 54
fax	+33 (0)5 63 70 26 44
e-mail	m.c.combes@wanadoo.fr
web	www.garrevaques.com

Les Buis de St Martin

Marssac sur Tarn, Tarn

Madame is a dear and loves having people to stay. The 19th-century manor, in its park on the banks of the Tarn, has been her home for 25 years; the gîte is in its own wing. How relaxing to wander down to the water's edge in this quietly special place. Inside, a charming minimalism prevails. The ground floor is terracotta, the first floor polished wood; muslin blinds hang at deep-set windows, walls are whiter-than-white. It's a contemporary look to suit a light and lofty space: furniture is wood, wicker or aluminium, there's a clean-cut sofa, a big bed covered in lemon-yellow with matching cushions, a few pictures, a simple rug. The galley-style kitchen and walk-in shower are chic and white; even the bedroom beam has been painted in Madame's favourite colour. Outside, your own garden with plunge pool and teak loungers. Little Marssac is delightful, and has the basic shops, and Albi and hilltop Cordes are close by. The area is filled with restaurants serving duck in all its forms, cassoulet, sheep's and goat's cheeses; the wines of Gaillac, less well-known than those of Bordeaux, are one of France's best kept secrets. *B&B also.*

sleeps	2-4.
price	€ 290-€ 1,000 (£190-£650).
rooms	1 double, 1 sofabed in living room, 1 shower room, 1 separate wc.
closed	Never.

booking details

Jacqueline Romanet

tel	+33 (0)5 63 55 41 23
fax	+33 (0)5 63 53 49 65
e-mail	jean.romanet@wanadoo.fr
web	perso.wanadoo.fr/les-buis-de-saint-martin/

map 16   entry 191

The Vineyard Cottage
Senouillac, Tarn

Thierry is a carpenter by trade: no wonder the little cottage has so much woody charm. It's a nest for two, secluded, shaded by young trees, surrounded by vineyards in an unspoiled southern corner. Inside: flagged floors, beamed ceilings, exposed stone walls, fine craftsmanship. The bed is carved, fitted and romantically curtained; the kitchen is rustic, with chunky timbers and exquisite granite worktop; the door to the shower has a carved bunch of grapes. Your one-bedroom house is small, solid and compact but has all you need to make you comfortable and happy: a walnut dresser stocked with crockery and glass, a sofa for two, pictures on the walls, electric heaters for cool nights, cassettes and CDs. Best of all, for hot days, your own plunge pool, fashioned from a huge oak wine vat – bliss in the private garden under the bamboos. There are sun loungers too, with fat cushions, and a barbecue for summer nights. The Cailhols live two minutes away, ready to help and advise. There are shops, markets and restaurants in Gaillac, a five-minute drive, and a bakery/patisserie in the village.

sleeps	2.
price	€ 275-€ 616.
rooms	1 double, 1 shower room.
closed	Never.

booking details

	Martine & Thierry Cailhol
tel	+33 (0)5 63 33 59 40
fax	+33 (0)5 63 33 20 67
e-mail	pugh@cocagne.com

Château de Broze – The Cottage
Broze, Tarn

The medieval château was occupied by the English during the Crusades and destroyed by Simon de Montfort. Its bakery survived and is now a delightful cottage; the bread oven is still in the sitting room. The old *boulangerie* is built of dreamy local white stone and looks due south, basking in day-long sun and giving fine views over ploughed fields and vineyards to the hamlet of Broze. The sitting room/kitchen is on the small side, but this hardly matters in summer as doors open onto the terrace, big and comfortable with teak chairs and wooden table, sun beds and a small, elegant plunge pool. There's croquet, too. Inside, wicker chairs and oak floors. A staircase leads up to the main bedroom where bed, floor and ceiling come in pretty pine and arched windows frame the view. An exterior stone staircase leads down to the second, small bedroom. This might sound complicated, but it's not, and the room is spotlessly clean with an attractive en suite shower room. Michelle and Andrew live next door; they know the area well and will advise. Market day in Cordes is Saturday; don't miss it. *Children over five welcome.*

sleeps	4.
price	€306–€1,115 (£190–£695).
rooms	2: 1 double, 1 twin, 2 shower rooms.
closed	Never.

booking details

	Michelle & Andrew Pugh
tel	+33 (0)5 63 33 59 40
fax	+33 (0)5 63 33 20 67
e-mail	pugh@cocagne.com
web	www.cottage-at-broze.com

map 16   entry 193

Château de Mayragues
Castelnau de Montmiral, Tarn

Superlatives cannot describe this remarkable cottage in its château grounds. It has everything: history, vineyards, atmosphere. The château is 14th century and, with its overhanging balcony circling the upper storey, is an outstanding example of the region's fortified architecture. Its authentic restoration over eight years won French-born Laurence and her Scottish husband Alan a national prize. Your home is, improbably, the château's old bakery; it is the prettiest home imaginable and has a south-facing terrace on which to relax with a glass of organic estate wine. It's cosy, light and simply but charmingly furnished – a mix of old and new. There's a living room with a wonderful new contemporary kitchen at one end, and a wooden stair to a tiny mezzanine with twin beds. The cool, roomy double has a blue and white theme with pretty checked curtains and new sisal on the floor; the shower room is excellent. Look out onto the 17th-century pigeonnier 'on legs'. Should you tire of being here, there's walking country all around, and the medieval hilltop village of Castelnau de Montmiral is well worth a visit. *B&B also.*

sleeps	2-3.
price	€305-€450.
rooms	1 family room for 3, 1 shower room.
closed	Never.

booking details

Alan & Laurence Geddes

tel	+33 (0)5 63 33 94 08
fax	+33 (0)5 63 33 98 10
e-mail	geddes@chateau-de-mayragues.com
web	www.chateau-de-mayragues.com

Enrouzié

Salvagnac, Tarn

This really is a home from home: the owners of the old farmhouse divide their time between the nearby bastide town of Salvagnac and here. The character of the rooms reflects Nuala's sunny personality, and the overall impression is one of friendly comfort and space. There are beautiful rafters in every room, new terracotta floors downstairs, stripped pine up, and the dreamy farmhouse kitchen is brilliantly equipped, with stacks of cookery books and lovely country crocks; the owner has quite a collection. You may help yourself to provisions, then replace them before you go. Furniture – some old, some modern – is country style, the bed linen is pretty and there are good prints and pictures on the walls. There's masses of space outside as well as in and the fenced garden is child-friendly, with even a lock to the pool area. There's also a handy summer kitchen, so you can lunch out here with ease – or just lounge with a cool drink. You have plenty of shops and restaurants close by… and the deep shade of the plum tree for outdoor dining in front of the house. Bliss.

sleeps	8-10.
price	€ 1,250–€ 2,350 (£875-£1,650).
rooms	4: 1 double with wc, 1 twin with wc, 2 family rooms for 3, 2 bathrooms, 1 shower room.
closed	October–April.

booking details

Nuala O'Neill
tel +33 (0)5 63 40 50 05
e-mail m.scott@wanadoo.fr

map 16 entry 195

Forcairenc – La Fermette, La Grange & La Bergerie

La Sauzière St Jean, Tarn

Angela and Geoff came here 10 years ago for the quiet life (and got it) and have renovated their 18th-century farmhouse with much sensitivity, and in style. They also have three gîtes, each entirely separate from the other, with roomy, light interiors and attractive, private, covered terraces for wining and dining. Each gîte is different and each has rustic charm. You get painted wooden furniture, patchwork quilts, pretty linen, pastel colours. The floors are stripped or stone-flagged, the beams old and painted, the beds are pine. Galley-style kitchens are compact, but have everything you need, and there's central heating for out-of-season stays. French windows open to that lovely terrace… keep going and you come to a shared and fenced pool with sun loungers and parasols for afternoon naps. Best of all are the majestic views: the countryside rolls away on all sides to hills, clumps of trees and, in full summer, fields of sunflowers. The whole place feels light, roomy, pleasingly simple – an easy spot to properly unwind. Angela knows this wonderful area well and will cheerfully advise.

sleeps	3 apartments for 4.
price	£200-£475 each.
rooms	2: 1 double, 1 twin, 1 bathroom.
closed	Never.

booking details

Angela Finn-Kelcey
tel +33 (0)5 63 33 50 70
fax +33 (0)5 63 33 50 70
e-mail angela.finn-kelcey@wanadoo.fr
web www.forcairenc.com

Couxe

Vieux, Tarn

This shimmering white-stone house stands on high ground. You can't miss it as you approach: sunlight bounces off the walls. Inside, a temple to the colour white, be it the walls, the handmade kitchen units, the painted beams or the stone that flanks the glimmering pool. It is unremittingly luxurious and contemporary. The enormous kitchen/dining room is full of the latest top-of-the-range equipment, cabinets are fronted with glass, framed black-and-white photographs hang on the wall. Bedrooms are big, flood with light, have white voile curtains and terracotta floors. Baths and power showers are immaculate... one bathroom is big enough for its own table and chairs (white, of course). Everything has been designed with a cool contemporary crispness. There's discreet up-lighting, sisal matting, modern prints on the walls and central heating for winter. Seek refuge from the sun on the covered terrace, or sunbathe by the pool on teak loungers. You are on the edge of a pretty village with a 14th-century church, and the views are stunning. Shops and restaurants are a 10-minute drive. *Changeover day Friday.*

sleeps	12.
price	£995–£1,975.
rooms	6: 3 doubles, 3 twins, 4 bath/shower rooms.
closed	Never.

booking details

	Mike Simler
tel	+33 (0)5 63 56 01 74
e-mail	mike.simler@wanadoo.fr
web	www.mikesimler.com

map 16   entry 197

Pechingorp

Castlenau de Montmiral, Tarn

The large stone farmhouse set in three and a half acres is reached by a small country track and has no close neighbours – peace and quiet are assured. You are surrounded by vines and open farmland, with the bastide village of Castlenau de Montmiral framed on top of the hill; it's floodlit at night – a magical sight. Pull up at a gravelled courtyard, where stone steps on one side lead to a wonderful covered terrace – the hub of the place – with a huge table at which to dine, wine, play games, chat. Beyond, a trim lawn encircles a big pool that gets day-long sun. Inside, good bedrooms, beamed ceilings, stone walls, wooden floors, powerful showers and a ceiling open to the rafters. Beds are comfy, walls are white, most rooms are light and airy, views are superb. It is an ideal property for two families as the house divides seamlessly into two (there are two rooms on one side, two on the other and both have their own sitting room and kitchen), so you won't feel on top of each other even for a moment. Gaillac with its wine and market is 20km away, the village and all you need are up the hill.

sleeps	8.
price	£725–£1,400.
rooms	4: 2 doubles, 2 twins, 4 bath/shower rooms.
closed	November–April.

booking details

	Mike Simler
tel	+33 (0)5 63 56 01 74
e-mail	mike.simler@wanadoo.fr
web	www.mikesimler.com

Château Cestayrols

Cestayrols, Tarn

A 15th-century château, a fortified house in a small bastide; stroll down to the boulangerie and pick up your morning croissants. This is a house of great charm, sensitively restored. You get peace and tranquillity in spades, a delightful walled garden (safe for kids) and a long, narrow, sun-trapping pool. Inside, a stone staircase rises in a cool and airy hall to a grand piano on the landing – baronial indeed! Pull straws for the master bedroom, enormous with white walls, cream drapes, sisal floors and views to the garden; the bathroom has a claw-foot bath. All bedrooms are light and airy, with wooden floors, old pine pieces, some open-stone walls. The first-floor salon, dominated by an immense fireplace with carved overmantel, has period chairs and a grandfather clock. Beamed ceilings and fresh white walls predominate. The kitchen and dining room are quarry-tiled and stone-walled; you have sparkling white units, dishwasher and oven. Beyond the village, vineyards, the medieval hilltop town of Cordes and the gorgeous river Tarn. Provisions are at Cahuzac, a 10-minute drive. *Changeover day Friday.*

sleeps	10.
price	£950–£1,850.
rooms	5: 3 doubles, 2 twins, 1 bathroom, 1 shower room.
closed	November–April.

booking details

	Mike Simler
tel	+33 (0)5 63 56 01 74
e-mail	mike.simler@wanadoo.fr
web	www.mikesimler.com

map 16   entry 199

Domaine de Villeneuve

Villeneuve sur Vère, Tarn

A *maison de maître*, a sublime house set in private parkland with ravishing views across meadows to an ancient church steeple; if you're lucky bells will chime. A place to come and hole up for a week in blissful isolation. The pool is flanked by rampant greenery with a rose pergola to one side, the terrace is sail-shaded with long views across open country. Inside, a sweeping wooden staircase, an enormous stone fireplace, oak and beamed ceilings and a *fleur-de-lys* tiled floor; the whole house swims in light. Mike, a collector, has a good eye. Acquisitions include an antique pram, a restored water trough, church pews and antique baskets. Upstairs, large airy bedrooms have voile curtains and wooden floors. One room has a marble fireplace, another a canopied wooden bed, and the room on the ground floor has floor-to-ceiling windows opening to the garden. Expect unremitting comfort: deep sofas, period furniture and old rugs. French windows lead from the well-equipped kitchen to a terrace that runs along two sides of the house. The medieval towns of Albi and Cordes are close by. *Changeover day Sunday.*

sleeps	12.
price	£950–£1,695.
rooms	6: 4 doubles, 2 twins, 4 bathrooms.
closed	Never.

booking details

	Mike Simler
tel	+33 (0)5 63 56 01 74
e-mail	mike.simler@wanadoo.fr
web	www.mikesimler.com

La Colombe

Donnazac, Tarn

There's a homely, welcoming feel to this beautifully restored stone house. Built on the edge of a vineyard-wrapped hamlet, it has rooms on three floors (and lots of stairs!). The front door takes you straight into a beamed kitchen – a warm, glorious mix of old and new, with a Rayburn, big bleached pine table and comfortable sofa, as well as all mod cons. A small corridor leads to a summer dining room, where French windows open onto the terrace. Up a flight of stairs from the kitchen is the main sitting room, overlooking the walled, secluded garden and new, lavender-fringed pool beyond. It's a charming, low-ceilinged room in cream and green with the palest beams. There are two bedrooms on this floor, each with an en suite bathroom, and two on the floor above. All are big, comfortable and full of light and character; the bathrooms, too, are roomy and cheerful with rugs and rattan chairs. The bustling medieval hilltop town of Cordes, which has a son-et-lumière and lots of summer festivals, is a 10-minute drive; Albi is not much further, with its fortified cathedral and museum devoted to Toulouse Lautrec. *Changeover day Friday.*

sleeps	8.
price	£725–£1,400.
rooms	4: 2 doubles, 2 twins, 3 bathrooms.
closed	Never.

booking details

	Mike Simler
tel	+33 (0)5 63 56 01 74
e-mail	mike.simler@wanadoo.fr
web	www.mikesimler.com

map 16   entry 201

Maraval
Cordes sur Ciel, Tarn

There's a feeling of remoteness here, although Cordes is no distance at all; only birdsong and the stream flowing beneath the house disturb the peace. Maraval stands at the end of a long, secret, country lane, an ancient farmhouse in 100 magical acres of woodland, cliffs and pasture. Behind, at the head of the valley, trees cluster steeply round the lawned garden and the lovely pool. The house itself is full of original features – massive beams, uneven floors, a creaky, eccentric staircase – and has white-painted walls and stunning views. Books, pictures, corner sofas and rugs make the split-level sitting room particularly homely and inviting. The kitchen, too, is a delight, with a vast open fireplace (and logs for cool evenings), an ancient farmhouse table, blue and white tiles and an armoire stuffed with crocks and glassware. Outside is a wonderful covered dining terrace. The large, pretty bedrooms are carpeted and furnished with rural antiques and comfortable beds; one bedroom suite is on the ground floor, with French windows onto the terrace; the other two are upstairs with the second bathroom. *Changeover day Sunday.*

sleeps	6.
price	£700-£995.
rooms	3: 2 doubles, 1 twin, 2 bathrooms.
closed	November-April.

booking details

	Mike Simler
tel	+33 (0)5 63 56 01 74
e-mail	mike.simler@wanadoo.fr
web	www.mikesimler.com

The Cottage
Cordes sur Ciel, Tarn

A treat to be staying in cobble-streeted Cordes – one of France's oldest bastide towns. English-born Gilles and Donna have poured love and energy into the restoration of this dear little one-up, one-down. You enter the kitchen and dining area, fresh with cream walls, pale beech units, old beams, lovely crocks and pots and pans; then up the coir-carpeted stair to a sunny, open-plan living area with the bedroom at the far end. It's a big, bright space with views that sail out over rooftops and valley. No gîte leftovers here, just simplicity and style. The walls are open-stone or cream, the floor is sisal, there's a sofa and a coffee table, curtains, pictures, magazines. A wrought-iron bed is covered by a pale blue quilt and the storage space is well-designed. You lack garden and terrace but the streets of Cordes are outside the door – and they're steep! Rampart walks, artisans' studios, shops, restaurants, a Saturday market, a sculpted-sugar museum – there's much to fascinate. Your young hosts run B&B two minutes down the hill and can offer you delicious food and wine whenever you choose not to cook. *Three more gîtes available. B&B also.*

sleeps	2.
price	From £250.
rooms	1 double, 1 bathroom.
closed	Never.

booking details

	Gilles Thacker
tel	+33 (0)5 63 56 88 95
fax	+33 (0)5 63 53 09 72
e-mail	gillesrace@aol.com
web	www.maisonbarbacane.com

map 16   entry 203

Château de Fourès
Campes/Cordes, Tarn

Swap stress for bliss at this gem of a cottage in the grounds of a 19th-century château. You'll be hard put to decide what to do first: relax by the waterlily ponds, set off for convivial Cordes, only a mile away… change into your whites for a game on the tennis court or take a dip in the pool (both shared with the owners). Or simply drink in the peace and views from your private roof terrace. The cottage has been beautifully restored by Madeleine, from Paris, and her Swiss husband Peter, who will respect your privacy but provide help when you need it. Furnishings are high quality, furniture is antique or new pine, the atmosphere attractive and light-filled. In the living room, exposed stone walls, a big rug on a terracotta floor, beamed ceilings, colourful cushions, a checked throw on the sofa, an open fire. Eat at the round table in the stunning, wooden fitted kitchen perfectly equipped, or outside on the shingled patio with its colourful flower beds. The light upstairs bedroom has wooden floorboards, pretty lace bedcovers on an antique bed and a door leading onto the roof terrace. Unbeatable value.

sleeps	4.
price	€ 550–€ 850.
rooms	2: 1 double, 2 singles downstairs, 1 shower room.
closed	Never.

booking details

	Madeleine Camenzind–Acory
tel	+33 (0)5 63 56 13 55
fax	+33 (0)5 63 56 13 55

Combe Nègre

St Marcel Campes, Tarn

A big-hearted family home, easily large enough to absorb its full complement of visitors. It stands on its own, 15 minutes from the nearest shops and restaurants: remote but not isolated. So the children can splash in the pool to their hearts' content, while you lounge. Follow the sun – or the shade – round the terrace with its long table, ample seating and barbecue. Inside, an interesting, higgledy-piggledy house with a lived-in feel. French windows lead into a large, bright kitchen with a big table and comfy sofa. Beech-topped units are filled with crockery and glassware, mismatched but of good quality, and there's TV, music and video. A beige carpet, a gold dralon suite with matching drapes and a beamy ceiling give old-fashioned comfort to the sitting room, and there are plenty of lights for reading and more French doors onto the garden. Carpeted bedrooms are plain and clean with white walls, stencils here and there, lots of hanging and drawer space, bookshelves with paperbacks. Rolling hills, forest and birdsong surround you, the area is heaven for walkers, and the kind owners live nearby if you need them.

sleeps	10.
price	£500–£1,200.
rooms	5: 2 doubles, 3 twins, 2 bathrooms, 1 shower room, 1 separate wc.
closed	Never.

booking details

	Ian & Penelope Wanklyn
tel	+33 (0)5 63 56 07 03
fax	+33 (0)5 63 56 07 03
e-mail	aurifat@wanadoo.fr

map 16   entry 205

La Croix de Fer
St Martin Laguepie, Tarn

It has the lot – stone walls, beamed ceilings, rolling views, ancient peace – but it is the way in which Jacqui and Francis have decorated this 18th-century converted barn that makes it sparkle. Step into a big, light living and kitchen area, with cream floor tiles, soft green sofa and chairs, a vase of dried flowers. On one side, the palest exposed-stone wall, on the other, white rough plaster; the space spills with light. The twin bedroom is soft lilac and lemon; Jacqui fell in love with the bed throws and linen, then designed the room around them. The double comes in cream and rose, with sofa, beams, a wrought-iron bed and windows on two walls with views of rolling hills. The house stands in 10 acres of grass and woodland, the silence broken only by birdsong. There are deckchairs, loungers, shady trees and a delicious terrace by the pool from which to worship the sun. Jacqui has thought of just about everything: fluffy towels in very good bathrooms, a music centre, books and a beautifully equipped, wooden kitchen. You can hire bikes in the local village, go riding nearby or walk your socks off in the Aveyron valley.

sleeps	4.
price	£300-£650.
rooms	2: 1 double, 1 twin, 1 bathroom, 1 shower room.
closed	November-April.

booking details

Jacqui & Francis Suckling
tel	+33 (0)5 63 56 25 20
fax	+33 (0)5 63 56 25 20
e-mail	suckling@wanadoo.fr

Rouyre – Braucol & Mauzac

Ste Cécile du Cayrou, Tarn

Golden boulders contrast with the springy turf surrounding this low, 18th-century stone farmhouse and its two attached gîtes. The terracotta roofs are deliciously mottled and there are far-reaching views over vineyards, sunflowers and corn. The gîtes have been named after a local variety of grape – Braucol and Mauzac – and have been imaginatively converted from an outbuilding. Open-plan interiors, walls of cream-painted plaster or stone and rugs on wooden floors give a light, airy feel. The kitchen areas are lavishly equipped, the living spaces bright and inviting, the sparkling bathrooms have little bottles of goodies. (Brian and Sandra-Anne ran a hotel in the Cotswolds and know how to spoil.) Braucol has three upstairs bedrooms, one with stunning views, two looking down over a wooden balustrade to the living area. Heavy curtains can be drawn to ensure privacy. Mauzac's double bedroom is on the ground floor; the twin is reached by a solid pine staircase. Each gîte has its own decked terrace with table and chairs, as well as full use of the farmhouse gardens and wonderful curved, deep pool. *Children over 8 welcome.*

sleeps	Braucol: 6. Mauzac: 4.
price	Braucol: €285–€1,010 (£195–£695). Mauzac: €255–€865 (£150–£595).
rooms	Braucol: 2 double, 1 twin, 1 bathroom, 1 shower room. Mauzac: 1 twin, 1 double, 1 bathroom.
closed	Never.

booking details

	Brian & Sandra-Anne Evans
tel	+33 (0)5 63 40 48 24
fax	+33 (0)5 63 40 48 24
e-mail	info@tarnprofonde.co.uk
web	www.tarnprofonde.co.uk

map 16   entry 207

Combenègre
Ste Cécile du Cayrou, Tarn

Anticipation rises as the small, unmade road winds its way through vineyards and gorgeous countryside. At the end of the track stands Combenègre, a beautifully proportioned 18th-century farmhouse in five hectares. To one side, with its own garden and built of the same rosy stone, is your gîte. Climb the outside stairs to its vast first-floor terrace and take in the full splendour of the views... Inside, a light-filled, open-plan room, beautifully designed and elegantly furnished. The uncluttered sitting area has deep, comfortable chairs, watercolours, rugs and masses of books; the kitchen/dining space is generously equipped and charming. Wooden stairs lead to an attractive mezzanine and fresh, airy bedrooms. White walls, stripped wooden floors and soft pastel fabrics create a restful air. There's also a large B&B suite in the main house. The Ritchies' sense of style spills over into the gardens and pool. Kirk and Sally have already made Combenègre very much their own, though they have only lived here a short while, and their friendliness and enthusiasm are infectious. Your nearest restaurant is a five-minute drive. *B&B also.*

sleeps	4.
price	€305–€765 (£210–£525).
rooms	2: 1 double, 1 twin, 1 shower room.
closed	Never.

booking details

Kirk & Sally Ritchie
tel	+33 (0)5 63 33 11 89
e-mail	contact@verevalley.com
web	www.verevalley.com

Le Moulin

Villefranche de Rouergue, Aveyron

A glorious place to come with a party of friends. Gaze into the waters of the ancient millpond and feel the stresses of modern life dissolve. Surrounded by 40 acres of woodland and orchid-dotted meadows, all you'll hear from this charmingly furnished mill are the woodpeckers and the rustling of trees. Eat on the terraces, in sun or shade, or take a dip in the lovely pool. There's tennis close by, windsurfing an hour away and fishing right here, on your own pond. The more energetic will explore this ruggedly beautiful region on foot or by canoe. The English owners have preserved many of the 18th-century mill's original features, from old beams in the living/dining room to the stone sink in the kitchen – which is smallish and beautifully planned, with dishwasher and every mod con. There's a spotless laundry room, too. On cool evenings, feast cosily by the immense stone cantou, then fall asleep to the murmur of the millstream from your deliciously canopied four-poster. In an area celebrated for its bastide towns, 13th-century Villefranche de Rouergue is a gem; market day is Thursday. *Not suitable for young children.*

sleeps	6-7.
price	€ 677-€ 1,585 (£425-£1,095).
rooms	3: 1 double, spare bed on landing, 2 twins, 1 downstairs, 1 bathroom, 1 shower room, 1 separate wc.
closed	Rarely.

booking details

	Edward & Sybil Roskill
tel	+44 (0)20 7703 4736
fax	+44 (0)20 7701 6158
e-mail	enquiries@la-belle-france.com
web	www.la-belle-france.com

map 16   entry 209

Monteillet-Sanvensa

Villefranche de Rouergue, Aveyron

Lounge in a hammock in the garden and luxuriate in the views of fields and the mini-hamlet of Sanvensa; walk across the Rouergue hills to the medieval towns of Bruniquel, Cordes and Gaillac; explore the nearby bastide town of Villefranche de Rouergue. The solid stone farmhouse provides a good centre from which to discover this rugged and fascinating *département*. The interior is basic but comfortable, furniture and colours rustic and old-fashioned. There's a large open-plan living room with Seventies-style chairs and brick fireplace, from which a section can be curtained off to make an extra bedroom. Upstairs is a large white bedroom under the gables, and a pretty smaller one with blue carpets. Delightful, eager-to-please Monique runs a B&B next door; she specialises in excellent, light, French cooking so why not join her and her guests for dinner in the courtyard one evening (book in advance). She will also put you in touch with local farmers to buy fresh produce and pick up bread for you in the mornings if you ask – or you could tread the one kilometre to the little village yourself. Great value. *B&B also.*

sleeps	5-8.
price	€300–€505.
rooms	2: 1 double, 1 family room for 3, sofabed & single downstairs, 1 bathroom, 1 separate wc.
closed	Never.

booking details

	Monique Bateson
tel	+33 (0)5 65 29 81 01
fax	+33 (0)5 65 65 89 52

La Mothe

Salles Courbatiers, Aveyron

Walkers, wine-buffs and wildlife lovers will adore this little-discovered corner of *la France profonde*, as the Aveyron is known. The road to the hamlet of La Mothe, in which the 200-year-old farmhouse stands, goes blissfully nowhere, and from the house you can stride out into rolling hills and woods. Inside the tone is ancient, authentic and comfortable. The Clarks, who live here for part of the year, have renovated the house with refreshing simplicity, showing off original stone walls, oak beams and fabulous original doors to lovely effect. There's a handsome vaulted kitchen with a large pine table and chairs, and you'll find food cupboards stocked with the basics for your stay. Enjoy the views from the first-floor sitting room with its stone fireplace, superb Louis XIII armoires, and delicious cream and apricot soft furnishings. Bedrooms have either pine or antique walnut furniture, and there's a huge sunny yellow attic room which children will love. Savour the wines from Cahors, Gaillac and Marcillac as you relax on one of the terraces (shaded or sunny) overlooking the valley below, then take a dip in your private pool.

sleeps	8-10.
price	€ 766–€ 2,234 (£480–£1,400).
rooms	4: 2 doubles, 1 twin, 1 quadruple attic room, 1 bathroom, 2 shower rooms.
closed	Never.

booking details

	Rosemary & Gordon Clark
tel	+44 (0)1296 747045
fax	+44 (0)870 056 1224
e-mail	gc@french-houses.demon.co.uk

map 16   entry 211

Château de Belcastel – Tourelle & Chambre du Comte

Belcastel, Aveyron

Lovers of history rejoice! Leave your car outside the castle walls, cross the carp-filled moat and greet the Middle Ages; the owners welcome you in an elegant, grassy courtyard. The architect of the 1975 restoration chose to leave parts undisturbed and these now form terraces for sitting, reading, dreaming. Views are to the village and the river below. Choose from one of two gîtes in this utterly romantic setting. Each is well-equipped with everything new, the furniture is carefully chosen, colours are warm and there are plenty of books and CDs. White, high backed sofas, a vast fireplace and terracotta floors in the larger gîte; pine furniture and a pink-walled kitchen in the smaller one in the tower. Both have balconies for al fresco meals. There's an additional kitchen in the tower for those who like to eat on the patio with a cascade running by, and a spiral staircase (not suitable for children) that leads down to the garden and pool, set into the castle wall. Tourists wander but the gîtes are private, there are local wines and delicacies in the castle shop and a *salon de thé. B&B also.*

sleeps	La Tourelle 2.
	La Chambre du Comte 2.
price	€ 1,300–€ 1,500 each.
rooms	La Tourelle: 1 double, 1 bathroom,
	1 separate wc.
	La Chambre du Comte:
	1 twin/double, 1 bathroom.
closed	January–15 March.

booking details

	Catherine & Pierre Toutain
tel	+33 (0)5 65 64 42 16
fax	+33 (0)5 65 64 61 41
e-mail	bienvenue@chateau-belcastel.com
web	www.chateau-belcastel.com

La Montarnie

Lescure Jaoul, Aveyron

A sleepy hamlet – the entire village is a farm – though a handsome young baker passes through twice a week to peddle his wares. It's picture-postcard pretty, cattle graze, birds sing, there are orchids in the meadows in spring. Relax on the wooden swing-seat in the shade of the walnut tree in your walled, suntrap garden; spot the wagtails nesting in the barn wall. The house dates from 1860, is stone-built, was once a barn and stands engulfed by a sea of greenery and wild flowers. It's a rustic little homestead furnished in a warm, contemporary style. Bedrooms are light and delightful, cool in summer, and with good views onto the garden. Downstairs: wicker dining chairs, a comfortable new cream sofa, CDs to listen to, books to read, an open fire (central heating, too). Baskets hang from beams and you eat at a long pine table where wooden church pews rest against stone walls. Rent bikes in nearby Najac, one of the loveliest old towns in the country of the Cathars. Fish, canoe, swim in the river, or head for historic Rodez and Albi. This is simple, rural France with few tourists on the radar. *Flexible changeover day.*

sleeps	4.
price	€ 360–€ 470.
rooms	2: 1 double, 1 twin, 1 bathroom, 1 shower room, 2 separate wcs.
closed	Rarely.

booking details

	Sarah & Charles Drury
tel	+44 (0)1981 240367
fax	+44 (0)1981 240327
e-mail	montarnie@amserve.com

map 16 entry 213

Montarsés de Tayrac

La Salvetat Peyralés, Aveyron

A huge, handsome 19th-century farmhouse and converted barn, perched on the top of a hill with glorious views – and a fine south-facing terrace from which to enjoy them. Jacques is passionate about pure-bred horses (see them grazing from your bedroom window), Jo also runs B&B (for up to 10 guests); both are warm and charming, love having guests – and their children – and are on hand should you need them. Roam the estate's 30 hectares of fields and woods, fish in the private lake, swim in another lake nearby, and, if you can prove your equine competence (and insurance), ride. Rooms are big and old-fashioned, furnished with a mix of antique and modern. There's a large dining room – blissfully cool in the summer heat – with great beams, and a newly-done salon with an impressive stone fireplace. Bedrooms are light and have stripped wooden floors, cream walls and open hanging space. The area is rich in bastide towns with their perfectly preserved arcaded market squares, including Villefranche de Rouergue and Najac. *House can be let for 10, 6 or 4. Prices on request. Winter lets available. B&B also.*

sleeps	7.
price	€ 270–€ 530.
rooms	4: 2 doubles, 1 twin, 1 single, 1 bathroom, 2 shower rooms.
closed	Never.

booking details

	Jo & Jacques Rieben
tel	+33 (0)5 65 81 46 10
fax	+33 (0)5 65 81 46 10
e-mail	chantelouve@club-internet.fr
web	www.ifrance.com/aveyronvacances

Maison La Grande Combe

St Izaire, Aveyron

This magnificent 17th-century stone farmhouse is the home of serene Dutch owners Nelleke, a psychologist, and her partner Hans. Full of enthusiasm and energy, they run relaxation and cookery courses and do B&B. You have your own little studio – poised at the end of the main house – with private entrance, patio and a view to die for. Furnishings are simple and new, walls are whitewashed, beams de rigueur. In the evenings you can cook in your own snug quarters, or join the other guests for a delicious, wholesome dinner in the main part of the house. Hans grows organic vegetables and fruit, some of which he bottles, and makes scrumptious bread; Nelleke is a splendid creator of jams. Walk the rugged Aveyron hills and wooded valleys, swim in the Tarn, visit romantic castles, explore the grounds, lovely with their secluded terraces with breathtaking views. Or just be. There's a library with a small fireplace to share, and a meditation room, and children are made extremely welcome. "I'll guarantee you'll come away from here feeling fantastic… it's a little paradise," says our inspector. *Shared washing machine. B&B also.*

sleeps	Studio 2-4; connecting room 2-3.
price	Studio from €336 for two; connecting room from an extra €280.
rooms	Studio: 1 twin/double & sofabed, 1 shower room. Connecting room: 1 family room for 3, 1 shower room.
closed	Rarely.

booking details

Hans & Nelleke Versteegen
tel	+33 (0)5 65 99 45 01
fax	+33 (0)5 65 99 48 41
e-mail	grande.combe@wanadoo.fr
web	www.la-grande-combe.nl

map 16   entry 215

Le Très Profond

St Antoine sous Terre, Aveyron

Many historians think of the notion of equality between the genders in Europe as starting with the Cathars in France. Here is evidence of an earlier beginning – 'his' and 'hers' cave entrances. Same size, different shapes – these twin entrances yield straight to the main hall, so they are merely symbolic of a gender equality that must have existed thousands of years ago. Such radical ideas came to grief, as we all know. Perhaps, even, men and women took it in turns to chase the woolly mammoth. Whatever – this is now the dinkiest little apartment with a hundred clever ways of bringing in natural light and creating air flow. (The great remaining wall is all that is left of a medieval attempt to draw air down into the bowels of the earth. It worked, but the invading English knights knocked most of it down in a fit of pique – they couldn't stand the French getting ahead of them technologically.) The great depth is proof against the fiercest summer sun and there is, anyway, always a deep pool of water in which to cool. Unusual and enterprising. *Only for use with night vision equipment – see a specialist.*

sleeps	Too many to count.
price	Only stone age currency accepted. If in doubt, bring a pebble or two.
rooms	One vast cavern, furnished with numerous large and small nooks, crannies and *niches*. No windows.
closed	Never, but sometimes difficult to access.

booking details

	Sue Terrain
tel	-(0) 99 438 # 456 *
fax	Broken, due to water.
e-mail	trog@profondeur-incroyable.fr.og
web	www.la-vie-sans-soleil.fr.og/club-cavern

HOW TO USE THIS BOOK

Explanations

Abbreviated address
...ect to be used for correspondence.

Italics
...ntions other relevant details e.g.
...B *also*, or when changeover day for
...-catering is not Saturday.

sleeps
...e lower number indicates how
...ny adults can comfortably sleep
...e. The higher is the maximum
...nber of people that can be
...ommodated.

price
...e price shown is per week
...d the range covers low season
...high season, unless we say
...erwise.

rooms
...give total numbers of each type
...bedroom e.g. double, triple, and
...al numbers of bathrooms. We give
...details only when they are separate
...m bathrooms.

closed
...hen given in months, this means for
...e whole of the named months and
...e time in between.

map & entry numbers
...ap page number; entry number.

symbols
...e the last page of the book for
...planation.

sample entry

WESTERN LOIRE

La Maison Aubelle - Tour, Gaudrez & Jardin
Montreuil Bellay, Maine-et-Loire

A 16th century nobleman's house in an old country town. It stands in secluded gardens flanked by high stone walls, renovated by craftsmen, thoughtfully equipped by Peter and Sally. The original apartments are Tour, Jardin and Gaudrez. Tour – in the tower, as you'd expect – is one flight up a spiralling stone stair; it has a beamed living room/kitchen with trim red sofas and wraparound views (below). The garden apartment, with terrace, is as neat as a new pin; white-walled Gaudrez has a 16th century window, discovered during restoration. The feel is airy, relaxing, comfortable; crisp linen, central heating and daily cleaning are included and the quality is superb. There's a terrace and games room for all and an appropriately large pool. If you can't face cooking, let the Smiths do it for you: they whisk up delicious meals five times a week, cheerfully served in the dining room in winter, on the terrace in summer. Peter and Sally are also on hand to advise, translate or leave you in peace. They run French courses, too. *Apartments rented separately or together. Children over 12 welcome. Shared laundry. Min. three nights.*

sleeps	Tour & Gaudrez: 4. Jardin: 2.
price	Tour & Gaudrez €775–€1,000; Jardin €675–€925.
rooms	Tour: 2 doubles, 2 shower rooms. Gaudrez: 2 doubles, 2 shower rooms. Jardin: 1 double, 1 bathroom, 1 separate wc.
closed	Rarely.

booking details

Peter & Sally Smith
tel	+33 (0)2 41 52 36 39
fax	+33 (0)2 41 50 94 83
e-mail	maison.aubelle@aubelle.com
web	www.aubelle.com

entry 71   map 7

Photography by Michael Busselle

languedoc-roussillon

Mas Manyaques – Apartments

Le Tech, Pyrénées-Orientales

A little bit of Eden in the south of France. This Catalan *mas* was built in 1789 and doubled as a mill. It is set in 25 acres of peace and quiet on the edge of the river Tech (the sound of which will lull you to sleep) and even though the valley is wooded, it opens up at the homestead. It's a very special place – it has its own little chapel – and as well as the pool there are swimming holes in the river: you can swim with the fishes, then try to land one for supper. The walking here is exceptional, so follow your nose and lose yourself in the hills for an afternoon. There are six gîtes in farmhouse style, all of which share the lovely decked pool, and all of which have their own private terrace. You have tiled floors, exposed beams, comfy sofas, chequered bed linen, good views, maybe a wood-burning stove in the kitchen; there's a simple, fresh feel. Outside, table tennis, swings and a barbeque area that tends to host convivial suppers… your young hosts are charming. If you want to take the whole place you can; just book early. Spain and the Mediterranean are 30 minutes away. Terrific. *Babysitting available. B&B also.*

sleeps	2 apartments sleep 6; 3 sleep 4; 1 sleeps 2.
price	For 6-8 £299-£849; 4-6 £199-£749; 2-4 £99-£449.
rooms	1 apartment with 1 double, 2 twins, 1 bath; 1 apartment with 2 doubles, 1 twin, 2 baths; 3 apartments with 1 double, 1 twin, 1 bath; 1 apartment with 1 double, 1 shower.
closed	Never.

booking details

Kim & Dominic Manley
tel +33 (0)4 68 39 62 91
e-mail dommanley@aol.com
web www.manyaques.com

4 Carrer San Vincenc

Eus, Pyrénées-Orientales

Small but impossibly sweet, this tiny village house has an uninterrupted view across the valley to Pic duCanigou. It was built in 1910, though you'd think it was older as the hill-stacked village dates to medieval times. Inside, an English cottage interior – best suited to the nimble – with snug bedrooms in pale yellows and whites. The twin is in what was the attic, the master has the view that stretches for miles. Both have doll's house bathrooms, one with a shower, one with a bath. Downstairs, a very pretty sitting room with wicker furniture, an exposed stone wall, a wooden floor and plenty of natural light. The kitchen is super. There are three terraces and patios so you can always catch the sun; breakfast on the balcony (in shifts if there are four of you), with its wrought-iron furniture and barbecue, or on the terrace where the grape arbour and the fig tree yield delicious fruit. You are 45 minutes from ski slopes and the Mediterranean, the region is packed with romanesque churches and there are four important cloisters nearby: Eus lies on a pilgrimage path of those travelling from Italy and northern Spain. *Children over 10 welcome.*

sleeps	4-5.
price	€ 300–€ 550
rooms	2: 1 double, 1 triple, 1 bathroom, 1 shower room.
closed	Never.

booking details

	John & Pauline Gordon
tel	+44 (0)788 9194507 (mobile)
fax	+44 (0)779 3564398 (mobile)
e-mail	ptimothy@amserve.com

map 16   entry 218

4 place de la Cellera
Thuir, Pyrénées-Orientales

Medieval outside, ultra-modern in. One of the owners is an artist, and her large abstracts embellish white walls. Number Four was the castle steward's house of this bastide town and the castle stood next door. Now there's a church, imposing and beautiful, to share this little square – an engaging setting. The redstone façade has been prettily and properly restored, right down to the gutters – green, ceramic, authentically Catalan. Inside, much is new: the clean sweep of wooden floor, the woodburner that heats most of the house, the quarry-tiled countertops in the kitchen, the iron stair that spirals from the ground floor up to the rooftop. Although the living room is dark, the bedrooms are large and light-filled; the dining room, too, is white, light and airy. Dine off a rococo-modern table with a glass top and matching metalwork chairs: the striking work of a sculptor friend. The good-sized kitchen is inviting and you could happily cook here. No garden but two terraces, one small, cosy and cool, the other on the roof, big enough for a barbecue and a table for six. The view from the rooftop sails over to the Pic du Canigou.

sleeps	6-7 + 1 cot.
price	€ 535–€ 1,000.
rooms	3: 2 doubles, 1 triple, 2 bathrooms, 2 shower rooms.
closed	Never.

booking details

	Ian Mayes
tel	+33 (0)4 68 38 87 83
e-mail	masstjacq@aol.com

Maison de la Place

Caixas, Pyrénées-Orientales

The restored Catalan stone cottage opens onto the little Place d'Eglise in the smallest village in France. Once you would have heard the church bells toll… today you can relish the peace. Given the house's age, the inside is surprisingly modern, with a lovely fresh, clean feel. The roomy living/dining room has tiled floors, comfortable cream sofas and an open fire; the sweet little kitchen – excellently equipped, with dishwasher – an older, more lived-in feel. There's a laundry room, too. Bedrooms are white with contrasting Persian rugs, one has a modern ironwork four-poster with soft white drapes. The beach isn't too far, the thermal baths are nearer, and the glorious, gently rugged Pic du Canigou is on the spot. (Visit the still inhabited 11th-century monastery of Saint Martin along the way.) Pop across the border to Spain and stock up on pots and paella, or laze by the walled pool at the owner's house where he runs B&B. If you like to cook, the shops are a 12-minute drive; if you feel sociable, book yourself dinner at Ian's. He's a great cook and an entertaining conversationalist. *B&B also.*

sleeps	5.
price	€ 399–€ 638 (£250–£400).
rooms	3: 2 doubles, 1 single, 1 bathroom, 1 separate wc.
closed	Never

booking details

	Ian Mayes
tel	+33 (0)4 68 38 87 83
fax	+33 (0)4 68 38 87 83
e-mail	masstjacq@aol.com

map 16   entry 220

Domaine de Sicard

Ribouisse, Aude

Heaven for nature lovers: in spring you hear nightingales. The farmhouse stands in 25 acres of woods and pasture, the Pyrenees lie at your door. The Van Vliets abandoned successful careers in Holland to find a stress-free environment in which to bring up their daughter; she's now left home, but they still look after a dog, cats and a horse called Stix. Wout devotes much of his time to drawing and painting. The charming and dynamic couple have renovated this ancient farmhouse stone by stone (the original dates from 1271) and turned one half into a holiday cottage. On summer days snooze in the garden among lilac trees, lavender and roses, then take lunch on your private terrace. The house is immaculate and there's an exquisite new wood-beam ceiling in the living/dining room. Furnishings are modest but comfortable in authentic 1960s style; bedrooms have wonderful views of the gardens and the mountains. The medieval towns of Mirepoix and Carcassonne are nearby, and there's horse riding, too. Great value.

sleeps	4.
price	€259–€434.
rooms	2: 1 double, 1 twin, 1 shower room.
closed	Never.

booking details

Wout Van Vliet

tel	+33 (0)4 68 60 50 66
fax	+33 (0)4 68 60 50 66
e-mail	domainesicard@hotmail.com

La Maison D'Oc
Villemoustaussou, Aude

Our inspector calls this small, three-storey house of delights "a nest for lovers". Your perfectly restored gamekeeper's cottage has a private walled gravel courtyard, attractive with flowers, teak chairs, stone barbecue and a splash pool; relax here with a glass of fruity Minervois after a day exploring medieval Carcassone, or the Canal du Midi. Or swim in the domaine's pool under the spreading cedar. A stable door leads directly into your living/kitchen/dining room; it may feel on the small side for four, maybe, but is is very attractively furnished in whites and blues and has a cleverly designed corner kitchen. There's a brilliant cooker with a small dishwasher underneath, a washing machine and a dryer – all sparkling new – and a traditional sink. Upstairs, a pretty mosaic frieze surrounds the gleaming white marble tiles of the generous shower room. The main bedroom on the second floor is indeed a romantic resting place; orange and yellow tones glow warmly next to mahogany, coconut matting and bamboo. You have plenty of storage space, and sweeping vineyard views. Gorgeous. *B&B also.*

sleeps	4.
price	€ 533–€ 990.
rooms	2: 1 double, 1 twin, 1 shower room.
closed	Rarely.

booking details

Christophe & Catherine Pariset

tel	+33 (0)4 68 77 00 68
fax	+33 (0)4 68 77 01 68
e-mail	cpariset@trapel.com
web	www.trapel.com

map 16 entry 222

Le Relais Occitan – Lo Barralier

Marseillette, Aude

Surrounded by sunflowers and vines, this fabulous old winery, with its giant oak vats, antique vineyard tools and incredible glass-paved cellar has been turned into a museum and four holiday cottages (two featured in this guide) by Anita and Jean Louis. It's been a labour of love, but labours of love are nothing unusual for this energetic and cultured Franco-Italian couple. Both writers and journalists – their passions are history and poetry – they are as likely to discuss troubadour verse as 19th-century winemaking techniques over a welcoming aperitif. All the cottages here, once the homes of the families working on the vineyard, have been refurbished with rustic simplicity; furniture, mostly pine, and kitchen crockery are basic, with a Fifties feel. Lo Barralier is the oldest and smallest cottage, once inhabited by the barrel-maker, and has a Languedocian staircase and a second-floor terrace with shimmering views of the vineyards and the Montagne d'Alaric. A huge covered barbecue area with a wood-burning oven for homemade pizza is yours to share; on Sundays there are pizza and wine parties, enjoyed hugely by guests. *B&B also.*

sleeps	2-4.
price	€300–€420.
rooms	2: 1 family room for 3, 1 sofabed on second floor, 1 shower room.
closed	Never.

booking details

	Jean Louis Cousin & Anita Canonica
tel	+33 (0)4 68 79 12 67
fax	+33 (0)4 68 79 12 67
e-mail	j-l.cousin@wanadoo.fr
web	perso.wanadoo.fr/relais.occitan

Le Relais Occitan – Lo Podaire

Marseillette, Aude

History and culture are what make the people tick here, so if watching TV or topping up your tan are what you're after, this is not for you. It's a delightful place run by delightful people, with an orchard, a vegetable garden (help yourself to produce), a splash pool for the children under the trees and plenty of loungers for you. Lo Podaire, the vine-cutter's house, has a walnut staircase and polished wooden floors, decorated with various objects brought back by Anita from her travels in far-flung places. Sip a glass of the domaine's extremely drinkable wine and dream on the views from the terrace of the little bedroom on the second floor. Lunch and dinner can be taken on the bigger terrace in front. There are bikes to borrow, steam baths in what used to be a huge wine tank, with aromatherapy, even cruises on the peaceful green waters of the Canal du Midi: Jean Louis' houseboat sets off every Wednesday. All these treats are on the house. Further afield are Cathar castles to visit and the medieval fairytale city of Carcassonne, perched above the Aude – a short drive. *B&B also.*

sleeps	2-5 + 2 children.
price	€ 365–€ 530.
rooms	2: 1 family room for 3, 1 childrens' twin, 1 sofabed, 1 bathroom, 1 separate wc.
closed	Never.

booking details

	Jean Louis Cousin & Anita Canonica
tel	+33 (0)4 68 79 12 67
fax	+33 (0)4 68 79 12 67
e-mail	j-l.cousin@wanadoo.fr
web	perso.wanadoo.fr/relais.occitan

map 16   entry 224

Pink Shutters

Ste Valière, Aude

A first floor patio balcony – perfect for breakfast and sundowners – links the two halves of this village house. This is a wonderful, easy place for two families to stay. There's a large, white, beamed kitchen/living room with music, radio, books and bright cushions, and a second living room with a yellow sofabed and wicker chairs round an open fire. Bedrooms have beautiful terracotta floors, white walls, plants, pale beams and vineyard views – the feel is fresh and modern. When not basking on the balcony pop across the (unbusy) street to your private walled garden with shady eating area, lawn, barbecue and raised fountain, which makes a delicious paddling pool for small feet. You have two bikes to spin off on, and Meg and Simon nearby (they have a B&B in Cazedarnes) for friendly advice. There's much charm in this village of viticulteurs; post office, restaurant, wine bar and tennis are a walk away. The gîte – once a 14th-century coach house – makes a charming staging post for the unspoilt beaches of the Languedoc, for Narbonne, Carcassonne, the Pyrenees, even Spain. *B&B also at Cazedarnes.*

sleeps	8.
price	£250–£600.
rooms	4: 3 doubles, 1 room with bunkbeds, 1 bathroom, 2 shower rooms.
closed	Rarely.

booking details

Meg & Simon Charles

tel	+33 (0)4 67 38 21 68
fax	+33 (0)4 67 38 21 68
e-mail	megsimon@wanadoo.fr
web	www.charles-french-gites.com

Hameau de Cazo – La Vigne
St Chinian, Hérault

Simple and quietly elegant, this little pink village house will delight all who eschew fussiness and clutter. And the dreamy views of vineyards and the red-earthed hills of the Montagne Noire clear the mind, too. In a small working hamlet, the three-storey house has been beautifully restored by Dutch owners Monique and Reinoud, who live in the next village. Neat box trees flank the front door and, inside, original patterned Languedocian floor tiles are enhanced by clean white walls and simple furniture. Dine around the large farmhouse pine table, or among the almond trees and lavender in the walled garden. Upstairs to colourful bedspreads and curtains, rust-red hexagonal floor tiles, and, in the double, an open fire. It's a romantic little home and a well-equipped one, too; there's everything you need, from central heating and two open fires to video and CD, dishwasher and coffee-maker. Walk in the Montagne Noire and the Mont Caroux, swim in peaceful rivers, or drink in simple village life (preferably with a glass of the local Minervois wine) while you watch sheep and goats lazily graze. St Chinian is a mile away.

sleeps	4 + 1 child.
	L'Amandier for 4–5 next door.
price	€275–€580.
rooms	2: 1 double, 1 twin, 1 bathroom.
closed	Never.

booking details

	Monique & Reinoud
	Weggelaar-Degenaar
tel	+33 (0)4 67 89 35 68
fax	+33 (0)4 67 89 35 68
e-mail	monique.degenaar@worldonline.fr
web	www.midimaison.com

map 16 entry 226

Paradix – Apartment One

Nissan lez Ensérune, Hérault

The handsome gateway is 19th century but the interiors are resolutely modern: old and new coexist effortlessly in this collection of four apartments (see next entry). This was once the *maison de maître* of a wine merchant and vines sweep in every direction. The stables and outbuildings have been imaginatively transformed by architect Colin and his Swiss wife, Susanna; they used to run an auberge in Tuscany, now they live here. Apartments have two storeys and a small patio garden; the rest – lawns, shady spots, chlorine-free pool – are to share. Inside: a minimalist look with the occasional cushion or Matisse print in colourful contrast to perfect white walls and pale terracotta floors; there's light, space, clean lines. Apartment One, the biggest, sleeping four, has an immaculate kitchen (with dishwasher), a large living/dining room with plenty of space in which to sit and read, and views to the lovely jasmine- and oleander-tumbled gardens that keep each apartment private. A yellow spiral staircase leads to luxurious but stylishly simple bedrooms, with beds dressed in fine white linen. *Shared laundry.*

sleeps	4.
price	€ 785–€ 970.
rooms	2 doubles, 2 shower rooms.
closed	Never.

booking details

	Susanna, Colin & Yvonne Glennie
tel	+33 (0)4 67 37 63 28
fax	+33 (0)4 67 37 63 72
e-mail	glennieauparadix@wanadoo.fr

Paradix – Apartments

Nissan lez Ensérune, Hérault

You can tell from the beautiful blue and white apartment kitchens that Colin Glennie was once a professional chef: they're so well equipped that even the most reluctant cook will be inspired. All is perfection in the apartments, the interiors a serene symphony of light woods and natural fabrics. Study, read or relax in the large, light living/dining rooms; the lighting is excellent, and central heating keeps you cosy and warm in winter. In summer, swim in the delicious pool, read under the plane trees, or stroll among the roses and oleander in the communal garden. Or set off for Béziers (don't miss the riotous four-day *feria* in August), the Oppidum d'Ensérune, the nearby site of a 2,600-year-old Gallo-Roman settlement, and the Canal du Midi, with its colourful barges. If you want a cheaper option, there's a first-floor studio for two, where striking blues and reds are offset by white walls. Come to Paradix if you're seeking a week of minimalist perfection in discreet and beautiful surroundings and a village you can walk to: Nissan is a lively little place with both market and shops. *Shared laundry.*

sleeps	3 apartments for 2.
price	€ 520–€ 790 each.
rooms	1 twin/double, 1 shower room.
closed	Never.

booking details

	Susanna, Colin & Yvonne Glennie
tel	+33 (0)4 67 37 63 28
fax	+33 (0)4 67 37 63 72
e-mail	glennieauparadix@wanadoo.fr

map 16   entry 228

Château de Grézan – Les Meneaux

Laurens, Hérault

Enter the battlemented gateway in the 'medieval' castle walls (those turrets are 19th-century follies), cross the cobbled yard and climb the old stone stairs. Les Meneaux feels big and somehow modern – yards of lovely, wide, original floorboards, high rafters, immaculate white walls and a fully-equipped kitchen that is definitely of the modern age. The flat is big, light and uncluttered, its paintwork picked out in blue, its sideboard full of perfectly chosen china. It has simple country furnishings, a pretty blue double bedroom, a smaller, spring-flowered twin and a sixth bed up on the mezzanine beneath the roof window. Outside the castle walls is the swimming pool, protected by palm trees and bamboo, where you can relax and eat, and beyond, a sea of vines beneath the great Languedoc sky. The garden, a superb mixture of wild and formal, has some fascinating native species and you can buy estate Faugères wine on the spot. Madame also does B&B, there's a restaurant within the walls and another cottage, so there will be others sharing the pool, which is stunning, and fine grounds. *B&B also.*

sleeps	4-6.
price	€ 515-€ 1,050.
rooms	3: 2 twins/doubles, 2 singles on mezzanine, 1 bathroom.
closed	Never.

booking details

	Marie-France Lanson
tel	+33 (0)4 67 90 28 03
fax	+33 (0)4 67 90 05 03
e-mail	chateau-grezan.lanson@wanadoo.fr

Château de Grézan – La Tour

Laurens, Hérault

La Tour is just inside the castle gate, by the pool, and its kitchen and bathroom fit within a circular tower – amazing. The antique-style oval windows and the 'arrow-slits' let in limited light from the outside world, but with great beams and old stones it's far more atmospheric than gloomy (and blessedly cool in high summer). A floral sofa and a couple of deep easy chairs still leave plenty of space on the tiled ground floor for a smart country table and a great carved armoire containing the crockery. To one side is the double bedroom with its soft-curtained bed and window opening onto the vines. The beamed twin room, behind a curtain on the mezzanine, gets air and light from the entrance hall and faces the old-fashioned bathroom in the tower at the other end of the gallery. The tower kitchen, off the living area below, is nicely equipped. An astonishing, wildly romantic castle setting, with a pool beneath the palms, a restaurant in the ramparts and holistic massage to tempt you. Madame Lanson has organised a fascinating wine trail especially for English speakers, so do take advantage of it. *B&B also.*

sleeps	2-4.
price	€ 400–€ 820.
rooms	2: 1 double, 1 twin on mezzanine, 1 bathroom.
closed	Never.

booking details

	Marie–France Lanson
tel	+33 (0)4 67 90 28 03
fax	+33 (0)4 67 90 05 03
e-mail	chateau-grezan.lanson@wanadoo.fr

map 16　entry 230

Le Château – Le Pêcheur & Le Peintre

Colombières sur Orb, Hérault

There's some serious fishing here: the rivers Orb and Jaur both pass 700m from the château (Sébastien, a fishing guide, is on hand to advise) and there are two lakes at Salvetat. Hence the name of the gîte, Le Pêcheur... fresh with whitewashed walls and sand-blasted beams, comfortable with CD systems and satellite TV. Le Peintre is so-named because of the painting courses that your hosts organise several times a year. (They are proud of their jazz and blues evenings, too.) This whole area is a national park, and although you can confidently expect very little to happen, there is much to do. The local walking is some of the best in France and you can stride out from the château and follow paths into the hills that rise behind. In autumn there are mushrooms to pick, in spring, wild flowers bring a patchwork of colour and the scent of rosemary hangs in the air. There's horse riding, cycling, kayaking, wine-tasting... Those who wish to shun such energetic pursuits can always rustle up a picnic in the summer kitchen by the pool, or find a swimming hole in the river. A great find.

sleeps	Le Pêcheur 5. Le Peintre 5.
price	Le Pêcheur & Le Peintre: each €600–€1,100.
rooms	Le Pêcheur & Le Peintre: each 2 doubles, 1 single, 1 bathroom.
closed	Never.

booking details

Thérèse Salavin & Chris Elliott
tel   +33 (0)4 67 95 63 62
fax   +33 (0)4 67 23 25 58
e-mail   christopher.elliott@club-internet.fr
web   www.gitesdecharme.biz

Le Château – Le Randonneur & Le Musicien
Colombières sur Orb, Hérault

A rural wonderland, lazy Languedoc at its best. Blow with the wind and you will chance upon hilltop villages, mountain streams, ancient vineyards, the Canal du Midi. And where better to stay than in an immaculately turned-out gîte on a château estate that's been in the family for 200 years? You are welcomed in the lovely *salle d'acceuil* – where the olives were once pressed – by Thérèse, who has poured her heart into restoring the old cellars, wine press and outbuildings. Across the courtyard, four stone dwellings side-by-side, each with its own private (though not secluded) terrace. Inside: brand new sofas on parquet or terracotta floors, perfectly equipped kitchens, double basins in most bathrooms, fresh bedrooms with cheerful fabrics and the odd antique. Thick walls keep you cool in summer and warm in winter – along with log fires and central heating. The gîtes are named after the activities of the region; Le Randonneur is the largest; one-storey Le Musicien, the most generously beamed; (below) it's also brilliantly geared up for wheelchairs. Tiny Colombières has an *épicerie* and a summer snack bar in the Gorges.

sleeps	Le Randonneur: 6; Le Musicien: 4–5.
price	Le Randonneur: € 550–€ 1,000.
	Le Musicien: € 700–€ 1,250.
rooms	Le Randonneur: 1 double, 2 twins,
	1 bathroom.
	Le Musicien: 2 twins, 1 bathroom.
	Extra bed for living room available
closed	Never.

booking details

	Thérèse Salavin & Chris Elliott
tel	+33 (0)4 67 95 63 62
fax	+33 (0)4 67 23 25 58
e-mail	christopher.elliott@club-internet.fr
web	www.gitesdecharme.biz

map 16 entry 232

Château de Murviel
Murviel lès Béziers, Hérault

New life and light among the old stones of this 15th-century village château with views that stretch over vineyards to the distant Pyrenees. Life centres around the cool, enclosed courtyard with its oleander, orange and lemon trees, fountain and summer kitchen. The Cousquers' careful renovation included sanding down old floors, creating new windows to the balcony and designing excellent bathrooms. Delicately coloured spaces are flooded with sunshine and in spite of grand dimensions – the dining room and iron-banistered stone stair are magnificent – the feel is not in the least intimidating. There are contemporary touches, comfortable sofas, a small but well-designed kitchen in the tower. The stone-floored pigeonnier has been transformed into a charming and simple bedroom – every pigeon hole clean and white-painted – with a dreamy bathroom. Tennis courts and scope for browsing in the village, lovely river beaches for swimming minutes away, wine-tasting all around and all the shops and bars you need in Murviel. The young caretakers will look after you well. *B&B also.*

sleeps	8-12.
price	€ 2,500–€ 4,000.
rooms	4: 3 doubles, 1 triple, 3 extra singles.
closed	January-February.

booking details

Yves & Florence Cousquer
tel	+33 (0)4 67 32 35 45
fax	+33 (0)4 67 32 35 25
e-mail	chateaudemurviel@free.fr
web	www.murviel.com

Prieuré Saint Martial

Alignan du Vent, Hérault

Two outdoor pools surrounded by vines and century-old oaks and pines, and a third inside under the rafters – bliss. There's a sauna and a fitness bench, ping-pong and bikes; the local village, with tennis and basic shops, is a 10-minute cycle. Old timbers and stones have been restored by perfectionist owners to create the very best in open-plan living. La Chapelle, the old chapel, is understandably vaulted, Le Pigeonnier, the dovecote, is a honeymooners' dream. Again, furnishings are contemporary and natural; smooth plaster walls and old terracotta floors are offset by splashes of colour in cushion, rug or painted cupboard. Big-check sofas harmonise with gleaming country antiques, kitchens are perfectly equipped (dishwashers, coffee machines, state-of-the-art ovens), and there's a beautiful painting on every wall. A studio is available for extra guests on a daily basis. Outside: a courtyard terrace for everyone, with a barbecue, and a garden that feels like a park, full of secret corners. And not a plastic table or chair in sight. *Babysitting available.*

sleeps	3 gîtes & 3 studios for 2.
price	€ 500–€ 1,000.
rooms	1 double, 1 bathroom each.
closed	Never.

booking details

Véronique de Colombe

tel	+33 (0)4 67 24 96 51
fax	+33 (0)4 67 24 99 49
e-mail	stmartial@aol.com
web	www.stmartial.com

map 16   entry 234

Prieuré Saint Martial – Preau & Ramonettage
Alignan du Vent, Hérault

Le Prieuré is near-perfect in winter, with open fires, central heating and three gorgeous pools maintained all year. Each of the 10 renovated buildings embraces a central courtyard fringed with oleander and bamboo, where you have your own piece of terrace – this is a place where you can be as private or as sociable as you like. Ramonettage, with its thick old walls, was part of the old mill, and, like all the gîtes, has a delightfully airy feel. All feels light, white and generous – and there's simply masses of space. Le Preau has a vast fireplace – you could hardly be cosier in winter – and two charming bedrooms with white beds, deep-red cushions and modern art in gilded frames. Véronique greets you with fresh flowers on arrival and will bring you bread and croissants if you ask her the night before; in summer, take breakfast on your terrace. The peace is a balm: just the distant hum of the tractor from the neighbouring *domaine viticole* and the chirping of birds. Raise yourself from your slumber to fish or swim in the Herault National Park – or head off for delicious sandy beaches, a half-hour drive. *Babysitting available.*

sleeps	Preau & Ramonettage each sleep 4.
price	€670–€1,350.
rooms	Preau & Ramonettage: 1 double, 1 twin, 1 bathroom.
closed	Never.

booking details

	Véronique de Colombe
tel	+33 (0)4 67 24 96 51
fax	+33 (0)4 67 24 99 49
e-mail	stmartial@aol.com
web	www.stmartial.com

Prieuré Saint Martial – Galerie & Terrasse

Alignan du Vent, Hérault

Always a charming detail to catch the eye, always a personal touch. There are 10 gîtes on this Languedocian domaine, each one different, each a delight. The de Colombes left Parisien lives for their southern slice of paradise and have been renovating and decorating these 18th-century farm buildings ever since. They have done an immaculate job. Hubert forages for paintings and antiques; Véronique takes care of the guests, and is charming. The gîtes for six have the most secluded terraces: that of Le Galerie catches the sun, north-facing Terrasse's stays deliciously cool. The lush rambling garden and the views belong to everyone. Le Galerie has a big kitchen with a vast fireplace, table and chairs, and its own gallery sprinkled with art. Terrasse has an all-white kitchen and bedrooms with fresh-painted French windows; one has an elegant wrought-iron four-poster hung with voile. Cheerful modern sofas, clean lines and carpeted bedrooms make for comfort without clutter. This is a peace-filled retreat, yet you are hardly in the sticks: Pézenas, with its narrow streets, shops, cafés and market, is a 10-minute drive. *Babysitting available.*

sleeps	Galerie 6. Terrasse 5-6.
price	€850–€1,700.
rooms	Galerie: 1 double, 2 twins, 1 bathroom. Terrasse: 1 double, 1 triple, 1 single, 1 bathroom.
closed	Never.

booking details

Véronique de Colombe

tel	+33 (0)4 67 24 96 51
fax	+33 (0)4 67 24 99 49
e-mail	stmartial@aol.com
web	www.stmartial.com

map 16   entry 236

La Maison Neuve

Bréau et Salagosse, Gard

If you are attracted by imaginative, contemporary decoration and ancient stones, you'll love this old farmstead in the wilds of the Cévennes. Interior designers Elizabeth and Paul bought it as a ruin after upping sticks with their four children and selling their British home. The layout is fascinating: rooms lead off a central hall downstairs and form internal balconies on the upper floors. Stone by stone, Elizabeth and Paul have tamed the building and its metre-thick walls, preserving original materials such as floor and roof tiles with passionate respect. Creaking nail-studded doors, gnarled roof beams and blackened stone fireplaces are a perfect foil for simple, decorative wrought-iron beds hung with voile, and Elizabeth's fine paint pigments, applied with rags to create an exquisitely soft look. You want for nothing: kitchen mod cons, CD and radio, towels for the pool, even cot, highchair and buggy are included. Laze in the fruit orchards, take a dip in your private pool. In season, Elizabeth can sell you home-grown organic sweet onions and raspberries. *House for four with central heating and small pool also available.*

sleeps	12.
price	€ 780–€ 2,200.
rooms	6: 3 doubles, 3 twins, 1 bathroom, 2 shower rooms.
closed	Never.

booking details

	Elizabeth Adam & Paul Wellard
tel	+33 (0)4 67 82 49 09
fax	+33 (0)4 67 82 49 09
e-mail	betjeadam@aol.com
web	www.ecoleisure.net

La Filature, Roquedur le Haut
Sumène, Gard

A stunning and remote mountain area with a fascinating history and a house that marries comfort and style. If you're a nature lover, La Filature, in a hilltop village with a permanent population of 12, has it all. The name, which means 'spinning mill', comes from the period when the silk industry boomed; cocoons were unwound in hot water by the women of this house. Look out for the tell-tale tunnel of white mulberry trees – the silkworms' staple diet – on one of the many stone terraces that make up the large and sloping gardens. The old stone house with its heavenly beams has been well restored and stylishly furnished by its (absent) English owner: stunning ethnic chair covers and wall hangings, a gleaming oak dresser, a pretty antique brass bed, a gilt-framed painting on a whitewashed wall. Pluck cherries, greengages and apples from the fruit trees, wander through the four-acre Spanish chestnut wood down to a stream, swim in the river Vis. In autumn look out for truffles, mushrooms and wild boar. The views here on the edge of the Cévennes National Park are memorable. *Children over five welcome.*

sleeps	6-10.
price	€399-€718 (£250-£450).
rooms	4: 1 double/twin, 1 twin on mezzanine, 2 family rooms for 3, 1 bathroom, 1 shower room.
closed	Never.

booking details

	Carmela Pearson
tel	+44 (0)1438 871364
fax	+44 (0)1438 871921
e-mail	carmpears@aol.com

map 17   entry 238

L'Ancien Pailler

Barjac, Gard

One appreciates the architect-owner's eye for space, light and design. Here is a superb conversion from hayloft, coach house and *magnanerie* (where silkworms were once raised) to perfect holiday home. There's a sitting room with fabulous thick stone walls, vaulted ceiling and massive fireplace – cool in summer, cosy in winter – then through an impressive archway to a kitchen/dining room that's light and airy with blue and white tiles and clever 'island' layout. A smaller living room has a TV and sofabed. Simple, natural materials run throughout – *terre cuite* floors, massive rafters, a spiral wooden stair. And where better to eat than under the shady veranda? This opens to a big, peaceful walled garden with lawn, fountain and pool – a wonderful treat, here, just off the main square of a beautiful, terracotta-roofed village. The pool, shaded by a fig tree, is shared with the owners, who live in a new house at the other end. Breakfast croissants are a step away; woods and fields lie all around. And if walking's too slow, there are bikes for hire in Ambroix. *Obligatory cleaning charge.*

sleeps	12.
price	€ 1,595.
rooms	4: 3 twins, 1 family room for 4, 1 sofabed in living room, 2 bathrooms.
closed	Rarely.

booking details

Joan Sturmer

tel	+33 (0)4 66 24 48 46
fax	+33 (0)4 66 24 43 41
e-mail	sturmer@bsi.fr
web	www.french-holidays-houses.com

L'Auzonnet

Les Mages, Gard

A magical place. One minute you're in an ordinary village street, the next you enter a cool dark stone tunnel and emerge into a sunlit, secret courtyard. Hydrangeas splash the walls with colour and a stone stairway leads up to the little apartment. It's enchanting. The kitchen/living area has delightful painted panelling, pine furniture and brightly coloured plates and bowls. Up on the mezzanine is a Wedgewood blue and white bedroom – light, pretty and open plan – and a shower room decorated with mosaics. The private terrace overlooks the Auzonnet river but you're also welcome to make the most of the wonderful garden. Cross the courtyard, go through another arch and you'll find yourself at the top of green, beautiful terraces dropping down to a small pool and the river. Sit and watch and you may see the hunched form of a heron or glimpse the blue flash of a kingfisher. This is the edge of the Cévennes National Park and is utterly secluded and peaceful. Lucy and Duncan, who have recently bought the house, are completely taken with it all and relish the relaxed pace of life. *Unsuitable for young children or the infirm.*

sleeps	2-4.
price	€ 420-€ 600 (£300-£425).
rooms	1 double, 1 sofabed downstairs, 1 shower room.
closed	Never.

booking details

	Lucy & Duncan Marshall
tel	+33 (0)4 66 25 39 98
e-mail	lucy@auzonnet.com
web	www.auzonnet.com

map 17   entry 240

Mije/Mas de Jandon

St Jean de Maruéjols et Avéjan, Gard

A beautiful collection of farm buildings encircled by meadow and field. The charming owners live on the other side of the courtyard and Monsieur, an architect, has renovated stylishly. You are on the ground floor, where ancient stone walls and low vaulted ceilings encase you. A small terrace, with barbecue, gives huge views; this is rural France at its best, the lane silent all day long, the landscape seemingly unchanged for centuries. Inside, everything pleases the eye – a big wooden bed, a delightful old fireplace, a long, antique table (the end drawer of which is an 18th-century highchair). The cool, compact interior has been decorated with white fabrics and painted furniture to soak up the light, the open stonework is eye-catching, and although the kitchen is tiny it is more than adequate for two. You can walk from the front door, visit markets, explore local (as yet unrestored) villages, canoe down the Gardon. Barjac, Ales, Uzès are all close and worth visiting. A perfect spot for a couple seeking a little style in the sleepy silence of rural France. *Upstairs gîte planned for 2005.*

sleeps	2 + 1 child.
price	€ 300–€ 350.
rooms	1 double, 1 bathroom.
closed	November–April.

booking details

Jean & Michèle de Margerie

tel	+33 (0)4 66 60 20 07
fax	+33 (0)4 66 60 20 15
e-mail	jdm1@worldonline.fr

Les Trémières

Fons sur Lussan, Gard

This little jewel of a house used to be the village bakery and upstairs, nurtured by the warmth from below, silkworms were bred to make the cloth for which this area used to be famous. It's just off the Place de l'Église of a delightful village, yet is blissfully quiet. Relax in the cottage garden overlooking fields behind, play the piano – or book yourself a yoga lesson with Marie or Robert who live next door (and run B&B). The couple had used the house for holidays for over 30 years before moving here from Paris in search of a simpler life. They've decorated gently, giving the gîte a homely rather than a sophisticated feel. Collections of antique irons and coffee grinders decorate the living/dining room/kitchen and there's an original washing plank by the old stone fireplace. Furniture is a mix of antique and modern, and the attic double bedroom has a sloping pine-clad ceiling and fitted carpet. Marie leaves homemade lavender soap, wine, flowers and other surprises for your arrival. Good swimming and canoeing are nearby on the river Cèze. *B&B also.*

sleeps	4.
price	€ 200–€ 460 (heating extra).
rooms	2: 1 double, 1 twin with separate entrance, 1 bathroom.
closed	Never.

booking details

Robert & Marie Freslon

tel	+33 (0)4 66 72 93 16
fax	+33 (0)4 66 72 93 16

map 17   entry 242

Haut Village
Vallabrix, Gard

It's not easy to photograph this stunning village house, sandwiched between the others of enchanting Vallabrix, but you'll have to trust us when we say that we know you won't be disappointed. The old honey-coloured stones embrace a private courtyard and pool, and there are countless delights: delicious views across the terracotta rooftops to distant hills, an interior among the best we've seen, deep peace. It's been beautifully restored by English owners Sheila and John (absent when you are here) and each has left their personal stamp on the décor. You'll find original African paintings and wooden artefacts collected by him on business assignments, and stylish soft furnishings crafted by Sheila. The L-shaped three-storey house has a bedroom and bathroom downstairs; a vast dining, living and kitchen area with creamy yellow walls leads to a geranium-bright terrace on the middle floor; and on the top level are attractive bedrooms with tiled floors and old pine furniture. Visit glorious old Uzès with its Saturday market – a celebration of everything southern, from sausages and snails to red peppers and Provençal prints.

sleeps	8.
price	€ 2,393 (£1,500).
rooms	4 twins/doubles, 3 bathrooms, 2 shower rooms, 1 wc, 1 poolside shower room & separate wc.
closed	October-April.

booking details

	Chris Hazell
tel	+33 (0)4 66 37 45 79
fax	+33 (0)4 66 37 14 78
e-mail	hazell.chris@wanadoo.fr

2 chemin de la Carcarie

Montaren, Gard

Arlette is the perfect hostess, friendly, interested and interesting – and cultured: her tortoises have Greek names. You'll meet them in the garden. Her little patch is the wonder of the house, and Arlette will happily walk you round, passing on the names of the plants and giving you the local gen. Views here take in the pretty village, which has a château. You are part of local life, yet close to Uzès, one of the most beautiful medieval towns in France (and where they filmed *Cyrano de Bergerac*). This 17th-century farmhouse is slightly shabby, but that is also its charm; if you want to sample French village life as the French live it, this is a good place to do so. Upstairs, a big bedroom sleeps four (two single beds are on a mezzanine), but the house is best for a couple and if you were going to share, you'd have to know each other well. Dried garden flowers hang from old beams in the dining room, but you eat on the terrace under a Provençal sun. Arlette lives in part of the house. You are private from her, but she is on hand to chat, advise, inform. No dishwasher, so bring your Marigolds.

sleeps	4.
price	€420–€580.
rooms	2: 1 double, 1 twin in loft, 1 bathroom.
closed	Never.

booking details

	Arlette Caccamo-Laniel
tel	+33 (0)4 66 22 52 14
e-mail	alaniel@freesurf.fr

map 17 entry 244

4 rue du 4 Septembre

Uzès, Gard

Glorious Uzès, the first Duchy of France, an architectural masterpiece – a town of towers, of vaulted stone walkways and narrow streets. The Wars of Religion came to the area, but in the 17th century prosperity returned, and magnificent houses such as this one were constructed in the grand style. Step in off the street and travel back a few hundred years. Here are vaulted limestone rooms, flagstone floors, a flurry of antiques, thick rich fabrics and genuine, old tapestries – one belonged to a duchess who fell on hard times. You have the choice of two apartments, rented separately or together. The one on the ground and first floors is the grandest and has a lovely terrace with olive trees, lavender, tables, chairs and barbecue; the second-floor apartment is reached via a private spiral stair. Both have magnificent old fireplaces and sophisticated bathrooms. The upstairs flat, however, is slightly less grand and has a simpler kitchen; it would be superb for a family. The market is a wonder of the Provençal world and it's on your doorstep – as are concerts, galleries, restaurants and delectable shops. *Secure parking five-minute walk.*

sleeps	Apartment 1: 4. Apartment 2: 4 + 1 child's bed.
price	Apartment 1 £450-£600. Apartment 2 £320-£400.
rooms	Apartment 1: 2 doubles, 1 bath, 1 shower, 1 separate wc. Apartment 2: 1 double, 1 twin with child's bed, 1 bath, 1 shower, 1 separate wc.
closed	Never.

booking details

Susie & David Nelson

tel	+33 (0)4 66 22 88 07
fax	+33 (0)4 66 22 87 35
e-mail	davidnelson445@aol.com

La Terre des Lauriers
Remoulins, Gard

The setting – six hectares of woodland stretching down to the Pont du Gard – is breathtaking. Sit by the river and marvel at this feat of Roman engineering as you watch for birds of prey – the estate was once a bird reserve. Gérard, the owner, is a delight: hospitality runs in his veins and as likely as not he'll invite you to an impromptu dinner or show you his collection of hats. He's even created a gym by the pool where you can work off any extra pounds gained in the area's fine restaurants. This century-old sheepfold has been restored with minimalist elegance – and entirely redecorated after a flood in 2003. There's a wonderful feeling of space, and some dramatic touches in the fine new furniture and the yellow and white *cuisine américaine*. A futuristic staircase leads up to air-conditioned, mezzanine bedrooms; the shower-bathroom is superb. You'll share the grounds, pool and excellent garden furniture with B&B guests and occupants of another cottage – there's simply masses of space – but you have your own terrace for dining that overlooks the private vineyard. *B&B also.*

sleeps	4-6.
price	€ 770–€ 850.
rooms	2: 1 double, 1 twin, 1 sofabed in living room, 1 bathroom, 1 wc.
closed	Never.

booking details

Gérard & Jasmine Cristini

tel	+33 (0)4 66 37 19 45
fax	+33 (0)4 66 37 19 45
e-mail	gerard.cristini@laterredeslauriers.com
web	www.laterredeslauriers.com

map 17   entry 246

Le Rocher Pointu
Aramon, Gard

It's easy to understand why André and Annie – whose ancestors were English – decided to cut their ties with Paris and move to this 150-year-old stone *bergerie*. Although bustling Avignon is just 15 minutes away, it's a haven of peace here, utterly secluded and reached via a windy track through pine scrub. There's a field with a donkey in front, and a vast thumb of rock behind, which gives the place its name. The apartment is the furthest of four which have been recently added to the main house where the owners do B&B; you share the grounds and lovely pool. Smart, small, delightfully compact, with old beams, Provençal tiles and some good antique furniture, your apartment has a tiny well-equipped kitchen off the dining/sitting room, and a split-level bedroom with a single bed on the top level and a double below. Both kitchen and shower room are attractively tiled. Relax on the terrace among the lavender and olive trees and slip into the pool with its distant views of Mont Ventoux, or watch the sunset dip behind the mountains. *Shared laundry. B&B also.*

sleeps	2 + 1 child.
price	€520–€693.
rooms	2: 1 double, 1 single on mezzanine, 1 shower room.
closed	Never.

booking details

Annie & André Malek
tel +33 (0)4 66 57 41 87
fax +33 (0)4 66 57 01 77
e-mail amk@rocherpointu.com
web www.rocherpointu.com

Les Bambous
Pujaut, Gard

The solemn chimes of the neighbouring church clock lull you to sleep. This snug getaway for two has the advantage of being bang in the middle of an unspoilt Provençal village – it's a short walk to the baker's for fresh croissants – and 10 minutes from the centre of historic Avignon. At weekends you might witness a wedding in the Mairie around the corner and women still wash clothes in the village's stone *lavoir*. Michèle and Joël, who lodge B&B guests in their house next door, have done up this tiny space beautifully and enhanced its exposed stone walls, beamed ceilings and terracotta floors. There's an old school desk and Joël's watercolours on the walls. The couple commissioned a well-known ceramicist to make the bright buttercup-coloured tiles in the kitchen area, and the lovely navy and yellow tiles that decorate the shower room. Cycle or walk in the hills around, relax in your private garden under the shade of the horse-chestnut. And when you don't feel like cooking, book in at the main house and join the Rousseaus and their guests. *Flexible changeover day. B&B also.*

sleeps	2.
price	€ 260–€ 335.
rooms	1 double, 1 shower room.
closed	Never.

booking details

Joël & Michèle Rousseau
tel	+33 (0)4 90 26 46 47
fax	+33 (0)4 90 26 46 47
e-mail	rousseau.michele@wanadoo.fr

map 17 entry 248

Photography by Michael Busselle

rhone valley –
alps & provence –
alps – riviera

La Ferme du Nant

La Chapelle d'Abondance, Haute-Savoie

A tale of two chalets. In summer you rent either or both of the two floors and look after yourselves; in winter, the place metamorphises into a catered chalet. Floor-to-ceiling windows span the front of the 200-year-old house pulling in the light; views are pure Heidi. Downstairs: a cosily restored living area with a wonderful central fireplace, country dining table and chairs and big open kitchen. Upstairs, past a collection of ancient wooden sledges: pine floors, halogen spotlights to illuminate white walls, sand-blasted timbers, big blue sofas. Two of the bedrooms are on the mezzanine – perfect for children; there's a long, rustic, south-facing balcony to catch the sun. Furniture is a mix of Savoyard and modern, with the odd giant pop-art portrait to add a sparkle. Bathrooms are white with mosaics. A trap door leads to a DVD cellar, a sloping garden has been reshaped to take a terrace and heated pool (the old cheese store makes great changing rooms), and the village is a six-minute walk downhill. The owners live on the top floor with their labrador; Susie also owns a horse – the riding here is wonderful. *Min. three nights in winter. B&B.*

sleeps	12-16 (or 6-8 + 6-8).
price	€570–€900 per floor (6-8 people).
rooms	Ground floor: 3 twins/doubles, 2 bathrooms, 1 shower room. First floor: 3 twins/doubles, 3 shower rooms. Extra beds available.
closed	Rarely.

booking details

	Susie Ward
tel	+44 (0)1872 553055 or +33 (0)4 50 73 40 87
e-mail	susie@susieward.com
web	www.susieward.com

Le Boën

Praz sur Arly, Haute-Savoie

Sporty families would be in their element – or anyone in love with the mountains. Your Canadian log cabin is young but looks like it's been here for ever; the family live above, you live below. In summer come for walks and wildflower pastures, golf, tennis and mountain bike rides. In winter, snowboard or ski: it's walking distance from the lift that whisks you up to the ski arena of Megève. The Bouchages are a skiing family and know every inch of terrain, so you are in the best hands. Inside, an L-shaped kitchen/lounge, white walls, tiled floors (heated for winter), old-fashioned sofa and armchairs, a table for six. The kitchen is a good size and newly equipped, and there are sliding doors to a terrace with plastic tables and chairs. (And swings and boules in the big garden, yours to share.) The main bedroom, with pastel bedding and extra bunks, has sensational views; the second bedroom is darker due to its high-up windows. There's a perfect alpine auberge in the village and others in nearby Prazaly, while Megève – the 'St Moritz of France' – has every shop and restaurant you could wish for, and a jazz festival in summer.

sleeps	5-6.
price	€ 483–€ 898.
rooms	2: 1 triple, 1 family room for 3, 1 bathroom.
closed	Never.

booking details

Josiane & Christian Bouchage
tel   +33 (0)4 50 21 98 14
e-mail   bouchagechris@aol.com

map 13   entry 250

Le Poulailler

St Félix, Haute-Savoie

This is an old chicken coop, not that the chickens would recognise their former home – only the original beams have survived the top-to-toe renovation. A simple place, light and airy, comfortably homely, spotlessly clean, brimming with all the bits and bobs you could need. The kitchen/sitting room is open plan with a ceiling that reaches to the eaves and a door that gives onto a small terrace where you can sit and gaze on distant mountains. There are neat tiled floors, a woodburner, lots of storage space and roller beds for two children. The bedroom, pale blue with red curtains, is compact but pretty. The Betts, who do B&B, know everything there is to know about the area; Denyse is a food writer, and if you don't want to cook, she'll steer you in the right direction. There's tennis in the grounds or you can head to Annecy, hire bikes and cycle round its glassy lake. The truly energetic can blow a little further east and head up an Alpine valley, or climb Mont Blanc. Geneva is close for a night on the town, but if you want to stay local you can stroll down to restaurants in St Félix. *B&B also.*

sleeps	2 + 2 children.
price	€450.
rooms	1 double, 2 singles for children in living room, 1 shower room, 1 separate wc.
closed	Never.

booking details

	Denyse & Bernard Betts
tel	+33 (0)4 50 60 96 53
fax	+33 (0)4 50 60 94 65
e-mail	les-bruyeres@libertysurf.fr

Les Granges

Bourg St Maurice, Savoie

Come here in summer and walk in flower-filled Alpine pastures to the tinkle of cowbells; come in winter to ski, virtually from the front door: you are surrounded by some of France's finest pistes. In a pretty mountain hamlet on the edge of the Vanoise National Park this chalet is cool in summer, cosy in winter, and always welcoming. Once the barn to the farmhouse next door, its three storeys have been skilfully converted to ensure its balconies – you can chase the sun or shade – are not overlooked; its one-metre-thick exterior walls ensure peace and quiet. The inside has been freshly decorated with high quality pine-panelled walls and floors, light furniture to match, a perfectly equipped kitchen. After an active day out, relax by the open fire in the beautiful modern sitting room with its high-backed pine settle, baby-blue and white striped cushions, clean cream walls, books. If you're here to ski, jump on the funicular just 100m down the lane to Les Arcs; in summer, walk in the mountains (look out for Alpine ibex). For dinner, pop into Bourg Saint Maurice for a taste of Savoyard cuisine. *Changeover day Sunday but flexible in summer.*

sleeps	8.
price	€ 640–€ 1,900; February is high season
rooms	4: 2 doubles, 2 twins, 1 bathroom, 1 shower room, 2 separate wcs.
closed	Never.

booking details

Yda & Rupert Morgan

tel	+44 (0)1576 300 232
fax	+44 (0)1576 300 818
e-mail	morganbellows@yahoo.co.uk
web	www.chaletlesarcs.co.uk

map 13   entry 252

Estourel, Le Mas Bleu

Rosières, Ardèche

You might first spot your neighbours through the mists of the steam bath or the bubbles of the jacuzzi. Le Mas Bleu (The Blue House), with its seven blue-shuttered, wisteria-clad apartments, may not be a typical Sawday choice, but it's certainly special. The 18th-century stone farmstead is superbly decorated and supremely peaceful, despite the presence of up to 30 other residents. It's slightly alternative, with a 'writer's café' in the grounds and some nude pool-bathing; there are Ayurveda and aqua treatments, too, and yoga. Children will love the sandpit, ping-pong, outdoor games and bikes to borrow. It's all run by an energetic and welcoming German couple: Anna, mother of two, and her partner Holger. They have restored the buildings with taste and sensitivity, keeping the exteriors, and the original beams, wherever possible. Estourel is the largest apartment, sleeping seven, with two storeys and a large covered terrace with magnificent views of vineyards and mountains in (almost) every direction. The highlight inside is a vast antique dining table, once used to cut lengths of silk, for which the area is famous.

sleeps	6-8.
price	€ 900-€ 1,100.
rooms	3: 1 double, 2 family rooms for 3, 2 shower rooms.
closed	Never.

booking details

Anna Niedeggen

tel	+33 (0)4 75 39 93 75
fax	+33 (0)4 75 39 92 79
e-mail	info@thebluehouse.net
web	www.thebluehouse.net

The Cottages at Le Bijou
Chomerac, Ardèche

Space, homeliness and the delight of being in the grounds of a château are yours in the little farmhouse and the pigeonnier. Both would make great places for families to stay, with their private terraces and their lawns leading to the lavender-fringed pool. The hub of the farmhouse is the big kitchen, where once the women made apricot jam; here are vast wooden beams, old bread oven and stone fireplace. Furnishings are modern and low-budget, with paint-washed pine, fitted carpets and brightly coloured walls; there's a large games room in the attic. Old farm implements decorate the white walls of the pigeonnier's sitting room; downstairs rooms – once the storerooms and stables – have great vaulted stone ceilings. Again, the décor is modern, with plenty of pine, primrose walls, framed prints and white floaty curtains. French doors lead to a small balustraded terrace. Roam the wooded mountains that surround you, visit the olive market at Nyons or the market in nearby Chomerac, canoe in the Ardèche gorges – and do try the delicious local chestnuts in autumn. *Flexible changeover day.*

sleeps	Petite Ferme: 8-9. Le Pigeonnier: 9.
price	€ 1,435-€ 2,155 (£900-£1,350) each.
rooms	Petite Ferme 4: 2 doubles, 2 twins, sofabed downstairs, 2 bathrooms, 1 shower & wc. Le Pigeonnier 5: 3 doubles, 1 twin, 1 single, 1 bathroom, 2 showers & 2 wcs.
closed	Never.

booking details

	Mark & Jo Cutmore-Scott
tel	+44 (0)777 555 6340 or +33 (0)4 75 65 07 50
e-mail	info@chateaudubijou.com
web	www.chateaudubijou.com

map 17   entry 254

Maison des Gardes, Rue du Centre
Allex, Drôme

Since the 11th century the stone houses of Allex, like those of the other *villages perchés* in this region, have huddled together around a castle high on a hill to keep enemies at bay. This remarkable house, built in the 16th century, was where the castle guards lived. The front walls were the defensive walls of the village and there was even a secret passage to the château. Built on three levels, linked by a staircase in the turret, it's deceptively large. Parisian owner Sophie's passion is collecting pottery cicadas, and you'll find them in all shapes and sizes throughout the house. Beautiful antique furniture, plush white sofas and a large stone fireplace give the vast and light sitting room an aristocratic air, while décor in the master bedroom is more experimental, with yellow rag-rolled walls and matching bedspread, and stencilling on the walls. French windows lead to a large roof terrace. This is the perfect house from which to experience the life of a lively, authentic French village in a beautiful corner of France. Artists and writers will love it.

sleeps	8.
price	€ 650–€ 780.
rooms	4: 2 doubles, 2 twins, 2 bathrooms, 3 separate wcs.
closed	December–Easter.

booking details

	Sophie Le Norcy
tel	+33 (0)1 45 78 99 61
fax	+33 (0)1 42 24 40 68
e-mail	le-norcy.s@wanadoo.fr

Salivet

Truinas, Drôme

Few places have it all, but this must be one. Breathtaking mountain views, a lovely owner and a fascinating building combine to make this a very special place. The honey-stone house stands where the oxen sheds and haylofts used to be; the ruins of the original farmhouse are still visible in the garden. Jane, an English artist who specialises in silk screen printing, lives next door; she and her architect partner have restored and furnished the place simply but beautifully with old beams, terracotta tile floors, whitewashed walls, stone fireplaces and antique furniture. On summer nights you can sleep on the roof terrace; during the day, sit on the terrace under the wisteria, snooze on the lawn under the weeping willow or cool off in the pool, shared with a second rented house next door. Jane runs courses on silk decoration to include a 'silk tour', which can be booked in advance; shiatsu and Qi Gong can be arranged for groups of 10. She sells honey, homemade jams and truffles in season, cooks fabulous meals on request and will supply walking itineraries, maps and flower guides to this beautiful area.

sleeps	6 + 1 cot.
price	€ 638–€ 1,244 (£400–£780).
rooms	4: 1 double, 1 double with cot, 2 singles, 1 bathroom, 1 shower room, 2 separate wcs.
closed	Mid-October–Easter.

booking details

Jane Worthington

tel	+33 (0)4 75 53 49 13
fax	+33 (0)4 75 53 37 31
e-mail	worthingtonjc@aol.com

map 17   entry 256

L'Amiradou
Mérindol les Oliviers, Drôme

The name comes from mirador or watchtower and you won't be disappointed by the view: a Cézanne from every window. The white granite flank of Mont Ventoux, herb-scented hills, vineyards and olive groves... the builder who helped Susan and Andrew renovate this farm labourer's cottage thought they'd made a mistake: the gîte, one level up from the house, has the best views. Many levels give the house and garden great character but make l'Amiradou unsuitable for the very young. Your hosts, who used to live in Paris, will be delighted to advise you on local trips, but otherwise leave you to yourselves. The pool is shared with them, but the south-facing pool house and barbecue, scented with lavender and honeysuckle, is all yours. You also have your own loggia and terrace. The house is immaculate, light and attractively furnished with good sofas and some antique pine; a vast baker's table separates the kitchen from the sitting/dining room. There's a log fire and central heating to keep you cosy in the colder months, and a perfectly equipped kitchen. Restaurants abound in the nearby villages.

sleeps	4.
price	€ 500–€ 1,000 (£360–£715).
rooms	2: 1 double, 1 twin, 2 bathrooms.
closed	Never.

booking details

	Susan Smith
tel	+33 (0)4 75 28 78 69
fax	+33 (0)4 75 28 78 69
e-mail	smitha@club-internet.fr
web	www.lamiradou.com

St Jean et Bel Air

St Croix à Lauze, Alpes-de-Haute-Provence

Luxury in the woods with huge views over the Luberon. This brilliantly restored 17th-century farmhouse is a real find for those seeking wilderness; strike out from the door on intrepid walks. Or simply gaze over fields and oaks to distant hills from the terrace by the gorgeous pool – floodlit for midnight swims. Jean-Pierre fell in love with a pile of old stones, put them back together, *et voilà*, paradise! You have three doubles in the main house, another bed on the mezzanine of the studio that adjoins. The feel is contemporary: the whitest walls, the palest tiled floors, a warm yellow throw on a sofa, a red leather armchair, paperbacks on white shelves, the odd rug. There's a modern open fireplace in the sitting room, a charming little dining room and a small kitchen with all you need. One bathroom has lovely yellow handmade tiles and a view from the tub. Bedrooms are strikingly simple and the master suite opens onto a terrace, so pull the bed out and sleep under the stars; people do. Restaurants are 10km away in Cereste, the shops are nearer. *At the end of long dirt track; arrange to meet owners on turn-off to Viens.*

sleeps	6-10.
price	€ 495-€ 1,905.
rooms	3 + 1: 3 doubles, 2 bathrooms; 1 studio for 4 with separate entrance, 1 double on mezzanine, 2 singles on ground floor, 1 shower room.
closed	Never.

booking details

Isabelle & Jean-Patrick Chesne
tel   +33 (0)4 92 79 08 42
fax   +33 (0)4 92 79 08 42
e-mail ijp.chesne@wanadoo.fr
web   www.gite-luberon.fluo.net

map 17   entry 258

Les Granges de Saint Pierre
Simiane la Rotonde, Alpes-de-Haute-Provence

Everything in this remarkably converted 14th-century grange – once attached to the Prieuré de Saint Pierre – is stylish and caring. Lavender-infused air, simple iron furniture, modern art, a fine use of colour, an inner terrace where lemons grow – it has a sense of peace and space. Arched doorways with new doors (and ancient locks) lead to big, light bedrooms with tiled floors and colourwashed walls. Bathrooms are sophisticated and stylish, in rust-red and white. You have a sunny, lofty, white-beamed living/dining room with cream drapes, canvas directors' chairs and big sofas in front of an even bigger fire. The kitchen is in the corner: terracotta-painted units, old country furniture, stripped floor. Rooms gather round a central terrace filled with geraniums, there's fruit in the orchards and chickens in the pen. Josiane, kind and intelligent, lives with her husband in the château next door where the magical pool half-hides in a walled garden. Simiane la Rotonde, once the regional capital of lavender, is a gem: a perched village with a 16th-century market place, surrounded by vast purple fields. A heavenly place. *B&B also.*

sleeps	6.
price	€630–€950.
rooms	3: 2 doubles, 1 twin, 3 shower rooms.
closed	Never.

booking details

	Josiane Tamburini
tel	+33 (0)4 92 75 93 81
fax	+33 (0)4 92 75 93 81
web	www.luberon-news.com/granges-st-pierre.html

Domaine la Condamine

Crillon le Brave, Vaucluse

Seven generations of wine-growers have breathed their first in this pretty 17th-century domaine, and Madame, an energetic businesswoman, organises tastings of her own delicious Coteaux du Ventoux. The apartment, at the far end of the farmstead, has its own entrance and a courtyard where you can dine on sultry evenings. Colours in the open-plan, colourwashed living area are soft and southern: terracottas, mellow golds, creams. The three bedrooms upstairs have stylish painted furniture, hand-painted decorative wall borders and magnificent views across the vineyards to Mont Ventoux. You'll have company around the pool, decked with loungers, fringed with grass and oleander, as Madame runs a large B&B; summer guests dine on the terrace of the main house. Visit the lively Monday market in nearby Bédoin or the larger one in Vaison la Romaine on Tuesdays, stock up on wine at the local *caves*, then come back and be creative in your well-equipped kitchen. There's lacework at Montmirail, Roman splendour at Orange… and doves, parrots and a black labrador on the estate. A lovely, peaceful spot for a family stay. *B&B also.*

sleeps	6.
price	€ 400–€ 600.
rooms	3: 1 double, 2 twins, 1 bathroom, 1 separate wc.
closed	Never.

booking details

	Marie-José Eydoux
tel	+33 (0)4 90 62 47 28
fax	+33 (0)4 90 62 47 28
e-mail	domlacondamine@hotmail.com
web	www.lacondamine.info

map 17   entry 260

La Lauzière

Puyméras, Vaucluse

A delightful 18th-century Provençal farmhouse with views on one side over Côte de Rhône vineyards. Wander around the garden and you will discover an orchard of cherry trees, the fruit of which you can munch in season. For 300 days a year sunshine beats down on this staggeringly beautiful land: the setting is spectacular. At the farmhouse: a pretty covered terrace and a gorgeous pool. It is a long, low stone-walled building with sea-green shutters on the walls and wrought-iron tables and chairs on the terrace. The interior is done in a contemporary Provençal style: white walls, colourful fabrics, terracotta floors and iron beds. Bedrooms have views of either pool or courtyard, while downstairs there is a choice of sitting rooms. Matisse prints hang on the walls, there's an open fireplace in the yellow-walled kitchen and central heating for winter. The typically Provençal village of Puyméras is a five-minute stroll – it has tennis courts, two bistro-cafés and a restaurant. Close by is medieval Vaison-La-Romaine with its Roman ruins and popular market. As for the walking – take your pick from mountain, valley and gorge.

sleeps	7.
price	€ 1,225–€ 2,450.
rooms	4: 2 doubles, 1 twin, 1 single, 2 bathrooms, 1 separate wc.
closed	Never.

booking details

Ralf Maurer

tel	+44 (0)20 7900 2359
fax	+44 (0)20 7900 2359
e-mail	mail@provenceliving.com
web	www.provenceliving.com

Les Convenents

Uchaux, Vaucluse

Pure Provence: the views from your green-shuttered, traditional stone *mas* are of vines, sunflowers and distant pines. Sarah and Ian, who do B&B in the adjoining house, stock the kitchen of the small gîte with basics – fruit, wine, olive oil – and often invite guests next door for a drink. They are also happy for you to share their pretty pool, but if you prefer the privacy of your own sitting out area (with barbecue) that's fine too. Inside, the feel is contemporary, light and bright; there's a dear little living/kitchen area with pale tiled floors, sandy walls, cheery blue and yellow curtains with matching cushions and throws, attractive cane armchairs, pale beams. The kitchen in the corner is cleverly designed to include oven, fridge and freezer. (If you need bigger pots and pans, these can be borrowed.) Up to two small but adequate bedrooms, whose yellow and blue bedspreads, cushions and curtains echo the furnishings downstairs. There's ping-pong, boules and bikes to borrow, and Vaison les Romaines, with restaurants and Tuesday market, is nearby. *Cot and high chair provided. B&B also.*

sleeps	4 + cot.
price	€ 485–€ 600.
rooms	2: 1 double, 1 twin, 1 shower room.
closed	Never.

booking details

	Sarah Banner
tel	+33 (0)4 90 40 65 64
fax	+33 (0)4 90 40 65 64
e-mail	sarahbanner@wanadoo.fr
web	www.lesconvenents.com

map 17   entry 262

Les Cerisiers – Les Tilleuls & Les Oliviers

Carpentras, Vaucluse

Almost too good to be true! An old stone farmhouse with sweeping views, Provencal décor, *tomette* floors, fine linen, helpful hosts and a gorgeous pool. You have it all, in a hamlet between Carpentras and Beaumes de Venise, surrounded by vineyards and orchards. Two-storey Les Tilleuls has its private piece of garden on the edge of the bigger, newly-landscaped one, with a barbecue, and lime trees for shade. Downstairs is open plan, contemporary and cool, with pale sofa and ironwork chairs, a corner kitchen, an open fire. Bedrooms are up: good big beds, white walls, beams. Bath and shower rooms sparkle. Les Oliviers, up an outside stair, is a dear little apartment with a roomy, sunny, open-plan feel. Relax on its balcony – on chic metal chairs – and sip Côtes de Ventoux as the sun goes down. Tory and Carol are full of enthusiasm for their new venture and have not stinted on a thing, be it air conditioning, central heating, crockery or towels for the pool. Go to Carpentras for its Friday market, Avignon for art and architecture. A sunny, civilised place to stay. *Dishwasher in Les Tilleuls. Shared laundry. B&B also.*

sleeps	Les Tilleuls: 6-7. Les Oliviers: 2-4.
price	Les Tilleuls €700–€1,700. Les Oliviers €400–€835 (+20% supplement p.p. for sofabed).
rooms	Les Tilleuls: 3 doubles, 1 with extra bed, 1 bathroom, 1 shower room. Les Oliviers: 1 double/twin, 1 sofabed in living room, 1 shower room.
closed	Never.

booking details

	Carol Chaplin & Tory Johnston
tel	+33 (0)4 90 67 76 10
fax	+33 (0)4 90 67 76 11
e-mail	info@les-cerisiers.com
web	www.les-cerisiers.com

Le Mas de Miejour

Le Thor, Vaucluse

You get the oldest part of this pretty Provençal farmhouse, with your own entrance and garden with barbecue. Frédéric and Emmanuelle came here to bring up their children (Frédéric turns potter in the winter months) and they share their home with both gîte and B&B guests. The atmosphere is utterly restful – white walls, wooden beams and ceilings, old hexagonal tiles on the floor. The kitchen is dominated by an ancient bread oven, perhaps originally pillaged from the 12th-century château nearby; well-equipped yet nicely old-fashioned and homely with its low ceiling, little windows and ancient tiles. Up steepish steps to the salon with comfy sofa and leather armchairs, and bedrooms... the double bed is huge and the white-tiled bathroom is small but fine. Views are over the garden or fields; Mont Ventoux lies beyond. The land here is flat with a high water table so the garden, sheltered by trees and the surrounding tall maize and sunflowers in summer, is always fresh and green. There's a lovely, fenced pool you are most welcome to share. *B&B also.*

sleeps	5.
price	High season: €850. Low season: €420–€570.
rooms	3: 1 double, 1 twin, 1 single, 1 bathroom.
closed	November–February.

booking details

	Frédéric & Emmanuelle Westercamp
tel	+33 (0)4 90 02 13 79
fax	+33 (0)4 90 02 13 03
e-mail	mas.miejour@free.fr
web	mas.miejour.free.fr

map 17   entry 264

Place Haute

Cabrières d'Avignon, Vaucluse

A timeless, pastoral landscape, with hill, village and fields bathing under a searing Provençal sun. The silence and the heat seem to coat the ear, the scent of sunburnt grass floats in the breeze. Your retreat in the village is a small, snug, stone cottage that is entered through an old archway in the village *lavoir* (the square where villagers used to wash their clothes). A flight of stone steps is flanked with potted plants, the terrace is shaded for cool summer suppers. Inside, encased by cooling walls, you find a picture-book interior: small sofas dressed in white, a pretty pine dresser, a round dining table, beamed ceilings and windows that give onto the village. The cosy double has steep stairs up from the (adequate but charming) kitchen to a mezzanine with a sofabed and a small balcony with views across ancient rooftops; the bathroom is curtained off. The twin downstairs has a couple of pillars, a vaulted ceiling and patchwork quilts on the beds. The village square is a stone's throw from the house, as is the Museum of Lavender; the nearest restaurant is a walk away. Spellbinding. *Children over 12 welcome.*

sleeps	4-6.
price	£250-£440.
rooms	2: 1 double with sofabed on mezzanine, 1 twin, 1 bathroom, 1 shower room.
closed	August.

booking details

	Anna Rose
tel	+44 (0)117 973 1857
fax	+44 (0)117 973 1857
e-mail	rose@fire-rose.co.uk

Mas des Genets

Saignon, Vaucluse

Set among vineyards and lavender fields just below the pretty village of Saignon, perched like a fort on turrets of white rock, this one-up-one-down is a peaceful retreat in the popular Luberon. Reached by a private drive, the pale-stoned extension (once a tractor shed) is part of an old farmhouse that has been skilfully converted by American-born Stephen and his English wife Meg. They live in the main part of the house and there's a second apartment for two next door. Each property has its own private terrace and lawn from which to take your fill of birdsong and mountain views. Inside, original beams, new terracotta tiles, modern pine tables and chairs, books, puzzles and games… even underfloor heating for winter stays. There's a functional kitchenette in one corner (with dishwasher and washing machine) and upstairs, a sunny bedroom with a big brass bed, sloping beamed ceilings and blue and green floral blinds. Take the footpath to Saignon, or walk in the Luberon hills. And don't miss the superb Saturday market in Apt.

sleeps	2.
price	€ 305–€ 535.
rooms	1 double, 1 shower room.
closed	Never.

booking details

	Meg & Stephen Parker
tel	+33 (0)4 90 04 65 33
fax	+33 (0)4 90 74 56 85
e-mail	masdegenet@aol.com

map 17   entry 266

Villa Agapanthe

St Saturnin les Apt, Vaucluse

Henrietta is a bit of a star, goes the extra mile and welcomes you with wine and flowers. Her 1975 one-storey villa is not the most striking of houses, but its spoiling interior and its beautiful garden compensate for any exterior shortfall. Inside, light, airy rooms hold the odd hidden treasure. There's a pink Art-Deco-style bathroom, a wrought-iron day bed in the sun room and a couple of cavernous white sofas in the sitting room. Big shuttered windows flood each room with light, and bedrooms are screened to keep mosquitoes at bay. Beds are dressed in fine linen, blue and green voile curtains billow in the breeze and sofas and armchairs are coloured by pink scatter cushions. Delicate floral friezes run along pale cream walls and bedroom views take in the garden, the village and its famous windmill, a ruined castle and the distant Roussillon hills. Outside, the garden bursts with life. There are pretty flowerbeds, Provençal herbs, lavender bushes, an olive grove and fig and cherry tress. A swimming pool will be ready by the summer of 2004, and you are bang in the centre of the village. Brilliant. *Children over 8 welcome.*

sleeps	6.
price	€ 850–€ 1,200.
rooms	3: 2 doubles, 1 twin, 1 bathroom, 1 shower room, 1 separate wc.
closed	Never.

booking details

	Henrietta Taylor
tel	+33 (0)4 90 75 49 64
fax	+33 (0)4 90 75 49 37
e-mail	henrietta@henriettataylor.com
web	www.henriettataylor.com

Rose Cottage

Saignon, Vaucluse

Luberon without the crowds. The centre of Saignon, perched precariously along a vast saddle of rock, is a minute's walk, but here you look onto a sleepy little square where cats roam and geraniums bloom. Australian owner Henrietta – she lives in the next village but will pop by should you need her – has created a refreshing mood of light and space through a blend of white walls and honey-coloured stone. Even the kitchen work surfaces are made of the soothing stone; no expense has been spared in bringing original features back to life. Old doors and ancient stone stairs have been superbly restored; terracotta floors are washed with lavender-scented water; a vaulted *cave* serves as a stunning utility room. Furniture is minimalist, much of it ironwork, and Henrietta has added charming touches like twigwork animals and handcrafted curtain rods. Bedrooms, with deliciously luxurious linen, are light and white; in the showers Salernes tiles, provide the odd splash of colour. The flagged kitchen is a happy place to chop and stir – and if you're not in the mood to cook you can dine in the restaurant next door.

sleeps	4.
price	€615–€920.
rooms	2: 1 double, 1 twin, 2 shower rooms.
closed	Never.

booking details

Henrietta Taylor
tel	+33 (0)4 90 75 49 64
fax	+33 (0)4 90 75 49 37
e-mail	henrietta@henriettataylor.com
web	www.henriettataylor.com

map 17   entry 268

Place de la Fontaine

Saignon, Vaucluse

Listen to the bubbling village fountain and the soothing murmur of the outdoor diners from the comfort of your white-linened bed. Your home is an ancient house in the central square of a lovely, lesser known Luberon village – a heavenly place to stay. Henrietta, its Australian owner, has decorated the immaculately limewashed three storeys with artistic flair, while respecting its old character. Soothing and sophisticated ochres and creams in the kitchen and living room are enhanced by delightful *objets* that Henrietta has picked up from craftsmen and *brocantes*. Kitchen floors and work surfaces have old wooden borders; beautiful crockery and modern gadgets are stored on free-standing ironwork shelves. Up a narrow, spiral stair to light, minimalist bedrooms with original wooden doors and beams, basketwork tables and simple concrete floors. The airy double on the third floor has a tiny flower-decked terrace that gives onto the beauty of Provence. In summer, relax with a glass of local wine; in winter, snuggle up on a sofa before an open fire.

sleeps	6-10.
price	€ 715–€ 1,000.
rooms	3: 2 doubles, 1 twin, 2 double sofabeds in living room, 1 bathroom, 1 shower room.
closed	Never.

booking details

Henrietta Taylor
tel	+33 (0)4 90 75 49 64
fax	+33 (0)4 90 75 49 37
e-mail	henrietta@henriettataylor.com
web	www.henriettataylor.com

Jas des Eydins
Bonnieux, Vaucluse

In open countryside with views to the Luberon hills, reached by a private lane, a blissful retreat. Recline on teak loungers by the pool, enveloped by the scent of roses and lavender. The 18th-century stone buildings, once a sheepfold and part of a Provençal farm, were restored by their architect owner and his elegant art historian wife. The style is luxurious and contemporary, a stunning mix of country antiques and modern pieces. There's a large, beautifully equipped kitchen and open-plan sitting room, and three charming and cosy bedrooms (one in an adjoining building) shaded by a trellis of old-fashioned roses. On hot summer days relax in the big garden and revel in views of Mont Ventoux; in the evenings eat on the large terrace to the song of the cicadas. There's a wonderful outdoor kitchen with chimney and built-in barbecue. Shirley and Jan live next door and are on hand if you need them, but also leave you to relax in peace. Escape the summer beaches to explore the enchanting hillside villages inland. *Twin bedroom in main house, with own entrance, at extra cost. B&B also.*

sleeps	6.
price	€ 1,250–€ 1,900.
rooms	3: 2 twins/doubles, 1 twin, 2 bathrooms, 1 shower room.
closed	November–mid-March.

booking details

	Shirley & Jan Kozlowski
tel	+33 (0)4 90 75 84 99
fax	+33 (0)4 90 75 96 71
e-mail	jasdeseydins@wanadoo.fr
web	www.jasdeseydins.com

map 17 entry 270

Mimosa & Magnolia

Éguilles, Bouches-du-Rhône

Wonderful to be within easy reach of Aix, yet in such a peaceful spot. From the pretty, one-acre hillside garden, full of big trees and flowering shrubs, there are views to the hilltop village of Éguilles. Down a few steps and hidden among the lush greenery, a big pool, surrounded by terrace and lawn. The garden is shared with the friendly, relaxed owners and their children who attend the international school in Aix, but there's plenty of room for all. The family live quite separately on the upper floor of the ivy-swathed house; it's about 50 years old and has a round tower where a double room is rented on a B&B basis. The apartments are on the ground floor, simply furnished, spotlessly clean. The bedrooms are cool and dark, the bathrooms functional and there's central heating for winter. Magnolia has a big sitting/dining room with a tiny galley kitchen; Mimosa's living room/kitchen opens onto a shady terrace with a barbecue. Though both kitchens have all that's necessary, they're not designed for cooking serious meals. Much better to take advantage of the restaurants in the thriving village — or in fashionable, irresistible Aix. *B&B also.*

sleeps	Mimosa: 4-6. Magnolia: 4-8
price	Mimosa: € 450-€ 850. Magnolia: € 600-€ 1,200.
rooms	Mimosa: 2 twins/doubles, 1 sofabed, 1 bathroom, 1 separate wc. Magnolia: 1 double/twin, 1 family room for 4, 1 sofabed, 1 bathroom.
closed	Never.

booking details

Chris & Aban McAndrew

tel	+33 (0)4 42 92 49 57
fax	+33 (0)4 42 92 49 57
e-mail	abanmcandrew@hotmail.com
web	www.chemindesbaoux.com

Appartment Quatre
Aix en Provence, Bouches-du-Rhône

A stylish bolthole in the centre of one of France's loveliest towns – all fountains and leafy squares. The building dates from 1900 and was designed for the Carmelite nuns, whose chapel stands next door. Step off a narrow pedestrianised shopping street to climb a wide and gracious stairwell up to a smart apartment. An immaculate façade, a cool Provençal interior: linen curtains billow in the breeze, the scent of lavender fills the air. There are tiled floors, shuttered windows and air conditioning, wicker furniture in the bedroom, a wild pink ceiling in the bathroom and a jacuzzi bath. The kitchen comes in green and blue and is well-equipped, so head to the market in the morning, then cook up a feast at night. In the sitting room you'll find a huge white L-shaped leather sofa and a round antique dining table. The feel is very much that of a home (albeit a rather smart one) with the latest glossy magazines lying about. Gabriele, a designer, is delightful. She will advise on just about anything, from where to get the best croissants to what's on at the opera. Perfect peace – even by day. *German spoken.*

sleeps	2.
price	€750–€950.
rooms	1 double, 1 bathroom.
closed	Never.

booking details

	Gabriele Skelton
tel	+33 (0)4 90 75 98 98
fax	+33 (0)4 90 75 98 99
e-mail	gabriele.skelton@wanadoo.fr

map 17 entry 272

La Petite Maison

Aix en Provence, Bouches-du-Rhône

A very pretty house in a secret garden that, given the surrounds, comes as quite a surprise. It has been in Christine's family for years; her grandmother lives next door and her sister – who charmingly welcomes guests – tends the garden that's walled, flowered and lush with colour. The whole house appears to open onto it and there is a lovely swimming pool in one corner. The inside is a stylish, contemporary take on a traditional villa, with terracotta tiles, white walls, a flowing sense of space. There are big comfy sofas, a long dining table with Provençal chairs, Moroccan lamps, books, toys. The attractive kitchen has sliding glass doors that lead to a huge veranda. Sunny bedrooms are simply white, with shuttered windows to keep you cool. There are wooden sun loungers for peace and quiet, and bikes on which to head off and fetch the bread. This is a fabulous place to stay, and not just in summer: you have logs and central heating to keep you snug in winter. You are in a new residential area yet five minutes from the centre of wonderful old Aix. Venture beyond the city walls to dreamy countryside and all things Van Gogh. *B&B also.*

sleeps	8.
price	£500–£1,100.
rooms	4: 3 doubles, 1 twin, 2 bathrooms.
closed	Christmas & Easter.

booking details

Christine & Martin Balandier-Brown

tel +44 (0)117 9621121 after 6pm or
+33 (0)4 42 26 62 51

e-mail christine.balandier-brown@bristol.ac.uk
until July 2004

Les Bréguières

Rousset, Bouches-du-Rhône

This is a 'find' in the proper sense of the word, a place beyond the designer's grasp: authentic, simple, refreshing. Madame, who lives in the house above, is warmly human yet assures your privacy, Monsieur spends his free time in the olive grove and you may, occasionally, bump into the grandchildren by the pool. Inside the old *cabanon* are simple wood and warm colours. All is homely and delightful – an L-shaped banquette, books, lovely old pine; there are terracotta tiles on the floor, pictures on the walls and French windows to fling open. The kitchen/living area is filled with morning sun; above is the bedroom on the mezzanine (with beams to be ducked). A giant cherry tree bows with fruit in a little piece of garden, vines and hills surround you, there are mountains in the distance, and the backdrop is dominated by Cengle de Sainte Victoire, a vast wall of white rock that rises mightily into the sky. The pool, all mosaic and terracotta, is reason enough to come to here. Ping-pong and boules, riding and golf are close by, and there's Aix for all things Provençal. Come and forget the world.

sleeps	2-4.
price	€ 487–€ 760.
rooms	2: 1 double on mezzanine, 1 twin, 1 bathroom.
closed	Never.

booking details

	Jean-Pierre & Sophie Babey
tel	+33 (0)4 42 29 01 16
fax	+33 (0)4 42 29 01 16
e-mail	jp.babey@club-internet.fr

map 17 entry 274

Le Bastidon

Fuveau, Bouches-du-Rhône

This is a dinky little house for two that stands in Monique and Michel's peaceful garden in the shade of the ancient oaks. It is quite delightful, absolutely tiny and deeply restful. The owners are lovely and there when you need them; Michel is a graphic designer and the interiors reflect his eye for fresh colour and clean lines. Make no mistake, the gîte is tiny! There's a bedroom with mirror, walls and rafters in cool white, a large bed with blue and white duvet and curtains to match, garden views and Michel's watercolours on the wall. The shower room sparkles with sea-green tiles and towels; the kitchenette is stylish, with small table and chairs. There's no sitting room, but outdoor furniture for warm days. There's also a superb pool with teak loungers and views off to Mont St Victoire, and *pétanque* and table tennis. Beyond, but hidden from view, is a golf course – you are a put's throw from the sixth hole, and a round or two can be easily arranged. Atmospheric Aix is close by, Cassis and its *calanques* not much further, and you can dine out every day if you choose at the auberge down the road.

sleeps	1-2.
price	€220 per week.
rooms	1 double, 1 shower room, 1 separate wc.
closed	July & August.

booking details

Monique & Michel Cassagne

tel	+33 (0)4 42 53 34 38
fax	+33 (0)4 42 53 39 93
e-mail	m-cassagne@wanadoo.fr
web	www.provencelocationaix.com

Séjours Découverte & Nature – Gîtes
Barjols, Var

Come for unfussy comfort and splendid seclusion. These two gîtes sit near yet out of sight of each other on the edge of a field – silent but for the hum of the cicadas. The one time animal shelters contain a twin bedroom each and a sitting/cooking/dining area with sofabed, round table and seating for four. Furniture is modern pine, walls are (mostly) exposed stone, curtains are checked; kitchens are well-equipped, with plenty of pans and crockery, washing machines, even dishwashers. Outside each is a small, private terrace with table and benches under a canopy of vines; behind the main house, an amazing circular pool. English-born Stephanie came to France in pursuit of a dream; she and Michel live at the big house, run B&B, make their own wine and have set up an exhibition of Roman artifacts in their house; vestiges of the property's former occupants are for ever being dug up. Both house and gîtes look over gently undulating farmland – hard to imagine a more unspoiled setting. Visit Cotignac for its markets, Barjols for its restaurants, the Abbaye du Thoronet for its music, Sillans for its *cascades*. *B&B also.*

sleeps	Gîte A: 2-4. Gîte B: 2-3.
price	Gîte A € 450. Gîte B € 400.
rooms	Gîte A: 1 double/twin, 1 sofabed in sitting room, 1 shower room. Gîte B: 1 double/twin, 1 single in sitting room, 1 shower room.
closed	15 October-15 April.

booking details

Michel & Stephanie Passebois
tel +33 (0)4 94 77 18 01
e-mail s.d.n.saint-jaume@wanadoo.fr
web perso.wanadoo.fr/sdn.saint-jaume/

map 18 entry 275

Pimaquet – La Vieille Ferme & La Magnanerie
Entrecasteaux, Var

The two old stone houses hunker down on the hill, separated by a shed and Mimi's office. In La Vieille Ferme the donkey once lived where the sitting room is – now filled to the beams with books, paintings and relics of Mimi's past. Outside, a vine heavy with grapes shades the terrace. Mimi – once a university lecturer – is a painter and a delightful, discreet hostess. Big bedrooms have a homely mix of old furniture and valley views; bathrooms are bright with handmade tiles, kitchens charmingly equipped. La Magnanerie (the old silk farm) climbs the hillside in four half-storeys; each level has a terrace under the shade of a majestic oak; in winter, a wood fire adds a cosy glow. Behind: a remarkable feature, a Roman irrigation canal – fast-flowing and pristine; Mimi pays £12 a year for the privilege of using it. This is a dreamy place to laze on languid summer days, in a shared garden shady with mulberry trees, lush with oleander. Then down to the cooling trout stream across the field, to swim, paddle or sit and read. Find shops, markets and restaurants in the twisting streets of Entrecasteaux.

sleeps	Vieille Ferme: 6-8 + cot. La Magnanerie: 6 + cot.
price	Vieille Ferme £600. La Magnanerie £100-£500.
rooms	Vieille Ferme: 1 twin, 2 family rooms for 3, 1 bath, 1 shower . La Magnanerie: 2 doubles, 1 twin, 1 bathroom, 1 shower room. Cots available.
closed	Vieille Ferme: mid-Sept–mid June. La Magnanerie: never.

booking details

Mrs June Watkins
tel +44 (0)20 8891 2656
e-mail junewatkins@lineone.net

Bastide des Hautes Moures

Le Thoronet, Var

A rough track deep in the Var forest leads to this exquisite 1780 *bergerie*. With the main house it stands in 15 acres of gnarled scrub oak, surrounded by cypresses and lavender; birds sing, butterflies shimmer. The cottage has been brought back to life in spectacular fashion, a monument to Catherine's flamboyant taste and passion for colour; she is also an assiduous seeker of antique and brocante finds. You have a vast, lofty, open-plan kitchen/dining/sitting room, decorated in anise green, and an amazingly pretty bedroom with a floral canopied bed and a yellow Provençal quilt. The bathroom is charming, the kitchen superb. Antoine was a restaurateur, so if you don't want to cook, he will; dine on stuffed vegetables, sea bass, fois gras. And you can breakfast with the B&B guests if you prefer (a small extra charge). Outside, your own small stone terrace with delightful wrought-iron tables and chairs. It's an easy drive to Aix from here and there's masses to do – once you've raised yourself from the teak loungers that flank the shared pool. Book early: word is spreading. *Children welcome during special children's week; call for dates. B&B also.*

sleeps	2-4.
price	€ 380–€ 910.
rooms	1 double, 1 sofabed, 1 bathroom.
closed	Never.

booking details

	Catherine Jobert & Antoine Debray
tel	+33 (0)4 94 60 13 36
fax	+33 (0)4 94 60 13 36
e-mail	jobertcatherine@aol.com
web	www.bastide-des-moures.com

map 18 entry 277

Les Pêchers

Ile de Porquerolles, Var

Wonderful Porquerolles! An off-season island retreat for a select few – and for many more in high summer. The pretty village and harbour are the nerve centre of island life; you can just catch the rooftops in the distance. Built in the 60s on the road to the lighthouse by the family who used to own the island, Les Pêchers stands in a big, nostalgically crumbly garden. Life is mostly lived under the bamboo awning of the large patio-terrace… you're wonderfully private here. The whole place has been recently redone: outdoors soft pink and lavender, indoors pale yellows and greens; sparkling bathroom, fabrics, tiles and children's beds all new. Bedrooms are comfortably furnished with quilts and big armoires guarding good blankets. The kitchen, well-equipped and with dishwasher, is just as comfortingly 'family', there's an extra fridge in the huge old cellar, and a new studio, with tiny bathroom and kitchen, that feeds off the salon. Cars are forbidden so hire your bikes to explore the pure white sandy beaches and cliffs, the vineyards and pheasant-thronged woods. A super place for a family holiday. *Linen can be hired locally.*

sleeps	8-10. Studio sleeps 2.
price	€ 800-€ 2,300. Studio € 400-€ 1,300.
rooms	3 + 1: 2 doubles, 1 family room for 2-4, 1 bathroom, 1 shower room, 1 separate wc; studio with 1 sofabed, 1 shower room.
closed	Rarely.

booking details

Christine Richet

tel	+33 (0)1 39 50 88 14
fax	+33 (0)1 39 50 88 14
e-mail	lespechers@freesurf.fr
web	www.lespechers.freesurf.fr

Hameau l'Autourière

La Garde Freinet, Var

The tortuous drive along a track to this ancient hamlet is worth the bumps. Climb the eight stone steps to your single-floor studio and you reach a haven of rustic cosiness. Warm rusts, creams and yellows enhance the feeling of comfort, as do the attractive ethnic artefacts brought back from Africa where Mrs Woodall, the English owner, used to farm before she made Provence her home. Ancient terracotta tiled floors, tiny windows and low beamed ceilings convey the great age of this stone *magnanerie* where silkworms used to be reared for the farmhouses next door. Mrs Woodall lives in one of them with Clio, her golden retriever, and often hosts a stream of friends, grandchildren and B&B guests. You may meet them in the magnificent pool among the trees, but if you want privacy there is plenty of space among the three-odd hectares of meadows, lawns and borders, skilfully tended by Mrs Woodall's green fingers. Visit medieval and fashionable La Garde Freinet, and walk the GR9 (Route des Crêtes) through the rugged Massif des Maures. *No children but babes-in-arms. B&B also.*

sleeps	2-4.
price	€ 420-€ 630 (£300-£450).
rooms	1 double with 2 single campbeds for children, 1 bathroom.
closed	Never.

booking details

	Mrs Philippa Woodall
tel	+33 (0)4 94 43 63 47
fax	+33 (0)4 94 43 63 47

map 18   entry 279

La Ferme de Guillandonne

Tourrettes, Var

This enchanting 200-year-old farmhouse is the height of country-hideaway chic. Earthy, stylish, magical, it stands under the sprawling embrace of an ancient oak (one of many) and is bordered on one side by a stream. You are wrapped in 10 acres of countryside. Rows of lavender run along on one side of the pool, while on the other a tunnel of wisteria leads down to a sun-trapping terrace. The interior is equally satisfying. Walls are washed in traditional colours – cool yellows, cosy reds, pale greens. There are old beams and a big arched window gives onto the terrace. One of the bedrooms has a magnificent high ceiling and a window that looks out onto a Chinese mulberry tree, another an original open fireplace and views over the pool. Marie-Joëlle, a former English teacher, and her husband, an architect, have renovated with a happy respect for the spirit of the place, for its history and the landscape that envelops it. You are in one of the loveliest parts of the Var and villages here have musical events running throughout the summer. This is a *bona fide* classic, a very special place. *B&B also.*

sleeps	6-7 + cot.
price	€ 1,000–€ 2,300.
rooms	3: 2 doubles, 1 twin, extra bed available, 2 bathrooms, 1 shower room, 1 shower room with separate entrance.
closed	Never.

booking details

	Marie–Joëlle Salaün
tel	+33 (0)4 94 76 04 71
fax	+33 (0)4 94 76 04 71

La Maison Blanche

Bargemon, Var

You're outside one of the prettiest, most fashionable villages of east Provence but here you see no one. Cradled by pine-clad mountains, this old farmhouse is surrounded by lawns, flower-filled meadows and orchards. In spring you'll hear nightingales and smell wild narcissi; in summer the fruit trees yield apricots, cherries and figs, all of which you're free to munch. The house has been completely renovated by the English owners, although they have kept old beams and some lovely hexagonal floor tiles. Furniture is mostly antique French and English, with some unusual items, like an ancient workbench-turned-sideboard in the dining room, and wooden doughboards at the heads of two of the beds. The charming end bedroom, once the hayloft, has a vine-clad balcony from which you can pluck grapes in the autumn. As bedrooms are reached by two staircases, the house is ideal for two families holidaying together. The village, with a weekly hiking party and a market, is a short walk up the hill. Then back for lunch on the huge terrace under the shade of the limes, and a dip in the heavenly pool. *Changeover day Thursday.*

sleeps	10.
price	£470–£2,050.
rooms	5: 1 double, 4 twins, 3 bathrooms, 1 shower room.
closed	Never.

booking details

	Janet Hill
tel	+44 (0)1628 482579
fax	+44 (0)1628 482579
e-mail	dsimons@onetel.net.uk

map 18   entry 281

30 rue Pierre Porre
Mons, Var

Come for the medieval hilltop village, perched above the forest like an eagle's nest. It's an echo of a France long lost, an architectural wonder beautifully preserved. Your house is medieval in parts with 17th- and 19th-century additions and a serenity borne of age. Bedrooms have a cultivated simplicity: a brass bed, fresh colours, a writing desk, a rooftop view; the main double is under the eaves and family watercolours add a personal touch. The kitchen is tiny yet perfectly equipped. Monsieur, whose mother spoke fluent Provençal, has been coming here since he was six. He and Madame are delightful; you may meet them in the garden where interesting bits of carved stone are scattered, some of them probably Roman. As for the views… the village is the second highest in the Var, and the vistas extend for miles, across wide stretches of forest and hill before falling off into a distant sea. There's no pool, but you won't give a fig. Don't miss the village square and its fountain; there's almost a feel of Ligurian Italy here. *Not suitable for young children due to steep stairs. B&B also.*

sleeps	6.
price	€ 450–€ 800.
rooms	4: 2 doubles, 2 singles, 2 shower rooms, 1 separate wc.
closed	Rarely.

booking details

	Ursula Mouton
tel	+33 (0)2 38 80 65 68
e-mail	u.mouton@free.fr
web	titmar.free.fr/Chambreshotes.htm

Les Palmiers

Cannes, Alpes-Maritimes

Don't be deceived by the Seventies facade; this ground-floor studio apartment is an absolute gem. From your bed you can watch the glistening waters of the Bay of Cannes and listen to the palm trees gently rustling in the breeze. Édith lives next door with her Scots terrier, Little Boy. Full of grace and tremendous kindness, she used to be a fashion model, which goes some way towards explaining her French flair and eye for detail. You will be charmed by the warm colours, antiques and fine fabrics – thick white bedspreads, cream curtains fluttering in the breeze. Fruit bowls and fresh flowers are beautifully arranged to ensure you feel pampered; there was even a plate of melon and Parma ham in the fridge when we visited. There are basic cooking facilities in the passage between the living room and the bathroom; sliding doors lead to a tiny, oleander-flowered terrace. The beach, local markets and glamour of Cannes are 10 minutes by bus and Édith will update you on all the local goings-on. *Minimum stay three nights. B&B also.*

sleeps	2.
price	€80–€125 per night.
rooms	1 twin/double, 1 bathroom.
closed	Never.

booking details

Édith Lefay
tel +33 (0)4 93 69 25 67
fax +33 (0)4 93 69 25 67

map 18 entry 283

La Maison

Vence, Alpes-Maritimes

One of the loveliest places in this book. Not the smartest or the most beautiful, just utterly authentic and sure of itself – its soul is not for sale, and it shines. It is a place to chance upon, as if the house were too modest to seduce you in advance. Those lucky enough to wash up on its shores find an old Provençal stone farmhouse that stands beneath the protective gaze of Le Baou, a sugar-loaf mountain. You are surrounded by wilderness. Hide away on the stone terrace under the shade of an old olive tree and gaze on distant hills, or stroll down to the waterfalls and swimming holes of the Cagne river. A delightfully unmanicured haven, where autumn leaves are free to drift. Bedrooms are simple and cosy, beds dressed in fine linen. One has whitewashed walls and a beautiful 18th-century 'built-in' cupboard, the other an antique desk and views through trees. There's a long refectory dining table in the kitchen and rush-matted chairs, and a tiny but utterly charming sitting room. Laurence, who lives next door with her two delightful children, is the real star: warm, cultured and full of life.

sleeps	4 + 1 child.
price	€300–€500.
rooms	2: 1 double, 1 twin, child's bed available, 1 bathroom.
closed	Never.

booking details

Laurence Thiebaut

tel	+33 (0)4 93 58 13 95
fax	+33 (0)4 93 58 13 95
e-mail	lamaisondelaurence@hotmail.com

WHAT'S IN THE BACK OF THE BOOK?

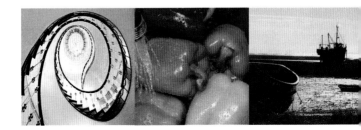

NATIONAL AND REGIONAL PARKS IN FRANCE

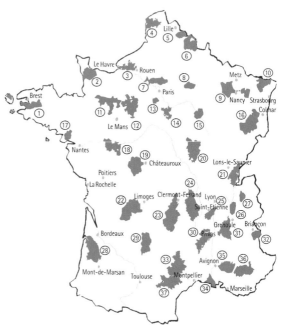

General De Gaulle signed the initial legislation for the creation of its National and Regional Parks in 1967. Forty national and regional nature parks in France now represent 11% of its landmass. Most are off the beaten track and are often missed by the foreign visitor. The motorway network is such that one swishes by huge patches of beautiful countryside without even realising it.

The National and Regional Parks charter promotes:

- Protection and management of natural and cultural heritage

- Participation in town and country planning and implementation of economic and social development

- Welcoming and informing the public, raising environmental awareness

There is a ban on hunting, camping, building and road construction in the six national parks: Cévennes, Ecrins, Mercantour, Port-Cros, Pyrénées and Vanoise. Access can be difficult but the rewards are considerable.

NATIONAL AND REGIONAL PARKS IN FRANCE

There are regional parks to be found in the mountains of Queyras (Hautes Alpes), the plains of Vexin (Ile de France), along the coast of Camargue (Provence), in the woodlands in the Northern Vosges (Alsace-Lorraine), in the wetlands of Brière (Western Loire) and off-shore in Port-Cros (Côte d'Azur).

All are ideal for rambles. Serious walkers can choose from the *sentiers de Grandes Randonnées* (GRs for short) which range through the parks and all park offices can provide maps of local walks.

There are grottos and museums to visit along with animal parks roaming with bison, yak, greater kudu and a pack of wolves. Activities include: horse-riding, cycling and bike rentals, canoeing and kayaking, canal boating, sailing, fishing, spa treatments, wine tours, bathing, rock climbing, handgliding, ballooning. There are packhorses in Livradois-Forez (Auvergne) and donkeys for hire in Haut-Languedoc (Languedoc). A range of activities make them ideal for children and a multitude of crafts are to be observed: clog-making, silk weaving, glass working, stone working in the Morvan (Burgundy), cheesemaking and pipe-making in the Haut Jura (Franche Comté).

www.parcs-naturales-regionaux.tm.fr

This central web site links to all the other parks. All have English language versions.

F. Mulet

FRENCH WORDS & EXPRESSIONS

French words & expressions used in this book.

armagnac	fiery spirit of distilled grapes produced in Gascony, not to be confused with cognac!
auberge	inn, hostel, guest house
bastide	several meanings: it can be a stronghold, a small fortified village or, in Provence, simply another word for mas
bergerie	sheepfold, sheep shed
brocante	secondhand furniture, objects, fabric, hats, knick-knacks
cabanon	cabin, chalet, or in Provence, cottage
cascade	waterfall, stream or torrent
caves	cellar
chambre d'hôtes	B&B
château	a mansion or stately home built for aristocrats between the 16th and 19th centuries. A castle, with fortifications, is a *château fort*
châtelain/e	lord/lady of the manor
coquillage	shells
cuisine arrière	scullery
cuisine américaine	kitchen/diner
dégustations	sampling or tasting
dépendance	outbuilding of château, farm etc
domaine viticole	wine producing estate
donjon	castle keep
épicerie	grocer's shop
fauteuil	armchair
feria	(Spanish) public holiday, festival
font caudière	hot spring
gardien	warden
gîte	self-catering holiday house, usually attached to owner's house or a farm
gîte	overnight dormitory-style huts/houses, often run by the local village or municipality, for cyclists or walkers (often with optional meals)
lavoir	washing place or wash house
longère	a long, low farmhouse made of Breton granite
magnanerie	silkworm farm
maison bourgeoise/ maison de maître	big, comfortable houses standing in quite large grounds and built for well-to-do members of the liberal professions, captains of industry, trade etc
maison paysanne	country cottage

FRENCH WORDS & EXPRESSIONS

a Provençal country house, usually long and low with old stone walls, pan-tiled roof and painted shutters

vigneronne — can be a tiny vine-worker's cottage or a comfortable house owned by the estate manager or proprietor

aux boules/
ue — bowling game played with metal balls on a dirt surface

and hôtel
e — town and city hall respectively

é au gras — market where you can buy foie gras and other delights

n — mill

boeuf — literally bull's eye window, i.e. small circular or oval window

— pineau – an alcoholic aperitif from the Charantes region made from wine and cognac

nier — pigeon-house or dovecote

eau — alcoholic drink made from apples

/potager — vegetable soup/vegetable garden

ir — press for olives/grapes/apples

— Auvergnat dialect for 'peak'

'accueil — reception room

d'eau — shower room

le séjour — living room

d'hôtes — dinner with the owners of the house

te — hexagonal terracotta floor tile

cuite — baked clay

de Jouy — classic fabric and wallpaper design, usually depicting rustic or court scenes in one colour on a white background

AVOIDING CULTURAL CONFUSION

En suite

'En suite' is not used in France to describe bathrooms off the bedroom and to do so can lead to confusion. To be clear, simply ask for a room *'avec salle de bains et wc'*.

Greetings and forms of address

We Anglo-Saxons drop far more easily into first-name terms than the French. This reluctance on their part is not a sign of coldness, it's simply an Old National Habit, to be respected, we feel, like any other tribal ritual. So it's advisable to wait for the signal from them as to when you have achieved more intimate status.

The French do not say *"Bonjour Monsieur Dupont"* or *"Bonjour Madame Jones"* – this is considered familiar. They simply say *"Bonjour Monsieur"* or *"Bonjour Madame"* – which makes it easy to be lazy about remembering people's names.

Eating out

Cutlery is laid concave face upwards in 'Anglo-Saxon' countries; in France it is proper to lay forks and spoons convex face upwards (crests are engraved accordingly). Do try to hold back your instinctive need to turn them over!

To the right of your plate, at the tip of the knife, you may find a knife-rest. This serves two purposes: to lay your knife on when you are not using it, rather than leaving it on your plate; to lay your knife and fork on (points downwards) if you are asked to *garder vos couverts* (keep your knife and fork) while the plates are changed – e.g. between starter and main dish.

Cheese comes before pudding in France – that's the way they do it. Cut a round cheese as you would cut a round cake – in triangular segments. When a ready-cut segment such as a piece of brie is presented, the rule is to 'preserve the point'.

Tipping All restaurants include tax and a 15% service charge; the words *service compris* indicate this on the bill. If a meal has been particularly good, leaving another few euros is customary as is leaving the small change from your bill if you paid in cash.

Children are welcome in most restaurants, even late into the evening.

TIPS FOR TRAVELLERS
IN FRANCE

Phonecard

If you are not wedded to a mobile phone buy a phonecard (*télécarte*) on arrival; they are on sale at post offices and tobacconists.

Public holidays

Be aware of public holidays; many national museums and galleries close on Tuesdays, others close on Mondays (e.g. Monet's garden in Giverny) as do many country restaurants, and opening times may be different on the following days:

Movable feasts in 2004 & 2005

New Year's Day (**1 January**)   May Day (**1 May**)
Liberation 1945 (**8 May**)   Bastille Day (**14 July**)
Assumption (**15 August**)   All Saints (**1 November**)
Armistice (**11 November**)
Easter Sunday **11 April 2004 (27 March 2005)**
Ascension Thursday **20 May 2004 (5 May 2005)**
Whit Sunday & Monday (Pentecost) **30 & 31 May 2004 (15 & 16 May 2005)**

Beware also of the mass exodus over public holiday weekends, both the first day – outward journey – and the last – return journey.

Medical & emergency procedures

If you are an EC citizen, have an E111 form with you for filling in after any medical treatment. Part of the sum will subsequently be refunded, so it is advisable to take out private insurance.

To call French emergency services dial 15: the public service called SAMU or the Casualty Department – Services des Urgences – of a hospital. The private service is called SOS MÉDECINS.

Other insurance

It is probably wise to insure the contents of your car.

Roads & driving

Current speed limits are: motorways 130 kph (80 mph), RN national trunk roads 110 kph (68 mph), other open roads 90 kph (56 mph), in towns 50 kph (30 mph). The road police are very active and can demand on-the-spot payment of fines.

One soon gets used to driving on the right but complacency leads to trouble; take special care coming out of car parks, private drives, one-lane roads and coming onto roundabouts.

Directions in towns

The French drive towards a destination and use road numbers far less than we do. Thus, to find your way *à la française*, know the general direction you want to go, i.e. the towns your route goes through, and when you see *Autres Directions* or *Toutes Directions* in a town, forget road numbers, just continue towards the place name you're heading for or through.

WALKING IN FRANCE

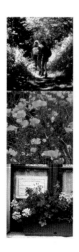

With over 60,000km of clearly marked long distance footpaths, or sentiers de Grandes Randonnées (GRs for short), and a fantastic variety of landscapes and terrains, France is a superb country in which to walk. Hike in the snow-topped glaciers of the Northern Alps, walk through the lush and rugged volcanic 'moonscapes' of the Auvergne, or amble through the vineyards of Burgundy, Alsace or Provence.

Stroll for an afternoon, or make an odyssey over several months. Some long-distance walks have become classics, like the famous GR65, the pilgrim road to Santiago de Compostela, the Tour du Mont Blanc, or the 450km long GR3 Sentier de la Loire, which runs from the Ardèche to the Atlantic. Wild or tamed, hot or temperate, populated or totally empty, take your choice: France has it all.

Wherever you are renting a house, there will almost certainly be a GR near you. You can walk a stretch of it, then use other paths to turn it into a circular walk. As well as the network of GRs, marked with red and white parallel paint markings, there's a network of Petites Randonnées (PRs), usually signalled by single yellow or green paint stripes. In addition, there are sentiers de Grandes Randonnées de Pays (GRPs), marked by a red and yellow stripe, and any number of variants of the original GR route which eventually become paths in their own right. Paths are evolving all the time.

The paths are lovingly waymarked and maintained by the Fédération Française de la Randonnée Pédestre (FFRP), which was founded in 1947 under another name. The federation is also responsible for producing the topo-guides, books for walkers containing walking directions and maps (see under Books).

The great reward for walkers is that you'll penetrate the soul of rural France in a way you never could from a car. You'll see quaint ruined châteaux, meet country characters whom you'll never forget, and last but not least, you'll encounter a dazzling variety of flora and fauna if you look for it. France has a remarkably rich natural heritage, including 266 species of nesting birds, 131 species of mammal, and nearly 5,000 species of flowering plants. Look out for golden eagles, griffon vultures and marmots in the Alps and Pyrenees, red kites and lizard orchids in the Dordogne, and fulmars and puffins off the rocky Brittany coast. There's no room for complacency, however, as hundreds of species are threatened with extinction: 400 species of flora are classed as threatened and about 20 species of mammals and birds are vulnerable or in danger of extinction.

When to go

The best months for walking are May, June, September and October. In high mountain areas, summers are briefer and paths may be free of snow only between July and early September. In the northern half of France July and August are also good months, but it's too hot at this time of year in the south. Southern France is ideal for a winter break, when days are often crisp and clear.

Maps

As mentioned in the cycling section, the two big names for maps are IGN (Institut Géographique National) and Michelin. IGN maps are likely to be of most use for walkers. A useful map for planning walks is the IGN's France: Grande Randonnée sheet No. 903 which shows all the country's long distance footpaths. For walking, the best large-scale maps are the IGN's 1:25,000 Serie Bleue and Top 25 series. Also look out for IGN's 1:50,000 Plein Air series which includes GRs and PRs, plus hotels and campsites. Unfortunately they cover only limited areas.

Books

The FFRP produces more than 180 topo-guides – guidebooks for walkers which include walking instructions and IGN maps (usually 1:50,000). Most of these are now translated into English so it's worth buying one of these to the area where you are going before you leave. Consult its web site too.

The Code du Randonneur

Love and respect nature · Avoid unnecessary noise · Destroy nothing · Do not leave litter · Do not pick flowers or plants · Do not disturb wildlife · Re-close all gates · Protect and preserve the habitat · No smoking or fires in the forests · Stay on the footpath · Respect and understand the country way of life and the country people · Think of others as you think of yourself

This obviously depends on the terrain, the length of the walk and the time of year, but here's a suggested checklist:

Clothing and equipment

Boots, sunhat, suncream and lip salve, mosquito repellent, sunglasses, sweater, cagoule, stick, water bottle, gaiters, change of clothing, phrase book, maps, compass, sense of humour, field guides to flora and fauna, waterproof daypack, camera and spare film, Swiss Army knife, whistle (for emergencies), spare socks, binoculars, waterproof jacket and trousers, emergency food, first-aid kit, torch.

CYCLING IN FRANCE

Two and a half times the size of the UK, France offers rich rewards to the cyclist: plenty of space, a superb network of minor roads with little traffic, and a huge diversity of landscapes, smells and terrains. You can chose the leafy forests and gently undulating plains of the north, or the jagged glacier-topped mountains of the Alps. Pedal through wafts of fermenting grapes in Champagne, resinous pines in the Midi, or spring flowers in the Pyrenees. You can amble slowly, stopping in remote villages for delicious meals or a café au lait, or pit yourself against the toughest terrains and cycle furiously.

You will also be joining in a national sport: bikes are an important part of French culture and thousands don their lycra and take to their bikes on summer weekends. (You can join the French cycle touring club on its organised trips if you wish – see under Useful Numbers section.) The country comes to a virtual standstill during the three-week Tour de France cycling race in July and the media is dominated by talk of who is the latest maillot jaune (literally 'yellow jersey' – the fellow in the lead). Cycling stars become national heroes and heroines with quasi-divine status.

Mountain bikes are becoming increasingly popular. They are known as VTTs (vélos tout terrain) and there is an extensive network of VTT trails, usually marked in purple. Cycles are available for hire in most towns and at most SNCF stations (useful as you can drop them off at another) and often offer special rates for a week's hire. The bikes are often not insured, however, so check if your travel insurance covers you for theft or damage.

When to go

Avoid July and August, if possible, as it's hot and the roads are at their busiest. The south is good from mid-March, except on high ground which may be snow-clad until the end of June. The north, which has a similar climate to Britain's, can be lovely from May onwards. Most other areas are suitable from April until October.

Getting bikes to and through France

If you are using public transport, you can get your bicycle to France by air, by ferry or via the Channel Tunnel. Ferries carry bikes for nothing or for a small fee. British Airways and Air France take bikes free. If you are travelling by Eurostar, you can store your bike in one of the guards' vans which have cycle-carrying hooks, with a potential capacity of up to eight bikes per train. To do this you need to reserve and pay extra.

CYCLING IN FRANCE

If you are travelling on French railways, some stations accept bikes free of charge, while others require you to register your bike, buy it a separate ticket, and it will travel separately. For information as to which trains accept bikes, consult the web site of the French railways (SNCF): www.sncf.com

A few mainline and most regional trains accept bikes free of charge and you can place them in the guard's van. These trains are indicated by a small bike symbol in the timetable. In the Paris area, you can take bikes on most trains except during rush hours. Certain central RER stations forbid the mounting of bikes onto trains. In the Rhone-Alps region, all local trains accept bikes free of charge. However, some trains limit the number of bikes to three.

Maps
The two big names are Michelin and the Institut Géographique National (IGN). For route-planning, IGN publishes a map of the whole of France showing mountain-biking and cycle tourism (No. 906). The best on-the-road reference maps are Michelin's Yellow 1:200,000 Series. IGN publishes a Green Series at a scale of 1:100,000. For larger scale maps, go for IGN's excellent 1:25,000 Top 25 and Blue Series (which you will also use for walking). You can buy maps at most Maisons de la Presse newsagents in France, or at Stanfords in the UK.

Repairs and spare parts
Bike shops are at least as numerous as in Britain and you should be able to get hold of spare parts, provided you don't try between noon and 2pm, when shops close for the all important business of lunching. Prices are often lower than in Britain and the US. However, if you have a non-French bike with non-standard metric wheels, it's advisable to carry spare tyres.

FLIGHT ROUTES

Ajaccio (Corsica)
Heathrow

Bastia (Corsica)
Gatwick

Bergerac
Southampton
Stansted

Biarritz
Stansted

Bordeaux
Birmingham
Dublin
Gatwick

Brest
Stansted

Carcassonne
Stansted

Chambery
Gatwick

Clermont-Ferrand
Gatwick
Stansted

Dinard
Stansted

Grenoble
Gatwick

La Rochelle
Stansted

Limoges
Stansted

Lyon
Birmingham
Edinburgh
Heathrow
Manchester
Stansted

Marseille
Gatwick

Montpellier
Gatwick
Stansted

Nantes
Cork
Gatwick

Nice
Birmingham
Bristol
Cork
Dublin
E. Midlands
Edinburgh
Gatwick
Glasgow
Heathrow
Leeds Bradford
Liverpool
Luton
Manchester
Stansted
Teesside

Nimes
Stansted

Paris Beauvais
Dublin
Glasgow
Shannon

Paris CDG
Aberdeen
Belfast City
Birmingham
Bristol
Cardiff
Cork
Dublin
E. Midlands
Edinburgh
Gatwick
Glasgow
Heathrow
Leeds Bradford

London City
Liverpool
Luton
Manchester
Newcastle
Southampton
Teesside

Paris Orly
London City

Pau
Stansted

Perpignan
Stansted

Poitiers
Stansted

Reims
Stansted

Rodez
Stansted

St Etienne
Stansted

Strasbourg
Gatwick
Stansted

Toulon
Gatwick

Toulouse
Belfast City
Birmingham
Cardiff
East Midlands
Edinburgh
Gatwick
Glasgow
Heathrow
Manchester
Southampton

Tours
Stansted

WHAT IS ALASTAIR SAWDAY PUBLISHING?

Twenty or so of us work in converted barns on a farm near Bristol, close enough to the city for a bicycle ride and far enough for a silence broken only by horses and the occasional passage of a tractor. Some editors work in the countries they write about, e.g. France; others work from the UK but are based outside the office. We enjoy each other's company, celebrate every event possible, and work in an easy-going but committed environment.

These books owe their style and mood to Alastair's miscellaneous career and his interest in the community and the environment. He has taught overseas, worked with refugees, run development projects abroad, founded a travel company and several environmental organisations. There has been a slightly unconventional streak throughout, not least in his driving of a waste-paper-collection lorry, the manning of stalls at jumble sales and the pursuit of causes long before they were considered sane.

Back to the travel company: trying to take his clients to eat and sleep in places that were not owned by corporations and assorted bandits he found dozens of very special places in France – farms, châteaux etc – a list that grew into the first book, *French Bed and Breakfast*. It was a celebration of 'real' places to stay and the remarkable people who run them.

The publishing company grew from that first and rather whimsical French book. It started as a mild crusade, and there it stays – full of 'attitude', and the more appealing for it. For we still celebrate the unusual, the beautiful, the individual. We are passionate about rejecting the banal, the ugly, the pompous and the indifferent and we are passionate, too, about 'real' food. Alastair is a trustee of the Soil Association and keen to promote organic growing and consuming by owners and visitors.

It is a source of deep pleasure to us to know that there are many thousands of people who share our views. We are by no means alone in trumpeting the virtues of resisting the destruction and uniformity of so much of our culture – and the cultures of other nations, too.

We run a company in which people and values matter. We love to hear of new friendships between those in the book and those using it, and to know that there are many people – among them farmers – who have been enabled to pursue their decent lives thanks to the extra income our books bring them.

Britain
France
Ireland
Italy
Portugal
Spain
Morocco
India...

all in one place!

On the unfathomable and often unnavigable sea of online accommodation pages, those who have discovered www.specialplacestostay.com have found it to be an island of reliability. Not only will you find a database full of trustworthy, up-to-date information about all the Special Places to Stay across Europe, but also:

- Links to the web sites of all of the places in the series
- Colourful, clickable, interactive maps to help you find the right place
- The opportunity to make most bookings by e-mail – even if you don't have e-mail yourself
- Online purchasing of our books, securely and cheaply
- Regular, exclusive special offers on books
- The latest news about future editions and future titles
- Notices about special offers, late availability and anything else our owners think you'll be interested in.

The site is constantly evolving and is frequently updated with news and special features that won't appear anywhere else but in our window on the worldwide web.

Russell Wilkinson, Web Producer
website@specialplacestostay.com

If you'd like to receive news and updates about our books by e-mail, visit the site and at the bottom of every page you can add yourself to our address book.

The Little Earth Book

w in its third edition and
as engrossing and
provocative as ever,
it continues to highlight
the perilously fragile
state of our planet.
£6.99
h edition available April 2004

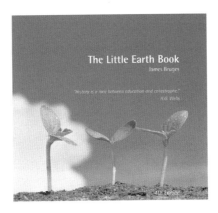

The Little Food Book

Makes for a wonderfully
:imulating read – one that
may change your
attitude to the
food choices you
make daily.
£6.99

The Little Money Book

Could make you look
at everything financial –
rom your bank statements
to the coins in
your pocket –
in a whole new way.
Available November 2003
£6.99

This fascinating series has been praised by politicians,
academics, environmentalists, civil servants – and 'general'
readers. It has come as a blast of fresh air, blowing away
confusion and incomprehension.

www.fragile-earth.com

SIX DAYS

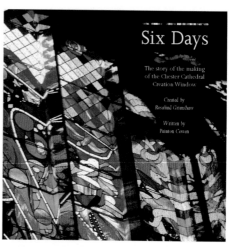

Celebrating the triumph of creativity over adversity

The inspiring and moving story of the making of the stained glass Creation window at Chester Cathedral by a woman battling with Parkinson's disease.

"Within a few seconds, the tears were running down my cheeks. The window was one of the most beautiful things I had ever seen. It is a tour-de-force, playing with light like no other window ..."

Anthropologist Hugh Brody

In 1983, Ros Grimshaw, a distinguished designer, artist and creator of stained-glass windows, was diagnosed with Parkinson's disease. Refusing to allow her illness to prevent her from working, Ros became even more adept at her craft, and in 2000 won the commission to design and make the Creation Stained Glass Window for Chester Cathedral.

Six Days traces the evolution of the window from the first sketches to its final, glorious completion as a rare and wonderful tribute to Life itself: for each of the six 'days' of creation recounted in Genesis, there is a scene below that is relevant to the world of today and tomorrow.

Extracts from Ros's diary capture the personal struggle involved. Superb photography captures the luminescence of the stunning stained glass, while the story weaves together essays, poems, and moving contributions from Ros's partner, Patrick Costeloe.

Available from Alastair Sawday Publishing £12.99

ORDER FORM UK

All these books are available in major bookshops or you may order them direct. **Post and packaging are FREE within the UK.**

		Price	No. copies
French Bed & Breakfast	Edition 8	£15.99	
French Hotels, Châteaux & Inns	Edition 3	£13.99	
French Holiday Homes	Edition 2	£11.99	
Paris Hotels	Edition 4	£9.99	
British Bed & Breakfast	Edition 8	£14.99	
British Hotels, Inns & Other Places	Edition 5	£13.99	
Bed & Breakfast for Garden Lovers	Edition 2	£14.99	
British Holiday Homes	Edition 1	£9.99	
London	Edition 1	£9.99	
Ireland	Edition 4	£12.99	
Spain	Edition 5	£13.99	
Portugal	Edition 2	£8.99	
Italy	Edition 3	£12.99	
Europe with courses & activities	Edition 1	£12.99	
India	Edition 1	£10.99	
Morocco	Edition 1	£10.99	
The Little Earth Book	Edition 3	£6.99	
The Little Food Book	Edition 1	£6.99	
The Little Money Book	Edition 1	£6.99	
Six Days		£12.99	

Please make cheques payable to   Total £ _____ _____
Alastair Sawday Publishing

Please send cheques to: Alastair Sawday Publishing,
The Home Farm Stables, Barrow Gurney, Bristol BS48 3RW.
For credit card orders call 01275 464891 or order directly
from our web site **www.specialplacestostay.com**

Title   First name   Surname

Address

Postcode   Tel

If you do not wish to receive mail from other like-minded companies,
please tick here ☐

If you would prefer not to receive information about special offers on our books,
please tick here ☐

FSC2

REPORT FORM

If you have any comments on entries in this guide, please let us have them. If you have a favourite house, hotel, inn or other new discovery, please let us know about it.

Existing Entry:

Name of property _____

Book title: _____

Entry no: _____ Edition no: _____

Date of visit: _____

New recommendation:

_____

Name of property: _____

Address: _____

_____

Postcode: _____

Tel: _____

Comments: _____

_____

_____

_____

Your name: _____

Address: _____

_____

_____

Postcode: _____

Tel: _____

Please send the completed form to:

Alastair Sawday Publishing,
The Home Farm Stables, Barrow Gurney, Bristol BS48 3RW
or go to www.specialplacestostay.com and click on 'contact'.

Thank you.

QUICK REFERENCE INDICES

QUICK REFERENCE INDICES

Groups of 10 & over

The following places can accommodate groups of 10 and over.
The North • 2 • Picardy • 5 • Burgundy • 13 • 22 • 25 • 27 •
Normandy • 32 • 34 • 36 • 37 • 38 • 40 • 41 • 42 • 53 • 59 • 60 •
Brittany • 67 • Western Loire • 71 • Loire Valley • 79 • 80 •
Poitou-Charentes • 94 • 95 • 96 • 102 • 103 • 105 • Limousin •
114 • 115 • Auvergne • 123 • Aquitaine • 125 • 132 • 133 • 138 •
142 • 145 • 148 • 149 • 151 • 154 • 155 • 158 • 160 • Midi-
Pyrénées • 167 • 168 • 169 • 170 • 182 • 183 • 187 • 188 • 189 •
190 • 196 • 197 • 200 • Languedoc-Roussillon • 217 • 223 • 224 •
227 • 228 • 233 • 234 • 235 • 236 • 237 • Rhône Valley – Alps •
249 • 253 • Provence – Alps – Riviera • 263 • 271 • 281

Meals can be arranged

These owners can either provide you with a meal (or a chef) in
your own gîte, or you may join them for dinner in their B&B.
Picardy • 5 • Champagne-Ardenne • 9 • Burgundy • 13 • 27 •
Normandy • 32 • 36 • 37 • 38 • 41 • 42 • 52 • Western Loire • 71
• 73 • Loire Valley • 77 • 79 • 88 • 89 • Poitou-Charentes • 94 •
95 • 96 • 102 • 103 • 105 • Limousin • 113 • 114 • 115 • 116 •
Auvergne • 120 • 121 • 123 • Aquitaine • 125 • 132 • 133 • 142 •
148 • 149 • 150 • 151 • 152 • 154 • 155 • Midi-Pyrénées • 163 •
169 • 170 • 172 • 175 • 176 • 177 • 178 • 179 • 180 • 181 • 182 •
183 • 187 • 188 • 189 • 190 • 191 • 196 • 197 • 198 • 199 • 200 •
201 • 202 • 203 • 213 • Languedoc-Roussillon • 217 • 229 • 230 •
233 • 239 • 248 • Rhône Valley – Alps • 249 • 253 • 256 • 257 •
Provence – Alps – Riviera • 262 • 266 • 270 • 275 • 276 • 277 • 284

Hosts wedding parties

The North • 2 • Burgundy • 14 • 27 • Normandy • 32 • 36 • 37 •
38 • 59 • 60 • Brittany • 67 • Western Loire • 71 • 73 • Loire
Valley • 87 • Poitou-Charentes • 102 • 103 • 105 • Limousin • 114 •
115 • Auvergne • 123 • Aquitaine • 125 • 132 • 133 • 135 • 148 •
149 • 151 • 154 • 155 • Midi-Pyrénées • 169 • 170 • 172 • 175 •
182 • 183 • 188 • 189 • 190 • 197 • 199 • 200 • Languedoc-
Roussillon • 217 • 223 • 224 • 229 • 230 • 233 • Rhône Valley –
Alps • 249 • 253 • 256 • Provence – Alps – Riviera • 262

Bikes for hire

Picardy • 3 • 5 • 6 • 7 • 8 • Champagne-Ardenne • 9 • Alsace • 11
• Burgundy • 14 • 15 • 16 • 17 • 18 • 19 • 20 • 21 • 27 • Paris-Ile
de France • 30 • Normandy • 31 • 34 • 35 • 36 • 37 • 38 • 49 • 51
• 52 • 55 • Brittany • 61 • Western Loire • 70 • 70 • 71 • 72 • 74 •
75 • Loire Valley • 83 • 87 • 88 • 89 • 90 • 92 • 93 • Poitou-
Charentes • 94 • 95 • 96 • 97 • 99 • 100 • 101 • 102 • 103 •

QUICK REFERENCE INDICES

INDEX - TOWN

INDEX - TOWN

INDEX - TOWN